Ninth Edition Introductory Course College Typewriting

D. D. LESSENBERRY   Professor of Business Education, Emeritus
University of Pittsburgh

S. J. WANOUS   Professor of Education, Emeritus
University of California, L.A.

C. H. DUNCAN   Professor of Business Education
Eastern Michigan University

S. E. WARNER   Head, Business Education
and Office Administration Department
University of Northern Iowa

ISBN: 0-538-20110-X
Library of Congress Catalog Card Number: 74-25416
2 3 4 5 6 7 8 H 1 0 9 8 7 6

Printed in U.S.A.

Published by

T11 **SOUTH-WESTERN PUBLISHING CO.**

CINCINNATI   WEST CHICAGO, ILL.   DALLAS   PELHAM MANOR, N.Y.
PALO ALTO, CALIF.   BRIGHTON, ENGLAND

CONTENTS

Basic Typewritten Communications

What Makes an Ideal Typing Book?

The ideal book provides the aids and materials that enable students, under the skillful guidance of an instructor, to learn how to type sufficiently well to meet the requirements of a job and to type personal papers. The student must bring to this task interest, desire, and the willingness to accept suggestions made by the book and the instructor. Thus, the triad:

```
              STUDENT
                △
INSTRUCTOR          TEXTBOOK
```

must work in close harmony. When this condition prevails, learning to type can move at a brisk pace.

How Is COLLEGE TYPEWRITING, Ninth Edition, Introductory Course, Organized?

The Introductory Course contains 75 lessons in 11 sections. Each section or set of two sections stresses one of the important phases of learning to typewrite:

- The letter keys
- The figure keys
- The most frequently used symbols
- Basic skill improvement
- Copy placement procedures
- Personal letters
- Business letters
- Tables
- Reports and outlines
- Measurement of basic and problem skills

In addition, there are included three special typing projects and a reference guide to frequently needed typing information. The students thus have an opportunity to concentrate on one part of the course at a time without the frequent interference of mixed or diffused goals.

What Unique Learning Aids Are Included?

The mere typing of a drill to gain either speed or accuracy will probably not result in achieving either goal. Each drill should be designed to single out some particular technique for improvement. COLLEGE TYPEWRITING, Ninth Edition, does exactly that. More than that, the drills are *stacked* to give substance to practice goals. Each lesson in this book contains one or more of these unique drills, spaced and repeated to give cohesiveness and unity to typing form.

When a new correspondence style or form is introduced, it is illustrated and presented as a problem. The various parts of the problem are labeled. Placement notations are included on the illustration. Complete directions for typing the solution are given in step-by-step order. Finally, when the students have completed the problem, they are told how to evaluate their solutions. In this way, they know immediately whether or not they have prepared an acceptable solution. As a result, early in the course, they can develop the habit of self-appraisal of their papers—a habit essential in an office typist.

After each group of related problems, materials for measuring student competency are provided; thus, both the instructor and the students can judge their progress from one group of lessons to the next.

Special Features

Some additional special features of this book are as follows:

1. Early emphasis is placed on the most frequently used letters, words, and two-letter stroking combinations to build stroking facility quickly.

2. Information on electric typewriters is given and variations in practice are made to accommodate electrics.

3. Two proofreading procedures are explained: *comparing* and *verifying*. Desirable procedures are laid down; then drills, ranging from spotting typographical errors to catching errors in meaning, are frequently provided to alert students to the kinds of errors they should look for in their typewritten work.

4. Guided writing and skill-comparison activities motivate the typist to work toward progressively higher goals and to practice on progressively more difficult copy.

5. Timed writings are triple-controlled and graduated in difficulty. Thus, the students move gradually and with certainty toward the office-level copy they will use.

6. Throughout the book, individual practice exercises are included, making it possible for the students to tailor practice to their needs by typing intensively the drill lines that emphasize the particular techniques and stroking sequences that give them the most difficulty.

7. Composing ability at the typewriter is developed through a logical sequence beginning with the typing of answers to simple questions to the typing of a variety of personal and business papers. A unique drill is introduced in which common letter-writing errors are identified and revisions are suggested. The students type the revised letter.

8. The copy is attractively arranged and spaced. Colored notations draw attention to important points. Clear, succinct directions are given at the beginning of each problem; and they are printed in distinctive type so that the student can readily distinguish what is to be read from what is to be typed.

9. Many full-size (or nearly so) illustrations give students accurate models from which to work and to use for comparison with their own solutions.

The authors express their grateful thanks to the instructors, students, and business workers who have contributed so generously to the content and organization of this book. Their recommendations and constructive criticisms have inspired the authors in preparing this Ninth Edition.

Lessenberry • Wanous • Duncan • Warner

1. Use 2 postal cards (or paper cut to 5½ by 3¼ inches).

2. Insert card; determine center; then set margin stops for a 48-space line.

3. Type the date on Line 3; then type the postal card message given below.

4. Remove the typed card; turn it message side down; insert the second card and type the same message.

> Because of the limited space on a postal card, the salutation and complimentary close are omitted.

		Words
1		
2		
3	March 30, 19--	3
4	TS	
5		
6	Norwell Products, Inc., foremost manufacturers	12
7	of electronic security and alarm systems, have	22
8	named us exclusive distributors of their complete	32
9	line of fine products.	37
10		
11	You will soon receive a catalog describing over	46
12	200 items for home and industrial use.	54
13	TS	
14		
15	PHILLIPS INTERNATIONAL COMPANY	60
16		
17		
18		
19		

Line 2
→Phillips International Company
24 East 40th Street
New York, NY 10016   6 / 10 / 14

Line 10 or 11

←——— 2″ ———→ Paradise Tours   17
4731 Pasadena Avenue   21
Tacoma, WA 98466   25
      —— 2 spaces

Addressing postal cards

SS and block both the return and the postal card addresses. Although the 2-letter state-name abbreviation for use with the ZIP Code is shown, it is still permissible to spell the state name in full or to use standard abbreviations.

Start the return address on Line 2, 3 spaces from the left edge. Start the address on about Line 10 or 11 and 2″ from the left edge.

Problem 2: Addressing Postal Card

1. Insert the first card typed in Problem 1 above, and type the address side of the card as illustrated.

2. Insert the second card typed in Problem 1 and address it to:

Pinkham & Lane, Inc.
7920 Sheppard Avenue
Brockton, MA 02401

Basic Typewritten Communications

Introduction

The general teaching/learning goals of this division of the book are to enable you:

- To type the letter, figure, and most commonly used symbol keys by touch, using from the beginning the kind of stroking techniques and mental approach that will add to your problem-typing competence as you progress through the course

- To use those techniques that have been found to be most efficient in shifting for capitals, in tabulating, in returning the carriage, and in handling other operative parts of your typewriter

- To use the basic rules underlying the arrangement of copy on paper and, further, to apply skill and understanding to the production of a variety of letters and reports

- To type from printed, script, corrected, and revised copy and also to compose on the typewriter simple letters, reports, and abstracts

- To proofread your copy for typographical accuracy and to evaluate its acceptability as a finished piece of work

How well you meet these goals will depend largely upon you. No one learns anything without a desire to learn. This desire must be coupled with a willingness to work through a series of organized lessons and to engage in self-study and evaluation.

If you are ready, the lessons presented in this textbook can help you meet the foregoing goals. The keyboard charts, illustrations, printed statements, and specially designed drills that are included in this division will help you to acquire touch-typing skill and efficiency in using your typewriter. The technique cues accompanying each drill tell you how to type it. Study the illustrations and printed statements. Read the cues, and apply them as you type the drills. Evaluate your growth by analyzing your performance and by noting your progress on the specially constructed timed writings provided in the book.

After you have built basic skill to an acceptable level, you will start applying it to typing letters, reports, tables, and other commonly used forms. As each new application problem is introduced, it is illustrated. Complete directions for typing the illustrated problem are given, and ample opportunity to apply these directions is provided by additional unarranged problems. Study the illustrations and follow the directions as you type the problems. In this manner, you will build the foundation needed for solving arrangement problems as you will encounter them in an office—without full directions and without close supervision.

Words

PHILLIPS INTERNATIONAL COMPANY
Manufacturer of
Electronic Equipment

24 East 40th Street
New York, NY 10016
Cable: PHICO
Telephone (212) 434-7891

Invoice

R. D. Dawson & Son Company
5781 East Greenwich Road
Springfield, MA 01106

Date Aug. 15, 19--

Our Order No. C-27145

Cust. Order No. TN-3197

Terms 2/10, n/30

Shipped Via East Bay Transport

8
13
19
21
27

Quantity	Description	Unit Price	Total
1	12-volt DC power converter	42.95	42.95
4	Universal car stereo power connectors	2.75	11.00
5	Photoelectric eye warning systems	31.45	157.25
4	100 ohm/volt AC/DC pocket multitesters	9.75	39.00
1	Auto tune-up analyzer	41.40	41.40
4	DC power timing lights	32.50	130.00
			421.60

35
45
53
66
73
82

83

Date

Sept. 1, 19--

Hemley & Green, Inc.
3907 Highview Avenue
Silver Spring, MD 20906

Statement of Account

PIC

PHILLIPS INTERNATIONAL COMPANY

24 East 40th Street
New York, New York 10016

Telephone (212) 434-7891

3

7
11
16

Date	Items	Debits	Credits	Balance Due
Aug. 1	Balance			365.00
4	Credit memorandum #4522		125.50	
9	Payment on account		239.50	00
23	Invoice #3381	721.00		721.00
25	Invoice #3410	255.05		976.05

17
21
27
33
40
46

GETTING STARTED

Arrange your work area

1. Clear the desk of unneeded books and papers.

2. Have the front of the frame of the typewriter even with the front edge of the desk.

3. Place this textbook to the right of the typewriter on a bookholder, or put something under the top to raise it to a better position.

4. Place blank sheets of paper to the left of the machine, with the long side of the paper even with the front edge of the desk.

5. Start each class by observing the foregoing directions.

Know your typewriter

1. Find on *your* typewriter each of the parts identified on the typewriter illustrated below. When you are asked to find a machine part, look at the illustration, find the part there; then locate that part on the typewriter you are using.

2. The numbers that are assigned to the machine parts on the illustration are used also on the detailed diagrams on Reference Guide pages i-ii at the back of this book.

3. While typewriters are similar in design, the location of a part may vary among different makes. When this is the case, refer to the operating manual for your typewriter.

4. Operating manuals furnished by typewriter companies show illustrations with parts identified.

The numbers shown in boldface in the textbook are those assigned to the machine parts illustrated below and on the diagrams presented on pp. i-ii.

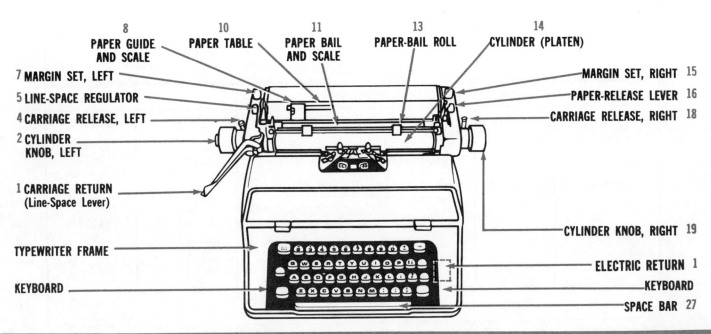

8 PAPER GUIDE AND SCALE
10 PAPER TABLE
11 PAPER BAIL AND SCALE
13 PAPER-BAIL ROLL
14 CYLINDER (PLATEN)

7 MARGIN SET, LEFT
5 LINE-SPACE REGULATOR
4 CARRIAGE RELEASE, LEFT
2 CYLINDER KNOB, LEFT
1 CARRIAGE RETURN (Line-Space Lever)
TYPEWRITER FRAME
KEYBOARD

MARGIN SET, RIGHT 15
PAPER-RELEASE LEVER 16
CARRIAGE RELEASE, RIGHT 18
CYLINDER KNOB, RIGHT 19
ELECTRIC RETURN 1
KEYBOARD
SPACE BAR 27

Tabulated business forms

Number of Copies. At least 2 copies (an original and a carbon) are made of invoices, credit memorandums, and similar forms. Usually, a single copy is made of a statement of account, which is merely a transfer of data already recorded.

Tabulator. Make full use of the tabulator for proper alignment of figures in the columns and to speed your work. For a column of numbers, set a tabulator stop at the point that requires the least forward and backward spacing. (Space forward for short amounts, back for long amounts.) Forms should be designed to allow a tab stop to serve for more than one item, as in the address and quantity items below.

Abbreviations. Periods may be omitted after abbreviations and in columns of figures where a rule separates the dollars and cents. Some customary abbreviations and symbols are gal., ft., ea., %, @, C for hundreds, M for thousands, # for *No.* The limited space on business forms makes it desirable to abbreviate names of months.

Capitalization. Usually, cap only the first word and any proper nouns or adjectives in an item.

Spacing. SS invoices, statements, credit memorandums, purchase requisitions and orders, and similar forms. (With only 2 or 3 single-line items, DS). If an item runs into 2 or more lines, indent the second and subsequent lines and DS between the items, as illustrated below.

Centering Items. There is no hard-and-fast rule for centering data in columns. Generally, short items (in columns other than the *Description* column) are centered visually. Exact centering is neither required nor recommended. Begin the descriptive items about 2 spaces to the right of the rule.

Problem 1: Purchase Order with Ruled Columns
(WB p. 105)

Use printed forms if they are available. If you must use plain paper, arrange the typewritten material on a half sheet as it would be on a printed form. *Do not type copy that would be printed on a form.*

PHILLIPS INTERNATIONAL COMPANY
24 East 40th Street
New York, NY 10016
Cable: PHICO
Telephone (212) 434-7891

Purchase Order

		Words
Order No.	5661	1
Date	Aug. 12, 19--	4
Terms	Net 30	11
Shipped Via	Reliance Transport	15

Middlesex Industries Corp.
45723 Peace Pipe Trail
Rockford, Ill 61103

Set margin stop

Set tab stop

Quantity	Cat. No.	Description	Price	Total	Words
12	22-126	12-volt DC power converters	22.95	275.40	33
8	22-077	10" x 2 1/8" x 5 1/8" DC power timing lights	24.95	199.60	40 / 47
8	27-129	Transistorized DC-to-AC power inverters	58.25	466.00	55 / 60
				941.00	62
Reset margin only when necessary	*Center visually; set tab stop*	*Set tab 2 spaces from the rule*	*Reset "Order No." tab stop only when necessary*	*Center visually; set tab stop*	

BY _____

PURCHASING AGENT

Insert paper

1. Adjust the **paper guide (8)** as directed on page iii, at the back of this book.

2. Pull the **paper bail (11)** forward—toward you—with your right hand.

3. Grasp the paper with your left hand, the thumb under the sheet, as shown below.

4. Drop the bottom edge of the paper behind the **cylinder (14)** and against the **paper guide (8)**. At the same time, bring the right hand to the right **cylinder knob (19)** and twirl the knob with a quick movement of the fingers and thumb.

5. Push the **paper bail (11)** back to hold the paper against the cylinder or platen; position **paper-bail rolls (13)** to divide paper into thirds.

Set margin stops

1. Some typewriters have hand-set margin stops; others have key-set margin stops. Note the illustration at the top of the next column. Determine whether your typewriter has hand-set or key-set margin stops.

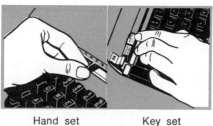

Hand set   Key set

2. Set the **left margin stop (7)** 25 spaces to the left of the center of the paper.

3. Set the **right margin stop (15)** at the end of the scale. As you will type copy line for line in the first lessons, you do not need the right margin stop to indicate the line ending.

NOTE: To set margin stops on *your* typewriter, refer to Reference Guide pages iii-iv.

Adjust the line-space regulator

1. Set the **line-space regulator (5)** on "2" for double-spacing the lines you are to type in Lesson 1.

2. When directed to single-space, set the line-space regulator on "1." When directed to triple-space, set the regulator on "3."

Line-space regulator

Take correct typing position

Note the following features of good typing position:

1. Sit back in chair; body erect

2. Feet on floor, one slightly ahead of the other

3. Fingers curved and upright; wrists low

4. Forearms parallel to slant of keyboard; elbows in comfortable position at sides

5. Eyes on copy

Take the correct typing position as illustrated below.

EYES ON COPY

FINGERS CURVED; WRISTS LOW

ELBOWS NEAR THE BODY; FOREARMS PARALLEL TO SLANT OF KEYBOARD

SIT BACK IN CHAIR; BODY ERECT

TEXTBOOK AT RIGHT OF MACHINE, ELEVATED FOR EASY READING

TABLE FREE OF UNNEEDED BOOKS

FEET ON FLOOR, ONE JUST AHEAD OF THE OTHER

Problem 4: Composing a Letter

Read quickly the following letter. It illustrates a number of errors commonly made by letter writers. The circled numbers in the body of the letter are keyed to the numbered comments below the letter. Compare the numbered statements and the comments.

On plain paper revise the letter, observing the numbered comments. Use a 60-space line and modified block style with open punctuation, as illustrated on page 137. Try starting on Line 15. If your revision of the letter is shorter, start your final copy lower.

November 15th, 19--
①

②
John M. Kingman, Pres③
Firestone Stores, Inc.
1472 Frontenac, SE④
Grand Rapids, MI 49508

Dear Mr. Kingman

Your letter about projectors was received by us on Nov. 1⑤ It⑥ affords us great pleasure⑦to tell you about the projectors this company⑧manu-factures.

It is my opinion⑨that our Model B fits the requirements outlined in your letter. This projector is described on page 12 of our catalog. ⑩It projects opaque material, glass slides, clippings, and postcards. Between you and I⑪this is the handiest projector you will be able to find just about anywhere. ⑫

The Model B sells for $375. An order blank is attached herewith⑬ for your convenience.⑭Hoping to hear from you soon, we are ⑮

Yours very truly

Jim Henderson, Sales③ Mgr.

Enc.⑯

You will not find it difficult to improve the foregoing letter. Before you rewrite it, consider each of these comments by number.

1 This form in the dateline is considered passé. (In the body of the letter, however, "the 15th" or "the 15th of November" would be correct.)

2 Use a personal title before the name of the addressee. It's essential.

3 Business titles should be spelled out.

4 SE is correct; however, S.E. (with periods) is more commonly used.

5 Spell out the name of the month.

6 The reader doesn't care when you received his letter. He may, however, be dismayed by your slow reply.

7 *Your* pleasure! What about the reader's pleasure?

8 *This company? We* is more personal.

9 Obvious. Unneeded.

10 Some may question the use of *It*, because the nearest antecedent is *catalog*. The catalog couldn't project, however, so the meaning appears clear.

11 *Between you and I* is a clumsy attempt to make the letter personal. Besides, it contains a grammatical error.

12 Sweeping statements don't convince; facts do.

13 Where else would it be attached?

14 You want him to *use* the blank. Say so.

15 Passé. An unconvincing closing. (The reader may buy the projector out of pity.)

16 *Enc.*, while acceptable, is perhaps less attractive than is *Enclosure*.

1A   Finger Position   For electric typewriters, turn ON-OFF switch to ON position.

Left hand   Right hand

1. With the help of the chart above, locate the left-hand guide or home keys on your typewriter: **A S D F**. Place the left-hand fingers on these keys.

2. Now locate the right-hand home keys: **J K L ;**. Place the right-hand fingers on these keys.

3. Take your fingers off the home keys. Replace them, saying the keys for each as you touch them: **ASDF JKL;**. (*Repeat.*)

4. To space after typing a letter or a word, operate the **space bar (27)** with a quick down-and-in motion of the right thumb.

5. Curve and hold the fingers lightly over the home keys. Hold the right thumb over the middle of the space bar. Keep your wrists low and relaxed.

6. Type the line below. Think and say each letter as you strike it.

```
ff jj dd kk ss ll a; sl dk fj a; sl dk fj a; fj fj
```

1B   Carriage (Element Carrier) Return

To space the paper forward (upward) and return to the beginning of the line, use the **lever (1)** on a manual (nonelectric) typewriter or the **return key (1)** on an electric typewriter, as described and illustrated below.

Manual (Nonelectric). Move the left hand, fingers bracing one another, to the carriage return lever and move the lever inward to take up the slack; then return the carriage with a quick wrist-and-hand motion. Drop the hand to typing position without letting it follow the carriage across. Return the carriage. Operate the space bar several times and return again.

Electric. Reach the little finger of the right hand to the return key; tap the key and release it quickly. Return the fingers to home position.

On Selectric typewriters, the return key returns the element carrier (not a carriage) to the left margin.

PHILLIPS INTERNATIONAL COMPANY

Manufacturer of
Electronic Equipment

24 East 40th Street
New York, New York 10016

Cable: PHICO
Telephone (212) 434-7891

Words
4

February 25, 19--

Universal Industries Corporation   10
19874 Chamberlain Drive   15
New Orleans, LA 70122   20

Attention line   Attention Training Department   26

Gentlemen   28

Subject or   SUBJECT: Standard Letter Setup   34
reference line

This is a sample of an outgoing letter from Phillips Inter-   46
national Company. Study this letter and conform as closely   58
as possible to the style illustrated. The various points   69
illustrated are fully explained in the report on letter styles   82
included in the handbook.   87

Type the attention line at the left margin, a double space   99
below the address. If you know the addressee's name, use it   111
above the company name in the address. Note that we also   123
prefer to have the subject line centered a double space below   135
the salutation. We should try in all our letters to make the   148
paragraphs of fairly uniform length and to keep reasonably   160
even right margins without overworking the hyphen.   170

The complimentary close should start at the midpoint, fol-   182
lowed by three blank line spaces and the signer's name and   193
title. Numbered enclosure notations are handled as shown   205
below.   207

Your cooperation in following these guides will be appreciated.   220

Very truly yours   223

Kathleen E. Hopkins

Mrs. Kathleen E. Hopkins   228
Communications Manager   233

FL   233

Enclosure   Enclosure   235
notation   M-306-A   237

1C Home-Key Stroking Practice

Type the lines as shown below. Think the letters as you type. Do not type line numbers or identifications.

Stroking Cue. Curve your fingers. Hold them lightly over the home keys. Strike and release a key quickly; then strike the next one the same way.

1 f j d k   ff jj ff jj fj fj fj dd kk dd kk dk dk dk fj dk fj   Return without looking up

2 s l a ;   ss ll ss ll sl sl sl aa ;; aa ;; a; a; a; sl a; sl

3 Home keys   dk fj dkfj a; sl a;sl dkfj a;sl a;sldk a;sldkfj a;   Think and say each letter

4 Home keys   all fall all fall ad lad ad lad as ask as ask fall

5 Space once after ;   a lad; as a lad; a lad asks dad; ask all; all fall

1D Location of H and E

1. Locate the new key on the keyboard chart, below.
2. Locate the new key on your typewriter keyboard.
3. Reach controlling finger to the new key a few times.
4. Type the location drill for that key as directed.

Type H with J finger

Type E with D finger

Touch **hj** lightly several times without moving the other fingers from their typing position. *Type Line 1, below, for tryout.*

Touch **ed** lightly several times, lifting the first finger slightly to free the *d* finger. *Type Line 2, below, for tryout.*

1E Location Drills for H and E   Type the lines as shown; then repeat them.

h   hj hj hj has hash lash dash hall halls shall shall

e   ed ed ed led fled led fled sale lake feel led sled

h e   he led a lad; he has a sled; he seeks a safe deal;

h e   she has; she has a desk; he has; he has had a desk

Space with a down-and-in motion

4. Keep margins reasonably even, balancing 554
appearance against ease of reading. 561
When necessary to divide a word, follow 569
the divisions shown in our company 576
word-division manual. 581

Complimentary Close 588

1. Start the complimentary close at the cen- 597
terpoint of the letterhead. 603
2. As with the salutation, no punctuation 612
follows the complimentary close. Capi- 619
talize only the first word. 625
3. The salutation and closing should agree 634
in formality. Examples: 639

(Tabulate with 6 spaces between columns)

Formal; Semiformal	Very Formal	
Gentlemen or Ladies	Sir or Madam	651
Dear Mr. Jones	Reverend Sir	658
Dear Ms. Wilson	My dear Mr.	663
	Ambassador	669
		671
Very truly yours	Respectfully	677
Sincerely yours	yours	680
Cordially yours		683

4. Do not end a letter with a phrase such 692
as "Thanking you, we remain" or "Hop- 699
ing to hear from you soon." 705

Signature Lines 711

1. Type the name of the dictator and his 719
or her title on all outgoing mail only. 727
Do not use a personal title before a male 736
dictator's name. We consider it courte- 744
ous for a female dictator to use Miss, 752
Ms., or Mrs. before her typewritten 760
name. 762
2. If, for example, James Cochran dictates 771
a letter for the signature of Walter 778
Adams, show this fact in a reference no- 786
tation: JC:xx (see Reference Initials, 797
No. 1). 799

Reference Initials and Enclosure Notations 816

1. Only the initials of the typist need appear 826
as the reference except as noted in No. 2, 835
above. 836
2. Attachments or enclosures in the letter 845
are noted by Enclosure typed a double 854
space below the reference initials. The 863
number of enclosures may be noted, but 870
this is optional. 874
3. If any serial-numbered documents are 882
enclosed, list their numbers below the 890
enclosure notation for better identifica- 898
tion. 899

Carbon Copies 905

1. Make all carbon copies on regular 8½- 913
by 11-inch white COPY paper. 919
2. When an interoffice memorandum is ad- 927
dressed to several individuals and carbon 935
copies will suffice, use onionskin for all 944
but the original copy. 949

Export Letters 955

1. A white onionskin copy of every export 963
letter must be sent to the Export De- 970
partment, regardless of the originating 978
department. 981
2. Type letters to Export District Repre- 989
sentatives in foreign countries on Form 997
M-205-E, green interoffice onionskin. 1005

Envelopes 1009

1. We prefer the large No. 10 envelopes for 1018
all letters on 8½- by 11-inch paper, even 1026
1-page letters. 1030
2. With half-size sheets and single onion- 1038
skin copies, use the small No. 6 envelopes. 1047
3. Do not address envelopes for the follow- 1056
ing unless the material enclosed is per- 1063
sonal or confidential: 1068
Interoffice correspondence 1074
District representatives 1078
Service representatives 1083
4. Address envelopes in block style, single- 1092
spaced, to agree exactly with the inside 1100
address. 1102

Problem 3: Sample Company Letter
(WB p. 103)

*Modified block style, open punctuation; 60-space line; date on
Line 15; correct errors*

Type the letter illustrated on page 137 as directed above.

1F Technique Practice: STROKING

Type the lines once; then repeat them.
Type at an easy, controlled pace.

Stroking Cue. Snap the finger quickly toward the palm of the hand as you release the key.

Home keys
```
all lads fall; ask a lad; a fall fad; ask all lads
```

h e
```
he had a sled; he sells desks; a shelf held a safe
```

All keys
```
she sells jade; he held a lead; he has had a sale;

sell all desks; see a hall safe; she has had jade;
```

1G Lesson Windup Remove paper; center carriage; turn off electrics.

1. Raise or pull forward the **paper bail (11)**. Operate the **paper-release lever (16)** with your right hand.

2. Remove paper with left hand. Return paper-release lever to normal position with right thumb.

3. Depress the **right carriage release (18)**; hold the platen knob firmly. Center the carriage (approximately).

LESSON 2

2A Ready to Type for each lesson in this section

1. Move front frame of typewriter even with edge of desk.
2. Adjust **paper guide (8)** and **paper bail (11)**.
3. Engage **paper release (16)**.
4. Set **line-space regulator (5)** on "1" for single spacing (SS).

5. Set **left margin stop (7)** about 25 spaces to left of center of paper; move **right margin stop (15)** to end of scale. *Note and use the numbers on the* **margin scale or paper-bail scale (11)** *for stop settings for this lesson and remaining lessons of this section.*

2B Preparatory Practice Type the lines as shown.

Typing Position. Sit erect; feet on floor; wrists low; fingers curved. (See illustration on page 3.)

Stroking Cue. Strike the keys sharply; release them quickly.

1 Home keys
```
fj dk sl a; fd jk fds jkl fdsa jkl; fdsa jkl; fjdk
```
2
```
fj dk sl a; fd jk fds jkl fdsa jkl; fdsa jkl; fjdk
```

DS (operate return twice)

3 h e
```
hj ed hj ed he she shed he held all hall shall has
```
4
```
hj ed hj ed he she shed he held all hall shall has
```

DS (double-space)

5 All letters
```
he led; she fled; he held a desk; she has had jade
```
6 learned
```
he led; she fled; he held a desk; she has had jade
```

TS (triple-space)

Some companies issue a communications handbook to typists, stenographers, and secretaries who handle correspondence. The following instructions on letter style are typical of those included in such handbooks. Assume that these guides have been taken from the handbook of Phillips International Company.

Problem 2: Leftbound Report on Letter Style

Use leftbound report style. SS and indent the enumerations from the left margin only; block the second and subsequent lines; DS between items. (Reference: page 121)

Words

LETTER STYLE 3
TS

Throughout our organization, letter style 11
DS
should be uniform. Use the style illustrated 20

in this manual. Note the following explana- 28

tory points: 31
TS

Dateline 34

1. Start the dateline at the centerpoint of 43
the letterhead. 47
2. If necessary, show the date dictated di- 55
rectly below the date of transcription. 64
3. Do not abbreviate the month nor use 71
end-of-line punctuation. 77
TS

Address 80

1. Use a complete address, with the ap- 87
proved two-letter abbreviations for state 96
names, and the ZIP Code. 101
2. Type the letter address in block style. 110
Use punctuation only with abbreviations. 118
If you have your correspondent's letter- 126
head, follow exactly the form and style 134
of the company name as shown. 140
3. When possible, address the letter to an 149
individual rather than to a company. 157
Use an appropriate personal title. 164

Attention Line 170

1. The use of an attention line is decreasing 179
in favor of No. 3, above. When used, 187
type it a double space below the address. 195
We prefer to have it flush with the left 204
margin. 205
2. The word Attention is followed by either 216
an individual's name or a title designat- 224
ing an individual or a group of people 232

(for example, Purchasing Agent or Per- 243
sonnel Department). 250
3. For the correct salutation with an atten- 259
tion line, see Salutation, No. 5. 268

Salutation 272

1. Type the salutation a double space below 281
the address or the attention line. 288
2. The salutation should agree with the ad- 297
dress: for a firm, Gentlemen or Ladies 308
and Gentlemen; for an individual, Dear 319
Mr. Smith or My dear Ms. Wilson. 332
3. We prefer open punctuation; therefore, 341
no mark follows the salutation. 347
4. Leave one blank line space above and 355
below the salutation. 360
5. Because a letter with an attention line is 369
addressed to a company, the preferred 377
salutation is Gentlemen. 384

Subject Line or Reference Line 396

1. When requested, type this information a 405
double space below the salutation. We 413
prefer to have it centered. 418
2. If desired, the subject title may be pre- 427
ceded by the word SUBJECT: (all caps 435
followed by a colon). 439
3. Some correspondents ask that our reply 448
state a file or case number. We prefer 456
to have this number typed as a subject 464
line. Such a notation is preceded by 471
REFERENCE: or RE: (all caps followed 479
by a colon). 481

Body of the Letter 489

1. We prefer block paragraphs. 495
2. Single-space all but very short letters 504
(two- or three-line letters of transmittal, 513
for instance). Double-space these very 521
short letters and indent the first line five 530
to ten spaces. 533
3. Keep paragraphs of proportionate length 542
if possible. 545

(Continued on page 136)

2C Left Shift Key Type each line twice SS; DS after second typing of line.

To type a capital letter controlled by a finger of the right hand, depress the **left shift key (28)** with the **a** finger without twisting the elbow or moving the other fingers from typing position. Hold the shift key down until you have typed the capital. Release the shift key quickly and return the finger to typing position.

    Ja Ja Ja Jake Jake Ha Ha Hall Hall La La Lake Lake
                                                              DS
    Jake led; Jeff fled; Hal fell; Les Hall; Jake Lake

2D Technique Practice: STROKING

Type each line twice SS; then DS.

Stroking Cue. Avoid sidewise (slanting) strokes. Hold the hands directly over the keys. Type with quick, sharp strokes.

 Incorrect finger alignment

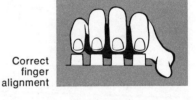 Correct finger alignment

1 **All letters learned are**
2 **used**

3

4

5

6

7

    Les leads; Jeff led all fall; Les has a safe lead;

    Lee led; Hal fled; Jake had a sale; he sells jade;

    Jeff Lake has a safe lease; Jake held a jade sale;

    Hal leads all jade sales; Les Lee heads all sales;

    Jess Leeds led all fall; he has held a shell sale;

    Jeff Leeds seeks a safe deal; Jake has had a deed;

    Les Kale had a hall desk; he has had a sales desk;

Return without looking up

2E Pica or Elite Type

Does your typewriter have pica or elite type? The first line shown below is in pica type; the second, in elite type. Compare your type size with those shown below:

10 pica spaces to a horizontal inch
12 elite spaces to a horizontal inch (2.5 cm)

in.		1		2		3	
cm	1	2	3	4	5	6	7	8	

Note that pica type is larger than elite type. As a result, there are 10 pica spaces to an inch; 12 elite spaces.

The cylinder or carriage scale range is from 0 to 110 or more on elite machines; from 0 to 90 or more on pica machines.

2F Center Point of Paper

When paper is inserted with the left edge at 0 on the cylinder or carriage scale, the horizontal center point of 8½″ by 11″ paper will be 51 (or 50 for convenience) on elite machines; 42 on pica machines.

Tryout. Remove the paper from the machine. Place the left and right edges together. Make a slight crease at the exact center at the top.

Reinsert the paper with the center at 50 for elite type or at 42 for pica type (unless your instructor directs you to use another center point).

Move the paper guide against the left edge of the paper. For ease in centering your copy later, check to see that the paper guide is in this position at the beginning of each practice period.

Prepare an original copy of each form or report. Erase and correct errors on problem copy.

Interoffice correspondence

An interoffice letterhead form is used for correspondence between offices or departments of a company. Printed headings on the forms, if positioned in the left margin, allow a one-inch margin setting to work for all the lines of the memorandum, including the headings. When typing an interoffice memorandum on plain paper, start the headings at the left margin to block on the left or space forward from the left margin as necessary to block the headings on the right.

Parts Omitted. Personal titles (*Mr., Mrs., Dr., Miss, Ms.*, etc.), the salutation, the complimentary close, and the signature lines are usually omitted.

Margins; Spacing. One-inch side margins are used.* Very short messages may be double-spaced for appearance; longer ones are single-spaced with a double space between paragraphs. Triple-space after the last line of the heading.

Reference Initials; Notations. Type reference initials at the left margin, a double space below the last line

of the message. Type other notations (*Enclosure, cc,* etc.) in the same position as in regular correspondence.

Envelopes for Interoffice Correspondence. When you use a regular envelope and no postage is required, type the words COMPANY MAIL in the space normally used for the postage stamp.

Use a personal title with the name in the envelope address. Use two lines, as shown below, unless the envelope is to go outside the building, in which case use the complete address.

* *Margin settings: pica, 10 and 75; elite, 12 and 90 (plus the adjustment figure).*

```
                                    COMPANY MAIL




        Mr. Frank Keefe
        Credit Manager
```

Problem 1: Interoffice Memorandum on Basic Rules of Dictating (WB p. 101)

Words

PHILLIPS INTERNATIONAL COMPANY
Interoffice Communication

24 East 40th Street
New York, NY   10016

		Words
Printed headings		
TO:	Letter Dictators	3
Omit personal title		
FROM:	Kathleen E. Hopkins, Communications Manager	12
DATE:	May 15, 19--	15
SUBJECT:	Basic Rules of Dictating	20

Omit salutation

1" side margins   Regardless of the dictation method used, the basic rules are the   33
same. These guides will improve the quality of your letters: 45

SS; DS between   1. Assemble needed materials before dictating. Make a mental out-   58
¶s and enumer-   line or jot down and organize ideas into a logical sequence.   69
ated items   Make sure to include all important information.   81

Start enumerated   2. Speak clearly, with special care on word endings for accuracy   93
items at left   in plurals and past tenses. After dictating a difficult or   105
margin; block   unusual word, spell it. Indicate paragraphs, too.   117
lines

Letters cost money. A good letter also <u>earns</u>. Help your secretary   132
Omit complimentary   to improve the quality of your letters.   140
close and
signature   xx   140

3A Ready to Type Review READY TO TYPE, page 6.

1. Align machine with edge of desk.
2. Adjust paper guide.
3. Insert paper; adjust paper bail.
4. Set machine on "1" for SS.
5. Set the left margin stop about 25 spaces to the left of the center of
the paper; move the right margin stop to the end of the scale.
6. Observe posture points, page 3.

3B Preparatory Practice each line at least twice

Type Line 1 twice SS; then DS after the 2-line group. Type the remaining lines in the same way.

Stroking Cue. Keep the fingers deeply curved and your wrists low and steady. Type with quick, sharp strokes.

a; sl dk fj ed hj a;sl fjdk edhj Ja Ja Ka Ka La La

Return quickly without looking up

he held she shell all fall hall led lead sell fell

Space once after ;

Lee fell; Hal had all; Jess Hall held a fall sale;

3C Location of I and T

Type I with K finger

Type T with F finger

Reach the *k* finger up to *i*; lift the *j* finger slightly for improved stroking control. *Type Line 1, below, for tryout.*

Straighten the *f* finger slightly; reach to **t** without arching the wrist. *Type Line 2, below, for tryout.*

3D Location Drills for I and T

Type each line twice SS; *DS* after the second typing of each line.

Keep the fingers curved over the home keys. Make short, direct reaches to such keys as *e*, *t*, and *i*.

1	i	ik ik ik if is his like dike file fill lid did hid
2	t	tf tf tf let take tall tale the hat that last late
3	i t	ik tf ik tf fit sit; if it is; if he is; it is the
4	Review	Kate had a late file; if it is the; the last list;
5	Review	I had a list; Keith has left his list at the lake;

Wrists and hands still

75D Problem Typing Measurement ㉚

Get Ready to Type	4′
Timed Production	20′
Proofreading	6′

Apply the standard rules for problems learned in earlier lessons. Erase and correct errors as you type.

Problem 1: One-Page Unbound Report

Full sheet; DS; SS table; leave 10 spaces between columns; last line of table is longest

	Words
COMPETENCIES OF BEGINNING	5
OFFICE WORKERS	8

(¶ 1) The following table shows the office — 16
competencies rated as essential for a begin- — 24
ning office worker, as reported by 161 organi- — 33
zations. Only the top five competencies are — 42
shown here. They were taken from a table — 51
listing 53 items.[1] (*Tabulate*) — 55

		Words
File alphabetically	84.5%	60
Handle telephone communications	80.7	67
Type envelopes	75.2	71
Use appropriate office procedure	74.5	79
Use manual or electric typewriter	73.3	87

(¶ 2) The ability to file alphabetically and — 94
the ability to use the telephone were rated — 103
highly by four out of five organizations in the — 113
survey. Nearly three out of every five of the — 122
organizations stated that the ability to use a — 131
manual or electric typewriter was essential. — 141
Fewer than one out of a hundred, however, — 149
stated that the ability to use an electric type- — 158
writer was more important than the ability — 167
to use a manual machine. — 172 / 176

[1] David L. Lemmer, "Office Skills Survey," — 184
The Balance Sheet, Vol. LIV, No. 8 (May, — 196
1973), p. 354. — 199

Problem 2: Second Page of Leftbound Report

Full sheet; number the page; DS

	Words
Be Natural	4

Nearly all the experts on letter writing say — 13
that the secret of doing this job well is to talk — 23

Supplies Needed: 1 ½-size and 2 full-size sheets.

	Words
to your reader. Be natural; pretend he's sit-	32
ting in your office. Talk to him face to face.	42
Give your letters the desirable human touch.	51
A recent article by Flesch states:	59

Express your natural feelings. If it's good — 69
news, say you're glad; if it's bad news, — 76
say you're sorry. Be as courteous, polite, — 85
and interested as you'd be if the addressee — 93
sat in front of you.[1] — 98 / 101

[1] Rudolf Flesch, "Write the Way You Talk," — 110
Reader's Digest (August, 1973), p. 122. — 120

Problem 3: Topic Outline

Half sheet inserted with long edge at left; 1½″ top margin; 45-space line; spread heading; provide the figure and letter designations for the appropriate lines; capitalize, space, and punctuate correctly; add accents for résumé with pen or pencil

	Words
applying for a job	7
the interview	11
preliminary preparation	16
making an appointment	22
learning about the job	27
analyzing yourself	32
conduct during the interview	38
dressing appropriately	44
being on time	47
answering questions	52
maintaining a friendly attitude	59
the written résumé	64
advance preparation	69
including factual data	74
listing references	79
material left with interviewer	86

3E Location of C and . (Period)

Type C with D finger

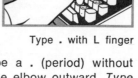

Type . with L finger

Reach down to **c** with the *d* finger without twisting the elbow in or out or moving the hand down. *Type Line 1, below, for tryout.*

Extend the *l* finger down to type a . (period) without moving the hand downward or the elbow outward. *Type Line 2, below, for tryout.*

3F Location Drills for C and . each line twice SS; DS after second typing of each line

Spacing Rule. Space once after . (period) used at the end of an abbreviation; twice after . at the end of a sentence except when it is the last stroke in the line; then return the carriage without spacing.

c   cd cd cd dcd call sick check clad lacks jack stack

.   .l .l .l l.l adj. alt. La. Ill. Hal led all sales.   Return without
                                                                  spacing after .

c .   Jack called. He lacks a check. Lt. Leach has it.

c .   His chief has a late file. Let Kit take the cash.

3G Technique Practice: STROKING each line once DS; repeat

Home-Row Stroking. Strike each key firmly; release it quickly, snapping the finger toward the palm of the hand.

Third-Row Stroking. Reach your finger to the third row (above home row) without arching the wrist or moving the hand forward.

First-Row Stroking. Make the reach to the first (bottom) row without moving the elbow in or out or changing the hand alignment.

All keyboard characters learned are used.

1	Home row	fj dk sl a; all fall; all lads fall; ask all lads;	Sharp strokes; quick release
2	h and e	she has jade; she leads all sales; she sells sleds	
3	i and t (3d row)	it is; he hit it; he is still ill; take this list;	Finger reaches
4	c and . (1st row)	Jack called Lee. His chief cashed all the checks.	
5	All letters learned are used	I see that Jack has the file. Keith has the list.	Still wrists and elbows
6	in Lines 5-8	I shall take this deed. Jack Hale is at his desk.	
7		Kit Hale has all the files. He has the last list.	
8		Lt. Leach said he cashed the checks that Kit left.	

LESSON 75

75A Preparatory Practice ⑤ each line twice

Alphabet Judge Vray promised to bring the portable screen for next week's quiz.

Subscripts They asked each of us to type these formulas: H_2O, H_2SO_4, and Na_2CO_3.

Figure/symbol Serial #81547 was stamped on the engine; Model #2093 (6) was below it.

Fluency Both speed and control will improve if you do your work well each day.

| 1 | 2 | 3 | 4 | 5 | 6 | 7 | 8 | 9 | 10 | 11 | 12 | 13 | 14 |

75B Technique Practice: STROKING ⑦ 1' writing on each line; compare GWAM

1 Long words   Government agencies and associations give help in developing programs.

2 Double letters Will Bill and Jess Phillips do well to pass up the offer from Russell?

3 Adjacent keys Twelve folk singers hope to buy an excellent bass viol and new guitar.

4 3d/4th fingers Polly was puzzled by six quaint wax dolls in an antique dealer's shop.

5 Direct reaches Young Lord Cecil received a large grant of undeveloped land in Africa.

6 Home row   Did Dale Flagg laugh after Sally asked that she look at the joke book?

| 1 | 2 | 3 | 4 | 5 | 6 | 7 | 8 | 9 | 10 | 11 | 12 | 13 | 14 |

75C Growth Index ⑧ one 5' writing; determine GWAM and errors

All letters are used.

	GWAM 1'	5'

¶ 1
1.5 SI
5.6 AWL
80% HFW

Almost anyone who works in an office needs special skills. They
are basic to success on the job. Equally prized are such qualities as
tact, loyalty, and enthusiasm. Because he does not attach enough importance to them, a worker will often fail to realize his aims. They are
needed, and they can be developed—just as the skills needed for a job
can be developed.

13 3 50
27 5 53
42 8 56
55 11 58
70 14 61
73 15 62

¶ 2
1.5 SI
5.6 AWL
80% HFW

"Tact," said Lincoln, "is the ability to describe others as they see
themselves." It is the lubricant that makes people work as a team, and
teamwork is an essential quality in getting through the complex affairs
of a busy office on time. Also needed is discretion. What one hears or
sees in an office must be held in the strictest of confidence. Remember,
you cannot be criticized for what you did not say.

14 17 65
28 20 67
43 23 70
57 26 73
72 29 76
82 31 78

¶ 3
1.5 SI
5.6 AWL
80% HFW

Generally, anyone expecting to advance in his company must like his
work. He must be willing to climb over an annoying hurdle or two to complete his job; for as one writer said, "In matters pertaining to enthusiasm, no man is sane who does not know how to be insane on the proper
occasion." Few factors are so damaging to company morale as the worker
who moves through his responsibilities in low gear.

14 34 81
28 37 84
43 40 87
57 42 90
71 45 92
81 47 94

1' GWAM | 1 | 2 | 3 | 4 | 5 | 6 | 7 | 8 | 9 | 10 | 11 | 12 | 13 | 14 |
5' GWAM | 1 | 2 | 3 |

LESSON 4

4A **Ready to Type** Review READY TO TYPE, page 6.

4B **Preparatory Practice** each line twice SS; DS after second typing of line

All strokes learned are used.

i t   ik ik tf tf dike fit that left lift jest tall tile   Eyes on copy

c .   cd cd .l .l sick lack lace call hack clad etc. La.

          Jack called; he has a check. Keith led this list.

4C **Technique Practice:** STROKING each line twice SS; DS after 2d typing of line

Strike each key with a sharp, quick movement of the fingers. The stroke should be downward toward the palm of the hand. Release the key quickly. Avoid pushing the key or raising the finger high over a key before striking it. Hold your fingers over the home keys. Raise them just enough to make quick, sharp strokes.

Striking the key   Releasing the key

All strokes learned are used.

1 Strike and release keys the chief had the file; he leads the skills class;   Return quickly with eyes on copy

2 quickly she had his aid; he held the jet; this is the list

3   it is; it is the; if it is; if it is the; if I had

4   I had the last list. Jack called; he had a check.

5   Jack cashed the check. Jeff had a safe cash deal.

6   Hal said Lt. Hale left the check file at his desk.

7   Jack Hill held the lead at the lake. He liked it.

4D **Right Shift Key** each line twice SS; DS after second typing of line

To type a capital letter controlled by a finger of the left hand, depress the **right shift key (26)** with the ; finger. Hold the shift key down until you have struck and released the key for the capital; then release the shift key. Return the finger to typing position without pausing. *Type the lines below for tryout.*

         Da Da Dale Dale Sl Sl Slade Slade Dale Slade Diele

         Dale has the list. Sid Fiske called. Alf led it.

74C Problem Typing Measurement ㉚

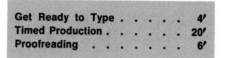
Problem 1: Two-Column Table

Full sheet; DS; reading position; SS heading; 12 spaces between columns; SS 2-line item and indent second line of an item 2 spaces

		Words
ESTIMATED RESEARCH AND DEVELOPMENT		7
EXPENDITURES | **IN COLLEGES AND UNI-**		13
VERSITIES		15
(In Thousands)		18
<u>Department or Agency</u>	<u>Amount</u>	29
Health, Education, and Welfare	$ 874,000	38
National Science Foundation	374,000	45
Defense––Military Functions	212,000	53
National Aeronautics and Space		59
Administration	119,000	65
Atomic Energy Commission	85,000	72
Agriculture	88,000	76
All other	<u>116,000</u>	82
	$1,868,000	84

Problem 2: Three-Column Table

Full sheet; DS; TS between groups; exact vertical center; spread the main heading; 6 spaces between columns

			Words
UNITED STATES EXPORTS			8
(In Millions)			11
<u>To</u>	<u>1970</u>	<u>1971</u>	16
Africa	$ 1,579	$ 1,694	20
Asia	10,082	9,850	24
Australia and Oceania	1,189	1,169	32
Canada	9,079	10,366	37
Other Western Hemisphere	6,532	6,484	45
Eastern Europe	354	384	51
Western Europe	<u>14.463</u>	<u>14.190</u>	59
	$43,278	$44,137	63

Problem 3: Business Letter with Table (WB p. 93)

Block, open punctuation; date on Line 15; 60-space line; SS and center table with 6 spaces between columns; 1 cc; address envelope

	Words
Current date | Miss Joyce Fessenden | 4865 West	9
Century Boulevard | Inglewood, CA 90304 |	17
Dear Miss Fessenden (¶ 1) I am pleased to	24
answer your letter about the future of job	33
openings. While no one can forecast the	41
future, some aspects of the job market can	50
be predicted quite accurately. (¶ 2) According-	57
ing to the U.S. Labor Department's Bureau	66
of Statistics, the five occupations with the	75
most openings each year during the 1970s are	84
as follows:	86

		Words
Stenographers/secretaries	247,000	93
Retail sales people	131,000	99
Hospital attendants	111,000	104
Mechanics/repairmen	89,200	110
Bookkeepers	74,000	114

(¶ 3) Apparently, automation has not affected 122
the need for secretaries. They are in great 131
demand today, and this demand will remain 139
with us. | Yours sincerely | Miss Amy Fitz- 147
gerald, Correspondent | xx 152/166

4E Continuity Practice: PHRASES AND SENTENCES   each line once SS; then each line once DS

All strokes learned are used.

1   file this lease; cash the check; tell the late lad
2   if he; if he is; if she; if she is; if he had this
3   she had a safe lead; if it fits; I shall see that;
4   Dick held a jade sale at Dike Lake late last fall.
5   This is the field test that Sid Dahl let Cal take.
6   Jack asked Cliff if he had set the last test date.

Type without
pauses between
strokes

LESSON 5

5A Preparatory Practice   each line twice SS; DS after second typing of line

All letters learned are used in each line.

she called; if it is; Cliff sells jade; I like it.
Cal let Al Hall take the jade; he is at Lief Lake.
Dick Jacks said that he let Les Lee take the file.

Type slowly
but steadily

5B Location of O and R

Type O with L finger

Type R with F finger

Reach the *l* finger up to type **o** without moving the hand forward or the elbow outward. *Type Line 1, below, for tryout.*

Reach the *f* finger to **r** without moving the other fingers from home-key positions. *Type Line 2, below, for tryout.*

5C Location Drills for O and R   each line twice SS; DS after second typing of line

All letters learned are used.

1 o   ol ol ol old old fold cold to took so sold do dole
2 r   rf rf rf rid risk sir air hair chair here are lard
3 o r   or for ford fork rock frock jar car soar cord roll
4 Review   Ceil Ford had their old car. She had a hard ride.
5 Review   He had the food for the fair. Rod heard the talk.

74A Preparatory Practice ⑦ each line twice; 1' writings on Lines 2 and 4

Alphabet   Marvin Bean required exactly a dozen jackets for the long winter trip.

Figure   Flight 697 will leave at 3:40 and arrive in Philadelphia at 12:58 p.m.

Figure/symbol   The interest rate on the 4-month note is $8\frac{1}{2}\%$; on the 1-year note, $7\frac{1}{4}\%$.

Fluency   Anyone who meets the public in the office must be tactful and patient.
　　　| 1 | 2 | 3 | 4 | 5 | 6 | 7 | 8 | 9 | 10 | 11 | 12 | 13 | 14 |

74B Typing from Revised Copy ⑬

Modified block, open punctuation; 60-space line; current date on Line 15; SS

This letter contains many errors commonly made by letter writers. Retype the letter as revised (WB p. 91)

Note the application
of these guides:

Words

Mr. Jasper Blair / 15892 Emmett Street / Beaumont, TX 77701 15

1	Use personal greeting.
2	Be concise.
3	Use personal pronoun.
4	Be concise.
5	Use short words.
6	Be concise.
7	Use simple words.
8–10	Be concise.
11	Reader knows ink is for press.
12	Use short words.
13	Be concise.
14	Use short sentences.
15	Use direct statements

Dear ~~Sir~~ Mr. Blair ① 18
②
~~Please be advised that~~ We, the people who helped put men on 25
the moon are working with problems closer to home. ③ We are ~~Our company~~ 37
~~is~~ science oriented~~, but at the same time, we~~ and are putting sci- 44
ence and its promise for the future to work ~~immediately~~ now. ⑤ 54
⑥
Our ~~company's~~ engineers have developed a new ~~kind of~~ 61
knitting ~~colossus~~ machine that can change patterns ~~more rapidly~~ faster ⑧ than 72
you can change sweaters. ~~Then, too,~~ They have ~~put together~~ also made ⑨ 81
today's most advanced newspaper ~~printing machine~~ press ⑩. The ink ~~for~~ 91
~~the press~~ ⑪ is computer controlled from one central location. 101
We are the world's largest ~~manufacturer~~ maker ⑫ of microcircuits. 111
~~We wish to inform you that these~~ ⑬ tiny circuits, ~~each of which~~ that 115
~~contains~~ 6,244 transistors, ⑨ They hand-size are used in electronic calculators. 131
~~that you can fit into your hand.~~ ⑭
Write for ⑮ We'll be glad 142
~~You may have~~ a copy of our annual report ~~by writing to~~ to send it free. 145
~~this company at the address above noted.~~

Yours very truly 148

Frank L. Moore 151/163

5D Location of Z and N

Type Z with A finger

Type N with J finger

Reach the *a* finger down to type **z** without moving the hand down or the elbow in or out. *Type Line 1, below, for tryout.*

Move the *j* finger down to type **n** without moving the other fingers from their home keys. *Type Line 2, below, for tryout.*

5E Location Drills for Z and N   each line twice SS; DS after second typing of each line

All letters learned are used.

1	z	aza za za za za haze jazz size zeal zoo doze froze
2	n	jnj nj nj nj nj an and then than can land hand not
3	z n	za nj za nj zone haze freeze fan ran rent kind den
4	Review	Fran Zier has land in this zone. The zoo is near.
5	Review	Zoe had lots of zeal and zest; this drill is done.

5F Spacing Summary   Type the line twice.

1. Space once after a period at the end of an abbreviation. Do not space after internal periods.

2. Space twice after . at the end of a sentence; once after ; used as punctuation.

3. At the end of a line, make the return without spacing after the final stroke.

Dr. Zier sent it c.o.d. Zoe called; Jane can act.

5G Continuity Practice: PHRASES AND SENTENCES   each line twice SS; then each line once DS

Continuity Cue. Type at a steady pace without pausing between strokes, words, or lines.

Stroking Cue. Type with your *fingers*, with minimum hand or arm motion. Use short, snappy strokes.

All strokes learned are used.

1	(From dictation)	to do; to do so; to do the; to do this; to do that	Short, quick strokes
2		it is; it is the; it is here; it is there; it does	
3		he can; he can take; he can seize it; in this zone	
4	(From the book)	The hard freeze forced the school to close at ten.	
5		Jake has size nine; he can send it to Scott c.o.d.	
6		Liz needs the land in this zone. Roz left at one.	

Problem 1: Letter with Centered Line

(WB p. 87)

Block style; open punctuation; 60-space line; date on Line 16

Words

Current date | Mrs Isabel Del Conte | 1728½   9
Simmons Avenue | Brockton MA 02401 | Dear   17
Mrs Del Conte (¶ 1) We can't promise to   24
make moving a picnic. No mover can. But if   33
a snag should develop during your move, we   41
guarantee you'll get more than a shoulder to   50
cry on. You'll get action, and you'll get it fast   60
because we want our service to live up to *(DS;*   69
center) YOUR EXPECTATIONS (¶ 2) The first   75
thing to do if you need help is to get in touch   84
with your Blue Star agent and tell the prob-   93
lem. Nine times out of ten the solution can   102
be worked out quickly. (¶ 3) If you need   109
more than local help, our toll-free hot line is   119
open to you. Pick up a phone--anywhere in   127
the country--and dial direct to Blue Star   136
Movers. We'll do our best to help you. So   144
when you need help or perhaps just a kind   153
word from people who care, call us. We want   162
to hear from you. | Yours very truly | LeRoy   170
R Fisher | Customer Relations | xx   177/189

Problem 2: Letter in Modified Block Style

(WB p. 89)

Modified block; mixed punctuation; 60-space line; date on Line 15

Words

Current date | The Honorable George Dens-   8
more | Mayor of the City of Scranton | City   16
Hall | Scranton PA 18510 | Dear Mr Mayor   25
(¶ 1) Used aluminum cans are worth as much   32
as $200 a ton. Unfortunately, many communi-   41
ties are just throwing them away; and that's   50
what we think should be stopped. (¶ 2) In   57
1970, we started a "Yes We Can" campaign   65

Words

to reclaim aluminum cans in the San Diego   74
and Dallas-Fort Worth areas. Since then, over   83
200 million cans have been reclaimed for re-   92
cycling in those cities alone. (¶ 3) We shall   100
pay as much as $200 a ton to any community   109
reclamation center for all the aluminum cans   118
it collects. We'll pay it because aluminum is   127
a practical packaging material for recycling.   136
(¶ 4) Read the enclosed brochure. Find out   144
how one community established its collection   153
center. We'll also send you a list of reclama-   162
tion centers. Just tell us you're interested. | 172
Respectfully yours | Lewis Archibald Man-   180
ager | Reclamation Division | xx | Enclosure   187/205

Problem 3: Personal Business Letter

Modified block style, mixed punctuation; 60-space line; start return address on Line 17; type enumeration double-indented with blocked lines

Words

10930 Waterman Street | Fort Worth Texas   8
76102 | November 17 19--   13

Allen & Howell Inc | 297 Causeway Boule-   21
vard | New Orleans LA 70212 | Gentlemen   29
(¶ 1) I am interested in buying a movie pro-   36
jector for general home use. Because I am   45
not an expert projectionist, the projector must   54
be easy to operate. In addition, I am inter-   63
ested in the following features: *(Enumerate)*   70
1. It should have instant playback, just like   79
TV. 2. It should be able to handle cassettes,   89
thus eliminating splicing and threading. (¶ 2)   97
Do you make a movie projector meeting the   106
foregoing requirements? If you do, please   114
send me a descriptive folder and let me know   123
where I may see a demonstration. | Yours   131
very truly | Miss Mary Ann Fielding   138/151

LESSON 6

6A Ribbon Control Lever

At the beginning of each practice period, set the ribbon-control lever to type on the upper part of the ribbon.

The **ribbon-control lever (22)** can be set to type on the upper, middle, or lower part of the ribbon (or, if there are 4 adjustments on the typewriter, in

stencil position). If there are only 3 adjustments, the typing will be done on the upper or lower part of the ribbon (or in stencil position).

When the ribbon control is in stencil position, the ribbon is disengaged.

6B Preparatory Practice   each line twice SS; DS after second typing of line

All reaches learned Roz called; Ed heard her. Flo thinks Jan is fine.

o r   so sold to told or for rod road role rock door oar

z n   size zone haze not daze kind seize one fizz on zoo

(From
Fluency dictation)   it is; if it is; to do; to do it; and to do; do so

6C Technique Practice: STROKING   each line twice SS; DS after second typing of line

Do not lean your hands over on the little fingers, or you will hit the keys with sidewise strokes.

Hold your hands directly over the home keys with fingers deeply curved. Strike the keys squarely.

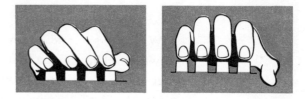

1 1st fingers   Jeff fir fine hen tin then join joint no nor north
2   He took tin to Jeff. Join the force in the north.

3 2d fingers   kind dent cite rake deck rack crack die died dried
4   Ken had a soft drink; he dried an oar on the deck.

5 3d/4th fingers sail loss hazed loaf load zeal hold salt jolt jail
6   Zoe can take the loaf; she had a jolt at the lake.

Hold the hands directly over the home keys

IF KEYS JAM

Key jamming is caused by striking a key before the preceding one is released or by a sluggish machine. To correct this fault, align fingers directly over the home keys and improve the timing of the strokes; or clean the typewriter.

To release jammed keys, proceed as directed at the right.

1. Use a special jammed-key release if your typewriter has this special key.

2. Depress the shift key; this sometimes works.

3. If the keys are still jammed, gently flick with your finger the stuck key nearest you; or push the keys slightly toward the platen to untangle them.

SECTION 11
Measurement: Basic and Problem Skills

LESSONS 73-75

Goal. In this section you will see how well you can type problems similar to those typed in prior lessons. Follow the directions given. Move quickly from one problem to the next.

Machine Adjustments. 70-space line; SS sentence drills; DS and indent ¶s 5 spaces; correct errors in all problem copy as you type. Circle uncorrected errors.

LESSON 73

73A Preparatory Practice ⑦ each line twice; then 1' writings on Lines 3 and 4

Alphabet	Ezra and John Voight played a number of quiet games with Clark Baxter.
Figure/symbol	Interest accumulated in 1975 to $436.08 when the rate increased by 2%.
Long words	Probability studies are particularly helpful in effective forecasting.
Fluency	You may find that some elements of their problems are hard to analyze.

| 1 | 2 | 3 | 4 | 5 | 6 | 7 | 8 | 9 | 10 | 11 | 12 | 13 | 14 |

73B Speed/Control Building ⑬

1. Type two 5' writings on the ¶s; the first for speed, the second for control.

2. Compare the *gwam* and number of errors on the 2 writings.

3. Proofread by comparing. Check with the original such words as *affect, success,* and *analyze.*

All letters are used.

	GWAM 1'	5'

¶ 1
1.4 SI
5.4 AWL
85% HFW

What we say and how we say it can influence those to whom we talk and write. The language that we use influences the reactions of our reader to us and to our thoughts. Therefore, how we think and express our ideas will significantly affect the success of our daily lives.

13 | 3 | 36
27 | 5 | 39
41 | 8 | 41
55 | 11 | 44

¶ 2
1.4 SI
5.4 AWL
85% HFW

All the top jobs in the modern world of business require an ability to write well——and the bigger the job, the more vital the writing skill. Sooner than you foresee, you may find yourself in a high-ranking job writing high-level letters and reports. Will you be ready and able?

14 | 14 | 47
28 | 17 | 50
42 | 19 | 53
56 | 22 | 55

¶ 3
1.4 SI
5.4 AWL
85% HFW

The writing flair that some people show is usually the result of years of careful effort. If you make a habit of analyzing the letters of others and also compose some yourself, you can develop a flair of your own. In fact, flair may be little more than word skill well applied.

13 | 25 | 58
28 | 28 | 61
42 | 30 | 64
56 | 33 | 66

1' GWAM | 1 | 2 | 3 | 4 | 5 | 6 | 7 | 8 | 9 | 10 | 11 | 12 | 13 | 14 |
5' GWAM | | 1 | | 2 | | 3 | |

Get Ready to Type . . . . . 4'
Timed Production . . . . . . 20'
Proofreading . . . . 6'

73C Problem Typing Measurement ㉚

On page 129, punctuation has been omitted in opening and closing lines. Provide those needed.

Type an original and 1 carbon copy of each letter. Correct errors; circle uncorrected errors.

Supplies Needed. Letterheads or plain paper; carbon paper; second sheets; appropriate envelopes.

6D Continuity Practice SENTENCE

Type each line 3 times SS. DS after the third typing of the line.

Continuity Cue. Type at a steady pace with fingers held directly over the keys.

All strokes learned are used.

1 He said that this is the size he sent to the fair.

No pauses between strokes

2 She can take the size she needs if it is in stock.

3 She had a zoo in this zone; she still has the zoo.

4 Fritz and Frank North do not like to ride at noon.

Type steadily

5 Jan lent a jar to Dan. Rod took the tire for Ann.

6 The staff thinks that Frank can find all the zinc.

7 Fern Thorne can take the late class at the school.

6E Sentence Guided Writing

1. Type each sentence twice without timing. Type at an easy, controlled pace. Avoid pausing after strokes and after words.

2. Type each sentence for 1 minute, trying to complete each sentence twice. (Your instructor may call the guide at the ½ minute to pace you.)

NOTE: Gross words a minute (*gwam*) are shown in Column 2 below.

All strokes learned are used.

		Words in Line *	GWAM 30″ Guide
1	Jane can take her to the fair.	6	12
2	I think the first act is too short.	7	14
3	Dick trained for the race at Lake Dietz.	8	16
4	Rod can teach the class; he can do the drill.	9	18
5	Nan can ride the horse; she can find the old road.	10	20

| 1 | 2 | 3 | 4 | 5 | 6 | 7 | 8 | 9 | 10 |

* How typewritten words are counted

Five strokes are counted as 1 standard typewritten word. The figures in the first column at the right of the copy show the number of 5-stroke words in each of the lines. The scale below the copy shows the word-by-word count (5 strokes per word) for each line.

To determine number of words typed in 1 minute

(1) Note the figure at the end of each complete line you typed during the writing. (2) For a partial line, note (from the scale below the drill) the point at which you stopped typing. (3) Add these figures to determine the total words typed in 1 minute (*gwam*).

72D Problem Typing Measurement ㉚ supplies needed: 3 sheets of plain 8½″ by 11″ paper

Get Ready to Type . . . . . . 4′
Timed Production . . . . 20′
Proofreading . . . . 6′

Problem 1: Second Page of a Topbound Report with Footnotes

Number page; DS. (References: style, pages 113-115; footnotes, pages 116-119); proofread; correct errors

	Words
(¶) Many business leaders believe the com-	8
puter to be the most remarkable development	16
of this decade. They say that it will bring	25
about the greatest changes in the entire his-	34
tory of mankind. A recent book on this sub-	43
ject states that: *(Double indent and SS the quotation)*	47

	Words
Computers are being used today to com-	54
pose music, write poetry, play chess or	62
tic-tac-toe, match men and women on the	70
basis of similar tastes, arrange class	78
schedules, keep airline schedules in order,	87
teach boys and girls how to read, sort	94
and route mail, and assist doctors in diag-	103
nosis and control of diseases.[1]	109

	Words
(¶) Another report states that the computer	117
can now be used to plan the logging of a	125
forest without causing either soil erosion or	135
the entire destruction of the forest. A simu-	144
lator can test the effects of a wide variety of	153
conditions in a matter of seconds.[2]	161
	164

	Words
[1] S. J. Wanous, E. E. Wanous, and Gerald	172
Wagner, Fundamentals of Data Processing	186
(Cincinnati: South-Western Publishing Co.,	195
1971), p. 4.	197
[2] "A Sixty-Year-Old Forest Simulated in a	206
Minute," Modern Data, Vol. 6, No. 7 (July,	216
1973), p. 27.	219

Problem 2: Short Unbound Report

DS; type the enumeration double-indented with blocked lines, SS. (Reference: pages 113-115) proofread; correct errors

	Words
ADDRESSING FOR OCR	4
(¶) The ZIP Code system of mail sorting was	12
started by the Post Office Department (now	20

	Words
the United States Postal Service Corporation)	30
on July 1, 1963. ZIP has been combined with	39
the Optical Character Reader (OCR) to pro-	47
vide electronic mail sorting in a number of	56
cities. The following guides for addressing	65
envelopes are compatible to OCR's reading	73
habits: *(Enumerate)* 1. All lines of the address	81
should be blocked at the left and single-spaced.	91
2. The last line of the address must contain	100
the city name, the state name or abbreviation,	109
and the ZIP Code. The Postal Service en-	117
courages the use of the two-letter ZIP abbre-	126
viations for state names (without periods or	135
spaces); however, these abbreviations may be	144
used only with ZIP Codes. 3. Addressee nota-	154
tions like Personal, Hold for Arrival, and	167
others should be typed a triple space below	176
the return address about three spaces from	185
the left edge in all caps or in caps and lower-	194
case, underlined. 4. Mailing notations, such	203
as AIRMAIL, REGISTERED, and the like, should	212
be typed below the stamp area and at least	221
three line spaces above the envelope address.	230

Problem 3: Leftbound Report with Table

Retype Problem 2 as a leftbound report, adding the copy given below. SS the lines of the table; leave 10 spaces between columns. Proofread; correct errors.

	Words
(¶ 2) There follow a few examples of state	237
names and their standard and ZIP abbrevia-	245
tions. Note that periods are retained in stan-	255
dard abbreviations. They are omitted in the	264
two-letter ZIP abbreviations.	269

			Words
California	Calif.	CA	274
Florida	Fla.	FL	277
Mississippi	Miss.	MS	281
Oklahoma	Okla.	OK	285

7A Preparatory Practice   each line 3 times SS; DS after third typing of line

All letters learned   Karl took the case; Jan needs it to send to Fritz.

Shift keys   Jack Steel and Ken Hale took the train to Red Oak.

Fluency (From dictation)   and the; and if the; and if it did; and it did the

Sit in an erect position

7B Technique Practice: DOUBLE LETTERS   each line twice SS; DS after second typing of line

Nonelectric. When typing double letters, do not allow full return of the key between strokes.

Electric. Allow time for the key to return to position before striking it again.

All letters learned are used.

soon took fool tool root cook door cool noon floor

fill till feel feet add jazz see class sheet steel

Al Steele took his class to the tool fair at noon.

Nell Coons can cross a street near the old school.

7C Location of U and W

Type U with J finger

Type W with S finger

Reach the *j* finger up to **u** without moving the other fingers from their home keys. *Type Line 1, below, for tryout.*

Reach the *s* finger up to **w** without moving the hand forward or arching the wrist. *Type Line 2, below, for tryout.*

7D Location Drills for U and W   each line twice SS; DS after second typing of each line

All letters learned are used.

1   u   uj uj uj us use due cue hut hurt fun sun nut nurse

2   w   ws ws ws wit with worn sworn how show win won when

3   u w   four sure just turn thus with work wish want would

4   Review   We know June wants to show the house to us at two.

5   Review   Zeke will join the hunt for the first week or two.

Quiet hands and wrists

72A Preparatory Practice ⑦ each line twice; then 1′ writings on Lines 1 and 4

Alphabet	Pete Fox and Sam Jay puzzled over the workbook acquired for geography.
Figure/symbol	Add the 4% sales tax of $7.22 (on $180.56) to Webb & Orr's bill #8390.
Drill on br	Brad's brother Bryant broke the bronze brooches and other bric-a-brac.
Fluency	The title to the land is now in the hands of the chairman of the firm.

| 1 | 2 | 3 | 4 | 5 | 6 | 7 | 8 | 9 | 10 | 11 | 12 | 13 | 14 |

72B Growth Index ⑧ one 5′ writing; determine GWAM and errors

All letters are used.

		5′ GWAM
¶ 1 1.5 SI 5.6 AWL 80% HFW	Some of the lessons in this textbook have developed a number of	3 | 43
	ideas on writing. Can you recall any of them? Here they are. Write	5 | 46
	as you speak; use ordinary words and phrases. Don't be pompous, fuzzy,	8 | 49
	or distant. Just remember, you have some ideas to send to a person who	11 | 51
	is human and agreeable. Write human, warm, natural letters.	14 | 54
¶ 2 1.5 SI 5.6 AWL 80% HFW	A look at some parts of letters will illustrate the foregoing	16 | 56
	points. Read this example: The rotary motor is so efficient and power-	19 | 59
	ful that more and more people are referring to it as the motor of the	22 | 62
	future. It operates like a fine watch and runs so quietly you cannot	24 | 65
	believe it. Ask your dealer for a demonstration very soon.	27 | 67
¶ 3 1.5 SI 5.6 AWL 80% HFW	Here is a good example: A good letterhead creates some magic about	30 | 70
	your name. It tells people what is special about you even before the	32 | 73
	letter itself says a word. That's why it is critical to make a good	35 | 75
	impression. Our letterheads are printed on paper that is very clear	38 | 78
	and magically opaque. Ask your supplier to show you samples.	40 | 81

5′ GWAM | 1 | 2 | 3 |

72C Composing a Short Summary ⑤ full sheet; unbound report style; DS

Compose as you type a short summary of the material in 72B, above. Proofread your copy, marking any necessary corrections. Retype in final form, providing an appropriate title for the summary.

7E Location of B and , (Comma)

Type B with F finger

Type , with K finger

Reach the *f* finger down to **b** without moving the hand from its typing position. *Type Line 1, below, for tryout.*

Reach the *k* finger down to , (comma). *Space once after a comma in a sentence. Type Line 2, below, for tryout.*

7F Location Drills for B and ,   each line twice SS; DS after second typing of each line

All strokes learned are used.

1	b	bf bf bf fbf bid fib fob bird bid bind bluff block
2	,	,k ,k ,k Kit, Ken, and Sue took a jet; I can, too.
3	b ,	to be, we can be, on the job, be sure, but it can,
4	Review	It will take us just two hours to cut these wires.
5	Review	Bud and Burt will count all the lots in this zone.

Center stroking in fingers

7G Continuity Practice: PHRASES AND SENTENCES   each line twice SS; then each line once DS

Continuity Cue. You have now learned the locations of and reaches to 19 letter keys. Type them without pauses between strokes and words.

Stroking Cue. Keep the correct hand alignment with the keyboard. As you make the down reaches, do not twist the hands or elbows out of position.

All strokes learned are used.

1 with us, and with us, he will, he will do the work

2 if we knew; if we knew how; if we know how to show

3 if it will, if it will be, but this, but this will

4 Bill holds a job with the new branch of this bank.

5 Liz went to New Wells in June; Buzz will join her.

| 1 | 2 | 3 | 4 | 5 | 6 | 7 | 8 | 9 | 10 |

Quiet hands and elbows

7H Technique Practice: LETTER RESPONSE   each line twice SS; DS after second typing of line

When typing one-hand words, type by *letter response* (think each letter); but pass from one letter to the next quickly. Speed up your typing by eliminating clumsy motions.

in as no at on are oil far kin set nil car ink add

was join face look dear kill wear hull trade farce

71D Problem Typing Review ㉚

Problem 1: Unbound Report with Spread Heading

Top margin, pica, 1½″, elite 2″; DS; spread the heading (References: style, pages 113-14; footnotes, pages 116-119)

Words

DATA PROCESSING 3

(¶ 1) Data processing is not new; it has been 11
around for centuries. Nor is the mechanical 20
processing of data a new development. In 29
fact, from the digital computer on his hands 38
and feet, man has progressed through the aba- 46
cus, the simple adding machine, and the elec- 55
tronic calculator to the modern electronic 64
computer. (¶ 2) In 1950, there were at most 72
15 electronic computers in use in the United 81
States. A recent book on the subject states 90
that by 1975 there will be 85 thousand in use; 99
and more than 3 million people will be needed 108
to operate them.[1] Another report states: 117
"The market for packaged computer software 125
and services, which totaled $770 million in 134
1972, will climb to $1.5 billion by 1982."[2] 143
(¶ 3) Computers were originally developed by 151
scientists and engineers to aid in the solu- 159
tion of problems involving large amounts of 168
computation. Today the computer is touching 177
the lives of virtually everyone; still, the evi- 187
dence shows that we have just begun to feel 195
its full impact. 199

202

[1] S. J. Wanous, E. E. Wanous, and Gerald 210
Wagner, Fundamentals of Data Processing 224
(Cincinnati: South-Western Publishing Co., 233
1971), p. 375. 236
[2] "Packaged Computer Software and Services 244
Regain Status," Computer Digest, Vol. 8, No. 256
6 (June, 1973), p. 1. 260

Problem 2: Second Page of a Leftbound Report

Type Problem 1 as the second page of a leftbound report. Omit the heading; number the page; DS (Reference: pages 113-115)

Problem 3: Second Page of a Report with a Table

Type the problem as the second page of a leftbound report. Number the page; DS; SS the table; leave 12 spaces between the columns (Reference: page 123)

Words

(¶) "The Age of the Industrial Revolution," 8
states Gilliam, "with its assembly lines and 17
fragmented tasks, built the greatest corpora- 26
tions and nations the world has ever known."[1] 35
Regardless of how we attempt to view this 44
age, one idea rises above all others. That 52
idea is the worth and dignity of the individual. 62
What has been employee reaction to our 70
recent preoccupation with technology? What 79
do employees really want? (¶) One company 87
making a study of this problem concluded 95
that wages are rarely at the bottom of any 104
discontent. The company rated job-satisfaction 113
factors in this order: 118

Factor	Rank	
Individual recognition	1	127
Interesting job	2	131
Job security	3	134
Company growth	4	137
Salary and related benefits	5	143

(¶) What is needed is a new concept designed 152
to enrich jobs at all levels in all depart- 160
ments. This concept is known as Work Itself. 169

173

[1] Marco Gilliam, "They Really Want to Do 181
a Good Job If We'll Let Them," Bell Tele- 191
phone Magazine Vol. 50 (January/February, 202
1971), p. 1. 205

LESSON 8

8A Preparatory Practice   each line twice SS; DS after second typing of line

1	All reaches learned	Tab, Al, and Jack worked for an hour; so did Zahl.
2	u w	use due jut hut hurt wit with sworn how show would
3	b ,	to bid, on the job, be here, this bill, to be safe
4	3d/4th fingers	zeal haze zone sale base loose lease saw slaw laws
5	(From Fluency dictation)	to be, to be the, if it be, to be sure, and is due

| 1 | 2 | 3 | 4 | 5 | 6 | 7 | 8 | 9 | 10 |

8B Technique Practice: STROKING   each line twice

Curve your fingers, not your wrists.
Hold your wrists low and steady.

WRONG
Don't buckle
your wrists

RIGHT
Hold the
wrists low

Lines 1-2. Adjacent-key reach controls, such as *re*, *oi*, *tr*, and the like, need special attention. Make exact reaches to the keys, keeping your wrists low and steady.

Lines 3-4. Make direct reaches to such strokes as *ce*, *ec*, *br*, *un*, and the like, without returning the controlling finger to home position. Center the stroking action in your fingers.

1	Adjacent keys	are her soil coil has said short trade heads sales
2		Hare has a fine tire on sale; it has a safe tread.
3	Direct reaches	once force deck check herbs broke unit fun sun run
4		Brad checked the deck but once and found the dart.
5	Double letters	roof tell stuff foot took shrill shall cross class
6		Buzz will cross the trail at the foot of the hill.

8C Sentence Guided Writing

1. Type each sentence for 1', trying to complete each sentence twice as time is called.

2. Think and type as words the easy, 2-letter words such as *to*, *if*, and *he*.

	Words in Line	GWAM 30" Guide
Burt will work at the bank in June.	7	14
I can show the old house to June at two.	8	16
I know we own just four of these bronze sets.	9	18
A lad can be what he likes if he likes what he is	10	20

1' GWAM | 1 | 2 | 3 | 4 | 5 | 6 | 7 | 8 | 9 | 10 |

LESSON 71

71A Preparatory Practice ⑤ each line twice

Alphabet	Jean and Gladys quickly won several prizes at the Foxburgh track meet.
Figure	In 1970, Lynn & Beard had 64 salesmen; in 1973, 298; and in 1975, 469.
Special symbols	I say the following problem is right: $360 \times 4 - 854 + 710 \div 12 = 108$.
Fluency	You will be glad to know that we think Ruth will be right for the job.

| 1 | 2 | 3 | 4 | 5 | 6 | 7 | 8 | 9 | 10 | 11 | 12 | 13 | 14 |

71B Review of Basic Manipulative Skills ⑤ Half sheet; 50-space line; DS; 1½″ top margin

Do each of the 6 basic typewriter manipulations called for in Problems 1-6, below.

1. Typing Outside the Margins. Begin the sentence below 7 spaces outside the left margin. When the bell rings, complete the sentence on one line.

Are you drinking at the fountain of knowledge-- or merely gargling?

2. Shift Lock. Type the sentence in correct form.

NOTE: For accuracy, type on the <u>control level</u>.

3. Aligning and Typing Over. Remove the paper; reinsert it. Type over the sentence in Problem 2.

4. Automatic Line Finder. Type the following sentence, using the automatic line finder to type the superscripts and subscripts.

Decrease the temperature of the H_2SO_4 to 32° F.

5. Horizontal Centering. Center the following heading:

MANIPULATIVE SKILLS

6. Spread Heading. Center the heading in Problem 5 as a spread heading.

71C Speed/Control Building ⑩

1. Type a 1′ writing for speed and a 1′ writing for control on the following ¶.

2. Type a 3′ writing for speed on the ¶. Try to equal your better 1′ *gwam*.

3. Type a 3′ writing for control on the ¶. Determine your *gwam* and number of errors.

All letters are used.

		3′ GWAM	
1.4 SI	Is it true that business competition today is just as keen as it was	5	37
5.4 AWL	fifty years ago? A lot of people think it is not. They say that compe-	9	42
85% HFW	tition is much less evident now than in the first half of the century.	14	47
	These doubters emphasize what they consider to be a great growth in firms	19	52
	that were once small and to the frequent merging of one company with	24	56
	another. They point, also, to the increase in government control and to	29	61
	taxes, two factors that limit competition to some extent.	32	68

3′ GWAM | 1 | 2 | 3 | 4 | 5 |

8D Tabulator Control   Type the drill twice.

To clear all tab stops

1. Move carriage to extreme left.

2. Depress **tab-clear key (31)** and hold it down as you pull the carriage all the way to the right.

To set tab stops

Move the carriage to the desired position; then depress the **tab-set key (23)**. Repeat this procedure for each stop needed.

Tabulating techniques

Nonelectric. Depress and hold the **tab bar (24)** [right index finger] or **key** [right fourth finger] until carriage has stopped.

Electric (and Some Nonelectric). Tap the **tab key (24)** [little finger] or **bar** [index finger] lightly; return finger to home-key position at once.

Clear all tabulator stops; set a tab stop 5 spaces, another 10 spaces, and still another 15 spaces to the right of the left margin.

Begin Line 1 of the drill at the left margin. Use the tab key or bar to type the remaining lines. Tab, release, and type quickly.

1 Margin   Liz sent cash to the bank; the bank wants a check.

2 Indent 5 *Tab once* ⟶ She will face the fact that a job takes work.

3 Indent 10 *Tab twice* ⟶ He took the old truck route to the fair.

4 Indent 15 *Tab three times* ⟶ Roz can be there for the fall show.

8E Continuity Practice: PARAGRAPH   Type the paragraphs (¶s) as directed; determine GWAM.

1. Clear tab stops; then set a stop for a 5-space ¶ indention. Use DS.

2. Depress tab bar or key to indent the first line of each ¶.

3. Type the ¶s as shown; then type 1' writings on each of the ¶s.

All letters learned are used.

		Total Words 1' GWAM
¶ 1 *Tab* ⟶ All of us need to know how to talk and write		9
1.0 SI 4.6 AWL 97% HFW well. We are sure to need these skills in school		19
and in the world of work, too. Learn both now.		28
¶ 2 *Tab* ⟶ To these skills, we can add the need to know		37
1.0 SI 4.6 AWL 97% HFW how to count. All jobs of the size we shall want		47
should teach us to think as we use skills, too.		57

1' GWAM | 1 | 2 | 3 | 4 | 5 | 6 | 7 | 8 | 9 | 10 |

Copy Difficulty. The ease or difficulty of copy to be typed is influenced greatly by 3 factors: (1) Syllable intensity (SI) or average number of syllables per word; (2) stroke intensity or average word length (AWL); (3) incidence of high-frequency words (HFW) or the percent of words used from among the 1,254 most-used words. In this section of lessons, the ¶s are *very easy*.

How to Determine GWAM. The ¶s are marked with the 4-word count shown in figures and with an in-between count of 2 words shown by a dot to aid you in determining your 1' **gwam**. If ¶ 1 is typed and a part or all of ¶ 2 in the 1' writing, use the *cumulative* total word count given in the column at the right, plus the count for the incomplete line shown below the second ¶.

70D Problem Typing: REPORT AND OUTLINE (25)

Problem 1: Leftbound Report with Table

Full sheet; leftbound manuscript style (top margin: 1½" pica, 2" elite); DS; SS the table; 10 spaces between columns (Reference: pages 113-115)

Words

WHO DECIDES ON TELEVISION PROGRAMS? 7

(¶ 1) **Many** people play a part in planning the 15 programs that appear on your television 23 screen: producers, advertising specialists, and 33 network leaders. Except for the news, how- 41 ever, no sponsored program is shown without 50 the approval of the company paying the bill. 59 The common practice is for the sponsor of the 68 program or his advertising agency to endorse 77 each program before it is telecast. (¶ 2) **The** 86 net result of the practice of sponsor approval 95 is that a very small number of companies de- 104 cides what you can see. About one third of 112 all the money spent on television programs 121 in a recent year came from a mere ten com- 129 panies. Together they spent $538,740,200 on 138 television advertising. These companies thus 147 decide to a considerable extent what programs 157 you can turn on. (¶ 3) **A** list of the top five 165 companies, with the amounts they spent on 173 sponsored programs during the aforemen- 181 tioned year, follows: 185

Procter & Gamble Co.	$116,032,400	192
American Home Products		197
Corp.	61,195,800	200
Sterling Drug, Inc.	56,398,200	207
Bristol-Meyers Co.	55,901,100	213
General Foods Corp.	50,578,300	220

(¶ 4) **While** the sponsor does approve the 227 programs, it is the viewer who really decides 236 what he sees. If he doesn't like a program, he 245 turns it off. The sponsor must consider this 255 in deciding what he will approve. 261

Problem 2: Outline

Half sheet inserted with long edge at the left; 44-space line; 1½" top margin; add designation numerals and letters for each order; use correct capitalization, punctuation, and spacing (References: outline style, page 115; centering on special-size paper, page 62)

Words

PROCEDURES OF DATA HANDLING 6

recording data 9

 using original source documents 17

 preparing punched cards and tape 24

 preparing magnetic cards and tape 32

classifying data 36

 using alphabetic code 41

 using numeric code 46

 using alphanumeric code 51

sorting data 55

creating new data 60

 programming to manipulate data 67

 performing arithmetic operations 74

  addition 77

  subtraction 80

  multiplication 84

  division 86

summarizing data 91

 consolidating data 95

 providing for information retrieval 103

LESSON 9

9A Preparatory Practice each line 3 times SS; DS after third typing of each line

All letters learned

Jack worked with Burt, Saul, and Fred; so did Roz.

Direct reaches

Lance found the wrecked cab and checked the tires.

(From Fluency dictation)

if he, if he is, if he is to do, if he is to do it

Make direct reaches for ce, ec, un, tr

Think words

9B Technique Practice: WORD RESPONSE each line twice SS; DS after second typing of each line

it fit he the then do so us for aid laid with such

an and land hand he she end lend own down of or an

(From dictation)

do so|for us|with the|and the|and then|it did land

Read word groups

9C Location of Y and X

Type Y with J finger

Type X with S finger

Reach the *j* finger up to type **y** without arching the wrist or moving fingers from home keys. *Type Line 1, below, for tryout.*

Reach the *s* finger down to type **x** without moving the hand downward. Reach with the finger. *Type Line 2, below, for tryout.*

9D Location Drill for Y and X each line twice SS; DS after second typing of each line

1 y

yj yj yj jay jay lay lay fly day say way sway yard

2 x

xs xs xs six fix fox next fixed lax sixth box jinx

3 y x

yes dry cry boy hay flax flex they next lynx ax by

4 Review

Clay Blyth can take the next tax case to Rex Knox.

5 Review

Rex says that he can fix the next box for Al Byrd.

70A Preparatory Practice ⑦ each line twice; then 1' writings on Lines 3 and 4

Alphabet	Rex Quig watched jet airplanes flying above the haze in the amber sky.
Figure-symbol	Hunt & Dwyer's $623.75 check (Check 1489) was delivered on January 19.
One hand	you were; only after you; refer my tax case; my opinion; extra reserve
Fluency	These two firms did hold the usual title to the visual aids they sold.

| 1 | 2 | 3 | 4 | 5 | 6 | 7 | 8 | 9 | 10 | 11 | 12 | 13 | 14 |

70B Skill-Transfer Typing ⑩ 60-space line; DS; 5-space ¶ indentions

1. Type two 1' writings on each ¶. Compare *gwam* and number of errors on the two ¶s.

2. Type a 3' writing on both ¶s. Compare the *gwam* with the better 1' rate on ¶ 1.

All letters are used.

		GWAM 1'	3'

¶ 1
1.4 SI
5.4 AWL
85% HFW
Straight copy

	1'	3'
Our economic system is one in which individuals have the	11	4	49
right to produce goods and services to be sold to the public	24	8	53
at a profit to the producer. As there are laws that govern	36	12	57
the operation of a business, our "free enterprise" system is	48	16	61
subject to those laws and thus is "free" just to the extent	60	20	65
that the laws allow.	64	21	66

¶ 2
1.4 SI
5.4 AWL
85% HFW
Script

	1'	3'
A business of any size is often owned by many people.	11	25	70
They buy stock in the hope of making a profit. If the busi-	23	29	74
ness prospers, any profits may be used to pay quarterly divi-	35	33	78
dends to the owners, expand a plant, or create new jobs. The	48	37	82
company managers must decide whether it is more beneficial to	60	41	86
return the profits to the owners or to use them for growth.	72	45	90

70C Typing from Corrected Copy/Composing ⑧ Full sheet; DS; unbound manuscript style

1. Type the ¶ below; then add a ¶ or two of your own, expanding on the thought in the first ¶.

2. Make corrections in your copy; provide an appropriate title; retype the ¶s.

Inthis fast- space age, even educated people can became rusty (moving) (highly) (obsolete) quickly. Since the post war students left college, the world's body of knowledge has doubled. Our leaders say that person out of college ⑩ years (devote must) at least ⑩ per cent of this time learn new things if he wants to compete in today's labor market. Their are countles ways in which the canbe done.

9E Location of V and P

Type V with F finger

Type P with ; finger

Reach the *f* finger down to type **v.** Hold the elbow in position and the hand in alignment. *Type Line 1, below, for tryout.*

Straighten the ; finger slightly and move up to type **p.** Avoid twisting the elbow out. *Type Line 2, below, for tryout.*

9F Location Drills for V and P   each line twice SS; DS after second typing of each line

1	v	vf vf vf vie view save salve sieve live loves have
2	p	p; p; p; pad paid pen spend spent paid prize plans
3	v p	vote van solve prove place drive drove prize stove
4	Review	Steve Prince will vote for the peace plan at five.
5	Review	A vote for Pat Vance is a vote for a low tax rate.

9G Continuity Practice: SENTENCE

Type each line 3 times SS; DS after the third typing of a line. Compute *gwam.*

Type at a smooth and steady pace. Hold the hands and arms quiet—almost motionless.

1	y	Syl Clay can pay Faye Kyle for the new style play.	
2	x	Knox can sell a box of flax seed to Rex next week.	**Type without pauses**
3	v	Dave Volk served on the leave board for five days.	
4	p	Pete has the pep, push, and poise for the top job.	
5	v p	Van pays in cash and saves; it proves a fine plan.	

| 1 | 2 | 3 | 4 | 5 | 6 | 7 | 8 | 9 | 10 |

9H Continuity Practice: PARAGRAPH

Type twice for practice; then type one or more 1' writings. Compute your *gwam.*

Sit erect. Keep your eyes on the copy as you type. Type at a steady, even pace.

All letters learned are used.

1.0 SI
4.6 AWL
95% HFW

If you plan to sell land lots, take the next trip in space, write jazz, or wash cars, find the bunch that thinks as it works. You do not need a seer to know that those who think will have a job.

69D Problem Typing: TWO-PAGE LEFTBOUND MANUSCRIPT WITH FOOTNOTES ⓪

Type the following copy as a 2-page manuscript to be bound at the left. Center the title over the line of writing. Number footnotes consecutively, typing each one on the same page as its reference number. (Reference: pages 113-114)

Use your stroke and line-space ruler as a guide in placing the heading on the first page, the page number (*folio*) on the second page, and the footnotes.

Words

HINTS ON MAKING A SPEECH   5

(¶ 1) The person who says that he does not   12
get panicky when he gets up to talk to an   21
audience is simply not telling the truth. To   30
be fearful is natural when one is confronted   39
by the unknown. Will the audience like me?   48
Will there be interest in my subject? Can   57
I put my talk over? These and other ques-   65
tions will race through your mind. The net   74
result is panic at the podium. Here are some   83
suggestions for minimizing that panicky feel-   92
ing and for giving an interesting talk.   100

Overcoming Fear   106

(¶ 2) Know your subject. Elson and Peck   117
state that the best way to conquer fear is by   126
complete preparation.[1] Select for your subject   136
some event with which you are very familiar,   145
or take plenty of time to gather material on   154
a new subject. Make that material part of   162
your life by relating it, with examples, to   171
your own experience. If you do this, you   180
won't fail to gain the self-confidence you need.   190
(¶ 3) Make contact with your audience. Fear   204
of his audience indicates a self-centered   214
speaker. He can reduce a good talk to shreds.   222
At the outset, ask the members of your audi-   230
ence if they can hear you clearly or see any   239
exhibits you may be using. This technique   248
takes the spotlight off you and places it on   257
the audience. (¶ 4) Be yourself. Another way   267
to minimize fear in speaking is to be your-   276
self. Talk from your own background, hon-   284
estly and enthusiastically. As Lamers and   293

Words

Staudacher state the case: "Have the courage   302
to be yourself. Give your speech your way.   311
If you make it an enjoyable experience for   319
yourself, your listeners will share your enjoy-   329
ment."[2]   330

Making Your Talk Interesting   342

(¶ 5) Be concrete. An interesting speech in-   351
forms. Monroe and Ehninger say that it   359
should be packed with facts and references to   369
actual experiences and events. Be careful of   378
becoming too detailed. Use round numbers;   386
select important data. Leave out irrelevant   395
and minute details and incidents.[3] (¶ 6) Be   404
clear. Confine your speech to three or four   414
main points; and develop each one in clear,   422
easily understood language. Whenever pos-   431
sible, use charts and diagrams to add clarity   440
to your talk. (¶ 7) Use humorous stories.   451
Generally, no tool of speech making is more   460
helpful than is good humor. Prochnow and   468
Prochnow warn, however, that a story must   477
always relate itself directly to the discussion.[4]   487
Never use an unrelated story to wake up an   495
audience——that's best done by waking up the   504
speaker.   506
  509

[1] E. F. Elson and Alberta Peck, The Art of Speaking (2d ed.; Boston: Ginn and Co., 1966), p. 37. *(23 words)*

[2] William M. Lamers and Joseph M. Staudacher, The Speech Arts (Chicago: Lyons and Carnahan, 1966), p. 5. *(25 words)*

[3] Alan H. Monroe and Douglas Ehninger, Principles of Speech (5th ed.; Chicago: Scott, Foresman and Co., 1964), p. 180. *(28 words)*

[4] Herbert V. Prochnow and Herbert V. Prochnow, Jr., The Speaker's Treasure Chest (Rev. ed.; New York: Harper & Row, 1964), p. 49. *(31 words)*

LESSON 10

10A Preparatory Practice   each line twice SS; DS after second typing of each line

All letters learned are used.

1 Review   Joyce Vaux won a prize for her work on the drives.

2 y x   by say yet year you your box boxed six sixth fixed

3 v p   five live serve save view pad prize plan pen spend

4 One hand   base you face pull fear join traced look bear hill

(From
5 Fluency dictation) he did, he did the, he did the work, if he did the
       | 1 | 2 | 3 | 4 | 5 | 6 | 7 | 8 | 9 | 10 |

10B Technique Practice: SHIFT KEY AND SHIFT LOCK   each line twice SS; DS after second typing of each line

Shift Keys. Hold the shift key down until you have struck the key for the capital; then release the shift key and return the finger to typing position without pausing.

Shift Lock. Depress the **shift lock (29)** and leave it down until you have typed the combination to be capitalized. To release the lock, operate the shift key.

1 Right shift   Scott Zier saw Vance Boone at the Trent Book Fair.
2   Charles Vale said he wrote to the Red Star Cab Co.

3 Left shift   Hale Jones asked Lance Poole to join her in Hayes.
4   John Hertz will paint the boats at June Lake soon.

5 Both shifts   Josh Wertz will see Lyle Branch in Oak Creek Park.
6   The Frank Bentz Co. will fix the desk for Jo Holt.

7 Shift lock   He saw each of the new shows on NBC, ABC, and CBS.
8   He joined the NEA and CBEA. He works for the IRS.

10C Sentence Guided Writing

Type each sentence for 1', trying to complete each one twice as time is called. (The ½' guides may be called to pace you.)

Technique Cue. All the words are typed with alternate (balanced) hands. Try to read, think, and type the words by *word response*.

	Words in Line	GWAM 30" Guide
She is to do the work for the town.	7	14
They paid for the field of corn with us.	8	16
Fiske paid for the work they did by the lake.	9	18
I own the land, but he paid for the work they did.	10	20

1' GWAM | 1 | 2 | 3 | 4 | 5 | 6 | 7 | 8 | 9 | 10 |

LESSON 69

69A Preparatory Practice (7) each line twice; then 1' writings on Line 1

Alphabet   Prizes for Albuquerque's next track meet will be given by Judson Hall.

Figure   Dial 649-5718 or 649-5709 to obtain your copy of this 32-page booklet.

Figure/symbol   Should the 6½% rate on Long's $3,250 note (dated May 18, 1974) be 8¼%?

Fluency   The auditor said the profit due you should have been paid much sooner.

| 1 | 2 | 3 | 4 | 5 | 6 | 7 | 8 | 9 | 10 | 11 | 12 | 13 | 14 |

69B Technique Practice: STROKING (5) each line twice

1 Long words   The unit has synthesized circuitry for clear, dependable transmission.

2 Left hand   A few extra seats were set up on the vast stage as dessert was served.

3 Right hand   Jimmy Polk pulled the oily junk down the hill, but Jon only looked on.

4 Direct reaches   A hundred unusual designs made the celebrated decorator justly famous.

5 Adjacent keys   Except for Bert and Ernie, we saw very poor relations between members.

6 Hyphen   He drew the step-by-step, door-to-door plans for our all-purpose soap.

| 1 | 2 | 3 | 4 | 5 | 6 | 7 | 8 | 9 | 10 | 11 | 12 | 13 | 14 |

69C Proofreading: READING FOR MEANING (8) Half sheet; 65-space line; 1½" top margin; DS

Type the following paragraph, filling in the blank spaces with the appropriate words selected from those listed at the left.

vis-a-vis
expenditure
concrete
decade
money
company
growing
leaders
dialogue
measure
life
expected
obligations
financial

There has been a _____ tendency in the past _____ for corporate _____ to use art in terms of their overall image _____ the complex requirements of today's society. The _____ of large sums of _____ may be difficult to justify because _____ results are difficult to _____. On the other hand, the _____ between management and society at large does emphasize some of the social _____ of modern capitalism. Is it not _____ to improve the quality of _____ for both the employees of a _____ and its public? Businessmen who look further than the next dividend recognize their responsibility to contribute more than mere _____ success.

10D Technique Practice: STROKING   Type the drill once as shown.

Lines 1-2. Reach directly to such strokes as *ce*, *br*, *un*, and the like, without returning the controlling finger to home position.

Lines 3-4. Type adjacent keys such as *re*, *poi*, and the like, by training your eyes to see quickly the correct letter sequences. Make each reach precisely.

| 1 | Direct | why lace once branch debt hunt lunch brisk aft nut |
| 2 | reaches | Herb Brill can hunt for the checks; he is in debt. |

| 3 | Adjacent keys | has poor suit buy oil cards talk point three treat |
| 4 | | start here; few buy silk; we were there; fast dash |

| 5 | Double letters | pool jazz roll off pass need Anne feel loss jarred | Distinct |
| 6 | | Anne stopped off at school on her way to the pool. | strokes |

| 7 | 3d/4th fingers | coax laws craze wax please loop size pop ooze ease | Quiet arms |
| 8 | | see a sloop of war; please wax the car; pass a law | and wrists |

10E Continuity Practice: PARAGRAPH

1. Type the ¶ twice for practice. Note any words that cause stroking difficulty.

2. Type the difficult words 2 or 3 times; then type one or more 1' writings on the ¶.

All letters learned are used.

1.0 SI
4.4 AWL
95% HFW

First, use your head on a job; then try your
hand at it. You will find that the sense of this
line pays off in the end. Size up each job; know
what you have to do next to do it with skill.

10F Individual Practice

1. Type each line once. Place a check mark before the lines that seemed difficult.

2. Type 2 or more times each line that you checked as difficult.

1	b	Burt, not Bob, will buy the new bonds at the bank.
2	z	Liz Zahl will join Zoe at the new zoo in our zone.
3	x	Tex Cox waxed that next box for Jinx and Rex Knox.
4	p	Pat Parks can help pay for part of the prize plan.
5	y	Kaye said you should stay with Faye for five days.
6	n	Ken Knolls has done the dance; now Sven can do it.

| 1 | 2 | 3 | 4 | 5 | 6 | 7 | 8 | 9 | 10 |

Problem 2: Footnotes; Magazine References

1. On a full sheet, type the copy below as a supposedly full second page of a leftbound report. Start on Line 25 (pica) or Line 32 (elite)in order to type the footnotes and leave at least a 1″ bottom margin. Use the style for leftbound manuscripts given on page 117.

2. In planning a manuscript page, save 2 lines for the divider line and the spaces above and below it, 3 lines (or at times 4) for each footnote to be typed on the page, and 6 lines for the bottom margin. (Reference: page 117)

Words

(¶) The new year will bring a search for 7
new methods of improving employee morale. 16
King concluded, after looking at a number of 25
plans to improve employee morale, that com- 33
panies need to provide "motivation through 42
the job itself, job enrichment and enlargement, 52
job rotation, and management by objectives."¹ 61
(¶) In addition, Goodfellow stresses the im- 69
portance of listening to employees in improv- 77
ing employee-employer relations. He states: 87
(*Double-indent and SS the quotation*) (¶) Listening 89
to employees is not to be confused with 97
interrogation. Nor is listening to employees 106
a haphazard, once-in-a-while, sporadic activity 115
to be carried on by anyone in personnel or 124

Words

industrial relations who happens to have a 133
spare hour. Carefully done, it must be part of 142
a regular system; and it requires a flexible, 151
alert management that has learned how to 160
make adjustments and corrections quickly 168
where required.² (*Reset margins*) 171
_____ SS 175
DS
¹ Paul A. King, "Personnel Trends '73: 183
Will the Executive Go AWOL?" Administra- 193
tive Management, Vol. XXXIV, No. 1 (Janu- 204
ary, 1973), p. 22. 208
² Matthew Goodfellow, "A Good Employee 215
Relations Checklist," Modern Office Proce- 228
dures, Vol. 18, No. 7 (July, 1973), p. 38. 237

68C Speed/Control Building (15)

1. Type each of the following ¶s as two 1′ writings, once for *speed* and once for *control*.

2. Type all 3 ¶s as a 5′ writing. Circle errors. Determine *gwam* and number of errors.

3. Proofread by comparing. Check with the original such commonly misspelled words as *desirable* and *device*.

All letters are used.

		GWAM
		1′ · 5′

¶ 1
1.4 SI
5.4 AWL
85% HFW

You have learned a great deal about typing in only a few months. | 13 | 3 · 44
You may not yet be striking all keys as rapidly or as precisely as you | 27 | 5 · 47
desire, but you have started a firm foundation upon which you can build | 42 | 8 · 50
even more skill. Like any other skill, typing requires continued effort | 56 | 11 · 53
to be maintained or improved; so set aside a daily practice time. | 69 | 14 · 55

¶ 2
1.4 SI
5.4 AWL
85% HFW

If you proceed with the typing program in college, your practice | 13 | 16 · 58
time will be scheduled for you. Even so, you will learn that a bit of | 27 | 19 · 61
extra practice each day may be just enough to permit your new skill to | 41 | 22 · 64
enter a prized category. Even if you do not continue with formal typing | 56 | 24 · 67
instruction, you can add greatly to your skill all by yourself. | 69 | 28 · 69

¶ 3
1.4 SI
5.4 AWL
85% HFW

A timed writing effort is superior to an untimed one. Timing can | 13 | 30 · 72
supply a little desirable pressure; it also can show you just how well | 27 | 33 · 75
you are doing. In school your teacher times you; if you decide to prac- | 42 | 36 · 77
tice on your own you should work under time pressure then, too. A | 55 | 39 · 80
timing record or tape is especially good to use for this fine purpose. | 69 | 41 · 83

1′ GWAM | 1 | 2 | 3 | 4 | 5 | 6 | 7 | 8 | 9 | 10 | 11 | 12 | 13 | 14 |
5′ GWAM | 1 | 2 | 3 |

LESSON 11

11A Preparatory Practice   each line 3 times SS; DS after third typing of each line

All letters learned   Bev Lentz picked this jazz show for our next year.

One hand   waste junk rest hulk treat you vase pill beat hunk

Fluency   (From dictation)   to do, to do the, if the, if he did, if he did the

| 1 | 2 | 3 | 4 | 5 | 6 | 7 | 8 | 9 | 10 |

11B Continuity Practice: SENTENCE   each line twice SS; DS after second typing of each line

He can do the drill in an hour or so, I feel sure.   **Keep on typing; do not pause**

Ned felt that the size of the vote would help Rod.

The tone of this fine harp has kept it at the top.

Rex Dix and Herb Cox saw a new show at the school.

| 1 | 2 | 3 | 4 | 5 | 6 | 7 | 8 | 9 | 10 |

11C Location of Q and M

Type Q with A finger

Type M with J finger

Reach the *a* finger up to type **q** without swinging the elbow out or arching the wrist. *Type Line 1, below, for tryout.*

Reach the *j* finger down to type **m**. Do not move the hand down; just your finger. *Type Line 2, below, for tryout.*

11D Location Drill for Q and M   each line twice SS; DS after second typing of each line

1 q   qa qa qa quit quite quote quaint quell queen quick

2 m   mj mj mj mat mist jam firm form harm come sum drum

3 q m   quiz quack quest qualm much must meet arm ham most

4 Review   Mr. Queen read the quaint myth on the blue mosque.

5 Review   Mark Quinn may make a quick trip to an old square.

LESSON 68

68A Preparatory Practice ⑦ each line twice; then 1' writings on Lines 1 and 4

Alphabet   Will Judge Alexander Vonrique permit the seizure of your bank records?

Figure   Your Certificates 36285A and 47190B bear the date of January 31, 1974.

Roman numerals   Type Roman numerals in capital letters: one I three III five V ten X.

Fluency   They are certain that a limit will be set on the resources to be used.

| 1 | 2 | 3 | 4 | 5 | 6 | 7 | 8 | 9 | 10 | 11 | 12 | 13 | 14 |

68B Problem Typing: REPORTS WITH FOOTNOTES ㉘

Problem 1: Footnotes on Partially Filled Page; Book References

For each footnote reference, use a superior figure (superscript) in the text. To type a superior figure: (1) operate the **automatic line finder or ratchet release (6)**; (2) turn the cylinder back (toward you) a half space; (3) type the figure and return the ratchet release and cylinder to normal position.

Study the illustration at the right; then, on a full sheet, type the *copy below* (do not work from the illustration) as the partially filled second page of an unbound report. Type the paragraph at the top of the page; the footnotes at the foot of the page, using the roll-back procedure (Reference: page 117).

Evaluate Your Work. Compare your solution with the illustration at the right. With a stroke and line-space ruler, check the top, bottom, and side margins of your copy. Proofread. Circle or correct errors.

2

According to a statement by Hailstones and Brennan, "By July of 1968, our total gold reserve had dwindled from its peak of $24.5 billion in 1949 to $10.7 billion."[1] Numerous measures have been proposed to reverse this process. In this regard, Warmke and others point out that since 1934, United States currency is not redeemable in gold to private citizens. It is redeemable, however, to foreign banks and business firms.[2]

[1]Thomas J. Hailstones and Michael J. Brennan, Economics, An Analysis of Principles and Policies (Cincinnati: South-Western Publishing Co., 1970), p. 280.

[2]Roman F. Warmke and others, Consumer Economic Problems (8th ed.; Cincinnati: South-Western Publishing Co., 1971), p. 150.

Words

According to a statement by Hailstones and Brennan, "By July of   13
1968, our total gold reserve had dwindled from its peak of $24.5 billion   27
in 1949 to $10.7 billion."[1] Numerous measures have been proposed to   41
reverse this process. In this regard, Warmke and others point out that since   56
1934, United States currency is not redeemable in gold to private citi-   70
zens. It is redeemable, however, to foreign banks and business firms.[2]   84

88

[1] Thomas J. Hailstones and Michael J. Brennan, Economics, An Analysis   104
of Principles and Policies (Cincinnati: South-Western Publishing Co.,   118
1970), p. 280.   121

[2] Roman F. Warmke and others, Consumer Economic Problems (8th ed.;   139
Cincinnati: South-Western Publishing Co., 1971), p. 150.   151

11E Location of G and ? (Question)

Type G with F finger

```
    4  3  2   1     1   2  3  4  ← FINGERS
  ! " #  $  %  _  &  ' ( )  *
  1 2 3  4  5  6  7  8 9 0  -
   Q W E R T Y U I O P ⅛ +
   A S D F G H J K L ; @ LOCK
   SHIFT Z X C V B N M , : ?  SHIFT
```

Type ? with ; finger

Reach *f* finger to type **g** without moving the other fingers from their home keys. *Type Line 1, below, for tryout.*

Shift to type **?**. *Space twice after ? at the end of a sentence. Type Line 2, below, for tryout.*

11F Location Drills for G and ? each line twice SS; DS after second typing of each line

1	g	gf gf gf go got fog fig rug dug flag right lug bug	Do not space after ? at end of line
2	?	;?; ?; ?; Is he? Is he next? Did Jo eat in town?	
3	g ?	Is Peg right? May Doug and I go? May I see Trig?	
4	Review	Does Marg have the right books for the new course?	
5	Review	Can George take a group of young boys to the camp?	

11G Continuity Practice: PARAGRAPH

Type each ¶ for practice; then type a 2′ writing on each one. Compute *gwam* (page 18).

Stroking Cue. Hold your hands directly over the keys with fingers curved. Strike the keys squarely.

All letters are used.

		2′ GWAM
¶ 1 1.0 SI 4.4 AWL 95% HFW	Of all the words that have been used to tell	4
	you how to type, none are so prized as those that	9
	point out the need of a clear, fixed view. Learn	14
	to know how to do what must be done each day.	19
¶ 2 1.0 SI 4.6 AWL 95% HFW	As you type, work for quick, firm strokes of	23
	all the keys. Do not press them, for that is the	28
	wrong way to do this job. Do not move your hands	33
	up and down or from side to side as you type.	38

2′ GWAM | 1 | 2 | 3 | 4 | 5 |

GENERAL GUIDES FOR TYPING FOOTNOTES

In a report, all statements of fact or of the opinions of someone other than the writer and all direct quotations taken from articles or books must be acknowledged with a footnote. Footnotes in full form give complete information on the references being cited, preferably typed with standard abbreviations to conserve space.

Generally, footnotes are placed at the foot of the page on which reference to them is made; or they may be grouped at the end of the report. Footnotes are single-spaced with one blank line between them. They are numbered consecutively throughout a report or starting anew with "1" on each page. These numbers are typed as reference numbers a half space above the line at the end of a quotation, after the author's name, or at the end of a statement of fact.

Although footnotes vary in length, the following system works well for determining the placement of footnotes:

1. Roll the platen down so that a one-inch bottom margin remains.

2. From this point, roll the platen up three spaces for each footnote, plus another for its blank line space. Make a pencil mark where you stop.

3. When you have typed the page to the pencil mark, single-space; type an underline one and a half inches long; double-space; indent to paragraph point; type the raised footnote number and the footnote.

4. Use the roll-back procedure even on pages only partially full.

Pica

GENERAL GUIDES FOR TYPING FOOTNOTES

In a report, all statements of fact or of the opinions of someone other than the writer and all direct quotations taken from articles or books must be acknowledged with a footnote. Footnotes in full form give complete information on the references being cited, preferably typed with standard abbreviations to conserve space.

Generally, footnotes are placed at the foot of the page on which reference to them is made; or they may be grouped at the end of the report. Footnotes are single-spaced with one blank line between them. They are numbered consecutively throughout a report or starting anew with "1" on each page. These numbers are typed as reference numbers a half space above the line at the end of a quotation, after the author's name, or at the end of a statement of fact.

Although footnotes vary in length, the following system works well for determining the placement of footnotes:

1. Roll the platen down so that a one-inch bottom margin remains.

2. From this point, roll the platen up three spaces for each footnote, plus another for its blank line space. Make a pencil mark where you stop.

3. When you have typed the page to the pencil mark, single-space; type an underline one and a half inches long; double-space; indent to paragraph point; type the raised footnote number and the footnote.

4. Use the roll-back procedure even on pages only partially full.

Elite

Problem 2: Leftbound Manuscript

NOTE: Miniature models of both the pica and elite solutions are given above. *Do not type from the models.* Study them; then type from the copy given below.

Top margin for pica type, 1½″, for elite type, 2″; left margin, 1½″; right margin, 1″; bottom margin, at least 1″; type enumeration as indicated on page 115, Problem 2.

Because of the wider left margin, the center point will be 3 spaces to the right of the point normally used.

GENERAL GUIDES FOR TYPING FOOTNOTES

(¶ 1) In a report, all statements of fact or of the opinions of someone other than the writer and all direct quotations taken from articles or books must be acknowledged with a footnote. Footnotes in full form give complete information on the references being cited, preferably typed with standard abbreviations to conserve space. (¶ 2) Generally, footnotes are placed at the foot of the page on which reference to them is made; or they may be grouped at the end of the report. Footnotes are single-spaced with one blank line between them. They are numbered consecutively throughout a report or starting anew with "1" on each page. These numbers are typed as reference numbers a half space above the line at the end of a quotation, after the author's name, or at the end of a statement of fact. (¶ 3) Although footnotes vary in length, the following system works well for determining the placement of footnotes: (*Enumerate*) 1. Roll the platen down so that a one-inch bottom margin remains. 2. From this point, roll the platen up three spaces for each footnote, plus another for its blank line space. Make a pencil mark where you stop. 3. When you have typed the page to the pencil mark, single-space; type an underline one and a half inches long; double-space; indent to paragraph point; type the raised footnote number and the footnote. 4. Use the roll-back procedure even on pages only partially full.

LESSON 12

12A Preparatory Practice   each line twice SS; DS after second typing of each line

Alphabet	Roz Groves just now packed my box with five quail.
q m	quite quilt qualm squirm milk mock much most smoke
Fluency (From dictation)	to do, to do the work, to go with, to go with them
Easy	He can do the job, but he should go with them now.

| 1 | 2 | 3 | 4 | 5 | 6 | 7 | 8 | 9 | 10 |

12B Backspacer

Use the **backspace key (30)** to fill in an omitted letter or to position the carriage.

Electric. Reach with the little finger (right or left depending upon key location); tap and release the key quickly.

Nonelectric. Reach with the appropriate finger; depress the key firmly; release it quickly.

Tryout Drill. Type the first incomplete word as shown in black; backspace and type in the missing letter (shown in color).

Type the remaining words in the same way.

a d mo t b nd thou ht bl nk dr nk cou d f re do e
  n   s   o   g   a   i   l   i   n

12C Technique Checkup: STROKING   each line twice SS; DS after second typing of each line

1	1st finger	Gregg Grout may yet try to get a toy gun for them.	Direct strokes
2	2d finger	Dick Dike said he did check the ice on Kech Creek.	Direct strokes
3	3d/4th fingers	Quartz and zinc were prized in this part of Spain.	Finger action
4	1st row	The men may get the bomb from the box in the cave.	Quiet elbows
5	Home row	Hal Hall held a sale. Alf shall add a half glass.	Light key contact
6	3d row	Trent wrote to Troy Trapp. He did not quote Ruth.	Wrists low
7	Double letters	Will Buzz and Gregg take some books to the troops?	Distinct strokes
8	One hand	as we saw, we look on, my grade, you were, see him	Letter response
9	Balanced hand	If they wish, he may make the forms for the disks.	Word response
10	Left shift	Kate Long and Pat Hunt will join them in New York.	Wrists low and quiet
11	Right shift	Fred, Don, Van, and Rod will go to Green Bay soon.	

| 1 | 2 | 3 | 4 | 5 | 6 | 7 | 8 | 9 | 10 |

LESSON 67

67A   Preparatory Practice ⑦ each line twice; then 1' writings on Lines 3 and 4

Alphabet   Will Dick Forman be quite happy visiting in Texas and Arizona in June?
Figure/symbol Send us a check for $273.84 now and another for $269.75 on January 10.
Double letters Nell Trapp will take a good look at the book Bill Boggs wants to sell.
Fluency   The real problem of your leisure time is to keep others from using it.
| 1 | 2 | 3 | 4 | 5 | 6 | 7 | 8 | 9 | 10 | 11 | 12 | 13 | 14 |

67B   Speed Building ⑧ three ½' and three 1' writings for speed; compare GWAM on best 1' and ½'

All letters are used.

1.4 SI
5.4 AWL
85% HFW

When typing, think the word; or think the sequence of letters if
the word is long or unusual. Adjust your speed to the kind of material
you are to type. Emphasize an even and flowing motion, and type without
pausing between one word and the next.

67C   Problem Typing: GUIDES TO TYPING MANUSCRIPTS AND FOOTNOTES ㉟

Problem 1: Topbound Report from Corrected Copy

Full sheet; DS; use topbound manuscript directions (Reference: p. 113); enumerations SS and double indented with blocked lines

Words

MISCELLANEOUS GUIDES FOR MANUSCRIPT TYPING TS   9

The following guides will be useful in the preparation of   23

manuscripts of two or more pages as well as for typing foot-notes: 37

1. Never end a pages with a hyphened word. Avoid having   48
    more than two consecutive lines end with hyphened words.   59
2. Never have one line of a paragraph at the bottom of at   72
    the top of a page.   76
3. Type footnote on the same page as its reference figures.   105
4. (Another acceptable practice is to place all footnotes at the end of the manuscript.) 115 / 122

3. Place a footnotes reference figure at the end of the material being cited. 134
5. Separate a footnote from the text by an inch-and-a-half   134
    underline, preceded by a single space and followed   145
    by a double space.   155
6. Single-space the lines of footnotes, but double-space   166
    between them.   169
7. Underline titles of complete publications; use quota-   180
    tion marks with parts of publications (magazine articles   192
    and the like).   194

12D Skill Checkup: STROKING

1. Type each sentence as a 1' writing, typing it as many times as you can until time is called.

2. Type Sentences 1, 3, and 5 for 1' each. Compare the *gwam* for the writings.

Stroking Cue. Think and type the easy words as words. Slow down for such words as *are*, *saw*, and *crossed*.

		Words in Line	1' GWAM
1	Is there a job for all of us to do?	7	14
2	Shoes of this size are too hard to find.	8	16
3	John saw the car just as it crossed the line.	9	18
4	If he is to do this work for us, he can do it now.	10	20
5	All of them know they must put first things first.	10	20
6	He knows they can do the work well on the new job.	10	20
7	In fact, a man with push can pass a man with pull.	10	20

1' GWAM | 1 | 2 | 3 | 4 | 5 | 6 | 7 | 8 | 9 | 10 |

12E Typing Checkup: CONTINUITY

1. Type each ¶ once for practice. Type each troublesome word 2 or 3 times.

2. Type a 1' writing on each ¶. Compute *gwam*.

3. Type a 2' writing on each ¶. Compute 2' *gwam* and compare it with 1' *gwam*.

4. Finally, type a 2' writing on both ¶s.

NOTE: Use the first-column *gwam* and the scale to determine the rate for 2' on single ¶s. Use the second 2' column and the scale to determine your 2' rate on both ¶s.

All letters are used.

		2' GWAM	
¶ 1	You will learn to type what you now write by	4	4
1.0 SI	hand. This is one of the prized end goals of the	9	9
4.8 AWL	course. This change will not be quick, but it is	14	14
95% HFW	sure to come. Just give it time, trust, and help.	19	19
¶ 2	The hope is that you can type as fast as you	4	24
1.0 SI	can think. This goal may not be reached, but you	9	29
4.6 AWL	should type at least three times the rate you can	14	34
95% HFW	write by hand. This is a sound claim, not a hoax.	19	39

2' GWAM | 1 | 2 | 3 | 4 | 5 |

Problem 2: Topic Outline Style

Full sheet; 2″ top margin; spread heading; 65-space line; vertical spacing and indentions from left margin as indicated

Words

T O P I C   O U T L I N E   5

TS

    I. IDENTIFYING DIVISIONS OF OUTLINES   16

DS

Reset margin———→ A. Roman Numerals for Major Divisions   24

B. Capital Letters for Subheadings (First Order)   34

C. Arabic Numerals for Items Under Subheadings (Second Order)   47

*2 spaces*_____ D. Lowercase Letters for Third Order Subheadings   57

DS

Align at right———→ II. CAPITALIZATION OF HEADINGS IN OUTLINES   66

Backspace into margin

A. Major Headings in All Caps   72

B. First-Order Subheadings with Important Words Capped   83

C. Second-Order Subheadings with Only First Word Capped   94

D. Third-Order Subheadings with Only First Word Capped   105

  III. SPACING AND PUNCTUATION IN OUTLINES   114

A. Spacing   117

Set tabs———→ 1. Horizontal spacing   121

———→ a. Title typed either solid or as spread heading   131

b. Other headings typed solid   138

c. Two spaces after identifying designation   147

2. Vertical spacing as indicated in this outline   157

B. Punctuation   160

1. Except for abbreviations, no end-of-line punctuation   171

in topic outlines   175

2. Appropriate end-of-line punctuation in sentence out-   186

lines   187

Problem 3: Outline of Leftbound Manuscript Style

Full sheet; 2½″ top margin; 65-space line; follow Problem 2 directions

Words

L E F T B O U N D   M A N U S C R I P T S   8

    I. MARGINS FOR LEFTBOUND MANUSCRIPTS   16

A. Top Margin   19

1. First page 1½″ for pica, 2″ for elite type   29

2. Other pages, 1″   33

B. Side and Bottom Margins (All Pages)   41

1. Left margin, 1½″   45

2. Right and bottom margins, 1″   51

   II. SPACING   54

A. Manuscripts for Publication, School Reports, Formal Reports   67

Double-Spaced   69

B. Business Reports Often Single-Spaced   78

C. Quoted Material of 4 or More Lines Single-Spaced   88

1. Indented 5 spaces from both margins (double-indented)   96

2. Quotation marks permissible but not required   106

D. Enumerations   109

1. Double-indented with blocked lines   117

2. Single-spaced with a double space between items   128

SECTION 2

Basic Skills Development

LESSONS 13-16

Machine Adjustments

1. Use a 60-space line, with the left margin set 30 spaces to left of center and right stop set at end of scale.

2. SS sentences and drill lines, with DS between groups of repeated lines.

3. DS ¶ copy. Set a tab stop for 5-space ¶ indention

Time Schedule. A time schedule for the parts of this lesson and those that follow is given as a guide for your minimum practice. The number of minutes for each part is shown within a circle. Vary the schedule if you feel you need more practice on one part, less on another Retype selected lines as time permits.

LESSON 13

13A Preparatory Practice ⑧ each line 3 times

Alphabet	Having just made six quick points, we simply froze the ball.
x and p	Dixon put six stamps on that box for the next postal pickup.
Fluency	He may pay the firm the usual price for the eight new forms.

| 1 | 2 | 3 | 4 | 5 | 6 | 7 | 8 | 9 | 10 | 11 | 12 |

13B Technique Practice: SHIFT KEYS ⑧ each line twice; see Shift Lock, in 10B, page 21

Keep the hands in home-key position as you reach the little fingers to the shift keys. Hold the shift key down until you have struck the key for the capital; then release the shift key and return the finger to typing position.

1	Left shift	Otto, Nate, Lyle, and I will go to Yellowstone Park in June.
2		Pat and Mary Young will meet Kate and Nancy Moore in Hawaii.
3	Right shift	Fred left for France, but Wes Quinn went to Spain with Eric.
4		Rodney Zahl won the Grant Ford award at the games in Quebec.
5	Both shifts	Ralph has gone to New York. Marv and Vince will go to Iowa.
6		Kirk Spitz will talk to the West Side Youth Club in January.

| 1 | 2 | 3 | 4 | 5 | 6 | 7 | 8 | 9 | 10 | 11 | 12 |

13C Technique Practice: RESPONSE PATTERNS ⑭ each line 3 times; Lines 1, 5, and 6 from dictation

Word Response. Some short, frequently used words (like to, **and**, **the**, and **work**) are so easy to type they can be typed as words instead of letter by letter. *Think and type the word.*

Letter Response. Many words (like **only**, **state**, **exceed**, and **extra**) are not so easy to type even though they are often used. Such words are typed letter by letter. *Think the letter; type it.*

Combination Response. Most copy is composed of both word and letter sequences that require variable speed: high speed for easy words, lower speed for hard ones *Learn to recognize the difference.*

1	Word	if he is	to go with	she did the work	he may show	to show the
2	response	Dixie may go to the firm to pay for the forms that Kent got.
3	Letter	only states jolly daze plump verve join extra upon great him
4	response	You exceeded the stated rate; only the street guard saw you.
5	Combination	to do my	and the date	it is only	and they care	if he saw the
6		and the joy	for she was	it is you	he did look	to see them go

| 1 | 2 | 3 | 4 | 5 | 6 | 7 | 8 | 9 | 10 | 11 | 12 |

Partial second page of unbound manuscript (pica type)

Paragraph headings. You have just typed a paragraph heading. It is indented, followed by a period, and underlined. Usually, only the first word or proper nouns and adjectives are capitalized.

Page Numbers

The first page need not be numbered; if it is, the number is centered a half inch from the bottom edge. On leftbound and unbound reports, the second and subsequent pages are numbered on Line 4 at the right margin. On topbound reports, all pages are numbered in first-page position.

LESSON 66

66A Preparatory Practice ⑦ each line twice; then 1' writings on Line 4

Alphabet	Jackie Bigsby is acquainted with an expert on Venezuelan family names.
Figure/symbol	Mr. Brook's note (due October 19) for $390 was discounted at 7% today.
Fractions	Is it correct for her to type $5\frac{1}{4}$ with 6 3/8, or should she type 5 1/4?
Fluency	Freedom is not worth having if it does not give us the freedom to err.

| 1 | 2 | 3 | 4 | 5 | 6 | 7 | 8 | 9 | 10 | 11 | 12 | 13 | 14 |

66B Technique Practice: SHIFT KEYS ⑧ each line twice without error or 3 times with no more than 1 error to a line

Left shift	Henry and I are going to Maryland in May, but Paul is going to Norway.
Right shift	Dick West left for Greece, but Clay Spillman went to France with Carl.
Both shifts	Henry Van Luen works for King Electronics, Inc., St. Paul, doesn't he?
Both shifts	"Get SPEED and ACCURACY," Mr. Fox wrote, "for real typewriting power."

| 1 | 2 | 3 | 4 | 5 | 6 | 7 | 8 | 9 | 10 | 11 | 12 | 13 | 14 |

66C Problem Typing: SPREAD HEADINGS AND OUTLINES ㉟

Problem 1: Centering Spread Headings

Half sheet; 2" top margin; DS; center each heading at the right as a spread heading as shown in the first heading

Centering spread headings

1. To center a spread heading, from the center point backspace once for each stroke in the heading.

2. From this point, type the heading, spacing once between the letters and 3 times between the words.

C E N T E R I N G   H E A D I N G S

MANUSCRIPT ON REPORT PREPARATION

SIMPLE REPORT STYLE

LEFTBOUND MANUSCRIPTS

SPACING OUTLINES

13D Paragraph Guided Writing ⑳ timed writings as directed

¶ 1. Type two 1' writings on ¶ 1. Determine *gwam* for the better writing. Use this as the base rate for setting a new goal as directed at the right.

New Goal. Add 4 *gwam* to your base rate. Note the 1' and ½' goals in your copy. Type three 1' writings at the new goal rate. Your instructor will call the ½' guides to pace you.

¶s 1-2. Type a 2' writing without the guides. Begin with ¶ 1 and type as much of ¶ 2 as you can. Determine *gwam*. Disregard errors temporarily.

All letters are used.

		2' GWAM	
¶ 1	As you size up the job of typing at a practical speed,	5	5
1.2 SI 5.0 AWL 94% HFW	keep in mind the thought that a gain results from the right	11	11
	mix of the mind and the hand. Your mind must always remain	17	17
	alert.	18	18
¶ 2	Good form is needed also; there is no question on this	5	24
1.2 SI 5.0 AWL 96% HFW	point. The hands should be held just over the keys. Every	11	30
	stroke must have quality. It must be quick, but it must be	17	35
	firm and sure. Your mind will tell you how to type.	23	40

2' GWAM | 1 | 2 | 3 | 4 | 5 | 6 |

LESSON 14

14A Preparatory Practice ⑧ each line 3 times

Alphabet Milford J. Zorn will give a trophy to the six quickest boys.

3d/4th fingers The producer is quite puzzled by my apparent lack of talent.

Fluency Did the clerks study the bids for the work on the city dock?

| 1 | 2 | 3 | 4 | 5 | 6 | 7 | 8 | 9 | 10 | 11 | 12 |

14B Technique Practice: SPACE-BAR CONTROL ⑩ each line at least twice

Operate the space bar with a short, quick, down-and-in thumb stroke in rhythm with typing the letters. Do not pause before or after making the space-bar stroke.

Left-hand ending the be is its quit send and for year off thing via new basic

Right-hand ending can when by any they to do will all with each you them thank

Combination endings The camera is so small that you can slip it into your purse.

Combination endings I think you can expect the prices to drop if she is elected.

| 1 | 2 | 3 | 4 | 5 | 6 | 7 | 8 | 9 | 10 | 11 | 12 |

65C Aligning and Typing Over ② Type the following line; remove the paper; reinsert and align. Type over the first and the last word in the line.

Our earnings are rising as the move from blue-collar jobs accelerates.

65D Problem Typing: UNBOUND MANUSCRIPT ㉟

Read the problem and study the illustrations below and on the next page. Then type the unbound manuscript as directed below. Indent the numbered items (*enumerations*) 5 spaces from the left and right margins (*double indention with blocked lines*), spaced as illustrated.

Full sheets; DS and indent ¶s 5 spaces; 1½″ top margin for pica, 2″ for elite; 1″ side and bottom margins; position page number as indicated in the manuscript

Make a light pencil mark at the right edge of the page about 1″ from the bottom and another about 1½″ to remind yourself to leave a 1″ bottom margin.

MANUSCRIPT ON REPORT PREPARATION
An Acceptable Style

Manuscripts or reports may be either single- or double-spaced, depending upon the type of report. School reports, formal reports, and manuscripts to be submitted for publication should be double-spaced. Business reports may be single-spaced.

<u>Margins</u>

Leave a bottom margin of about one inch. Leave one-inch top and side margins on all pages with these exceptions:

1. For the first page of an unbound or leftbound manuscript, leave a top margin of one and a half or two inches.
2. On all pages of a leftbound manuscript, leave a left margin of one and a half inches.
3. For the first page of a topbound manuscript, leave a top margin of two or two and a half inches; the second and subsequent pages, one and a half inches.

Indent the first line of a paragraph either five, seven, or ten spaces. Quoted matter of four lines or more is single-spaced and indented five spaces from the left and right margins, preceded and followed by one blank line space.

<u>Headings</u>

<u>Main headings</u>. The main heading is typed in all capitals and centered over the line of writing. Secondary headings are typed a double space below in capitals and lowercase, followed by a triple space. If no secondary heading is used, the main heading is followed by a triple space.

<u>Side headings</u>. Side headings (like <u>Margins</u> and <u>Headings</u> in this manuscript) are typed at the left margin with no terminal punctuation and are underlined. Main words are started with a capital letter. Two blank line spaces precede and one blank line space follows a side heading.

First page of unbound manuscript (pica type)

14C Technique Practice: STROKING ⑭ each line at least twice

1	Direct	fund any group fourth accept number broil young grinder thus
2	reaches	Irv Munce must bring records of any debts to Herbert Breece.
3	Adjacent	toil mask trap condemn wreck bulk pole wears sad buys cavern
4	keys	Was there a wreck where the fast New Hope traffic builds up?
5	Double	book dinner little abbey occur possible account apply effort
6	letters	Will Buzz and Lee carry the supplies across the street soon?
7	Awkward	exact copy; was pleased; excess debt; extra point; next size
8	reaches	I am pleased to get extra copies of opposing points of view.

| 1 | 2 | 3 | 4 | 5 | 6 | 7 | 8 | 9 | 10 | 11 | 12 |

14D Paragraph Guided Writing ⑱

1. Type 1' writings on each ¶ below as directed in 13D, page 28.

2. Type a 2' writing, beginning with ¶1 and typing as much of ¶2 as you can.

All letters are used.

		2' GWAM
¶1 1.2 SI 4.8 AWL 94% HFW	The major aim of this book is to help you learn how to type. Its second aim is to help you improve how you write, for you will not always be able merely to copy all the work you need to prepare. You will have to compose, also.	6 12 18 23
¶2 1.2 SI 4.8 AWL 94% HFW	As you practice to learn how to type, try to develop a writing skill, too. The next time you are asked to compose a paper for class, size up the job and set about writing it on the machine. It may be quite slow at first, but keep on.	29 35 42 47

2' GWAM | 1 | 2 | 3 | 4 | 5 | 6 |

LESSON 15

15A Preparatory Practice ⑧ each line 3 times

Alphabet	One judge was baffled as five boys quickly mixed the prizes.
Shift lock	We hope to read TO RACE THE WIND and TIME OUT FOR HAPPINESS.
Fluency	Major cities are rich with problems but poor with solutions.

| 1 | 2 | 3 | 4 | 5 | 6 | 7 | 8 | 9 | 10 | 11 | 12 |

64D Problem Typing: SIMPLE REPORT STYLE ㉕

Problem 1: Report with the Line Length Specified

Full sheet; 65-space line (center − 33, + 32, + 3 to 7; center heading on Line 10 (pica), Line 13 (elite); TS; then DS the ¶s with 5-space ¶ indentions; proofread by comparing

SIMPLE REPORT STYLE

TS

	Words
	4

To this point, you have typed most of your papers with a line 16
length specified (60 or 70 spaces), regardless of whether your 29
machine had pica- or elite-size type. You will now learn to type 42
reports according to standard conventions of manuscript layout, 55
based on the number of inches in the margin instead of the number 68
of spaces in the writing line. 74

When standard conventions are followed, pica and elite solu- 86
tions will differ somewhat. If one-inch side margins are used, 99
for example, an elite line will contain 78 spaces and a pica line 112
will contain but 65 spaces. As a result, more copy will fit on a 125
page of elite type. 129

If side margins of one inch are desired, ten pica spaces 141
should be allowed in each margin. On the other hand, users of 153
elite type should allow 12 spaces. 161

METRIC EQUIVALENTS	
	Centimeters (cm)
1 inch	2.5
1½ inches	3.75
2 inches	5
10 pica spaces	2.5
12 elite spaces	2.5
6 vertical line spaces	2.5
8½- by 11-inch paper	21.5 by 28

Problem 2: Report with the Margin Width Specified

Retype the report in Problem 1, using a top margin of 2″ (pica) and 2½″ (elite) and side margins of 1″ each.

Evaluate Your Work. With a stroke and line-space ruler, check top and side margins.

LESSON 65

65A Preparatory Practice ⑦ each line twice; then 1′ writings on Line 4

Alphabet	Dick will make a quick flight to La Paz, Bolivia, next July or August.
Figure	A 2-act play, held at 95 East 47 Street on June 16, began at 8:30 p.m.
Figure/symbol	Lehman & Warden's catalog lists item #482 at $960 (less 10% for cash).
Fluency	A man should want work enough to do and strength enough to do it well.

| 1 | 2 | 3 | 4 | 5 | 6 | 7 | 8 | 9 | 10 | 11 | 12 | 13 | 14 |

65B Special Characters and Symbols ⑥ each line twice; in Line 4, write the letter l with a pen

Abbreviations	The c.o.d. shipment to Maxwell & Bond, Inc., was sent f.o.b. New York.
Equation	Use x for <u>times</u>, − for <u>minus</u>, and = for <u>equals</u>: 450 x 7 − 670 = 2480.
Degrees	The melting point of gold is 1063° C.; but that of potassium, 63.5° C.
Formula	The beam loading formula she used was: $\dfrac{bdf^2}{6\ell} = W$ (W = load in pounds).

15B Technique Practice: TABULATOR ⑦

Clear all tabulator stops; set a tab stop 5 spaces, another 10 spaces, and still another 15 spaces to the right of the left margin.

Begin the first line of the drill at the left margin. Use the tab key or bar to type the remaining lines. Tab, release, and type quickly.

Margin   Typing beats writing with a pen, so learn how to type right.

Indent 5 ——*Tab once*——→ No typewriter is made that can do your writing for you.

Indent 10 ——*Tab twice*——→ We all must learn to say just what we want to say.

Indent 15 ——*Tab three times*——→ Typing skill is a highly prized writing tool.

15C Technique Practice: STROKING ⑩   each line twice; Line 1 from dictation

1 Fluency   it is | if it is | to do the | and did it | if they go | if they do go

2 Long words   practice condition choice luxury visit country respect happy

3 un   sun sunk bun bunt burn runs lung hunt rung trunk young under

4 One hand   As we agreed, John erected extra seats.   Jim saw only a few.

5 Balanced hand   Did the girls do the work?   The men may find the right firm.

6 Combination   He based his case on the data he got from the tax statement.

15D Paragraph Guided Writing ⑱

1. Type 1' writings on each ¶ below as directed in 13D, page 28.

2. Type a 3' writing, beginning with ¶ 1 and typing as much of ¶ 2 as you can.

All letters are used.

	3' GWAM

¶ 1
1.2 SI
5.0 AWL
96% HFW

      Believe it or not, some things in life are still free,   4 | 35

the respect of close friends, the luxury of a day or two in   8 | 39

the quiet country, or the practice of free choice. Perhaps   12 | 43

you now know how much value these things do add to a life.   16 | 47

¶ 2
1.2 SI
5.0 AWL
96% HFW

      You can also extend a helping hand or a kind word to a   19 | 50

fellow who needs it, enjoy a clear breeze, or visit with an   23 | 54

old friend. These things, and many more, cost nothing. As   27 | 58

you may know, a happy condition comes from a state of mind.   31 | 62

3' GWAM | 1 | 2 | 3 | 4 |

SECTION 10

Reports, Outlines, and Composing

LESSONS 64-72

Goal. The lessons in this section will enable you to type simple reports and outlines in attractive and acceptable style. You will also increase your skill in composing at the typewriter.

Machine Adjustments. 70-space line; SS sentence drills; DS and indent ¶s 5 spaces; space problem copy as directed. For problems and ¶ copy, use an adjusted right margin.

LESSON 64

64A   Preparatory Practice ⑦   each line twice; then 1′ writings on Lines 2 and 4

Alphabet	The explorer questioned Jack's amazing tale about an unknown vicinity.
Figure	In 1965, 213 clerks were working here; in 1970, 842; and in 1975, 947.
Figure/symbol	Roth's sold 1,469 meals @ $2.75 per plate and 830 pieces of pie @ 50¢.
Fluency	He may work for many weeks on the eight forms for the city land panel.

| 1 | 2 | 3 | 4 | 5 | 6 | 7 | 8 | 9 | 10 | 11 | 12 | 13 | 14 |

64B   Skill-Transfer Typing ⑧   65-space line; 1′ writing on each line; compare GWAM

		Words
Straight copy	A majority of the club women questioned the chairman's authority.	13
Figure	Flight 746 left Copenhagen at 9:35 a.m. and arrived at 10:28 p.m.	13
Script	When you write, relax; the real secret is to talk to your reader.	13
Corrected copy	He ~~said~~ maintains that #a wide vocbulary i⌒s vital to*g forc*ful writ⌒ing.	13
Proofreading	Is a letter does'nt found just like your, change it until if does.	13

64C   Speed/Control Building ⑩

1. Type a 1′ writing for speed and a 1′ writing for control on the ¶ below.

2. Type a 3′ writing for speed on the ¶. Try to equal your better 1′ *gwam*.

3. Type a 3′ writing for control on the ¶. Determine your *gwam* and number of errors.

All letters are used.

1.4 SI
5.4 AWL
85% HFW

	GWAM 1′	3′	
One must plan to devote a good deal of time to the process of secur-	14	5	40
ing his or her first full-time job. It may be a false step to grab the	28	9	45
first job that is offered. Recognize the importance of actually forming	43	14	50
a plan that will get the best job available. Expend all possible time	57	19	54
and effort to discover where the job openings are. Telephone friends and	72	24	59
members of your family. Keep an eye on the daily papers. And remember	86	29	64
that the services of the public and private employment agencies can be	100	33	69
of immense help in your quest.	106	35	71

1′ GWAM | 1 | 2 | 3 | 4 | 5 | 6 | 7 | 8 | 9 | 10 | 11 | 12 | 13 | 14 |
3′ GWAM | 1 | 2 | 3 | 4 | 5 |

15E Individual Practice ⑦

1. Type each line once. Place a check mark before each line that seemed difficult.

2. Type 2 or more times each line that you checked as difficult.

1 p x   mix pack toxic group fixed price wrap place coax plate sixth

2 q m   quit most acquit room quick game liquid warm qualm may quake

3 z y   lazy graze fry sieze yet freeze lonely azure your zone money

4 n t   count ton nothing string thing went sent lent slant not lint

5 b u   but buy bunch number lumber jumble rumble rubber built blunt

6 v ?   Can Vince vote? Can Merv go? Did Dave move? Did Vi drive?

LESSON 16

16A Preparatory Practice ⑧ each line 3 times

Alphabet   Pride in his work quickly gave Jim Fitz his next big chance.

q and m   Mark Quinn is not quite sure he can take my next major quiz.

Fluency   A light touch is the right touch to use to build good skill.
            | 1 | 2 | 3 | 4 | 5 | 6 | 7 | 8 | 9 | 10 | 11 | 12 |

16B Skill Checkup: STROKING ⑫

Type a 1′ writing on each sentence, typing it as many times as you can until time is called. Determine *gwam*.

Stroking Cue. Keep your eyes on the copy. Make low, quick reach-strokes. Keep the hands and arms quiet.

		Words in Line
1	Can men differ, yet have the same goals?	8
2	Many young people are looking for new ideals.	9
3	Some are trying to put these ideals into practice.	10
4	The rules under which men have lived are being changed.	11
5	In sum, this whole problem is being attacked on many fronts.	12
6	We must expand our horizons and work for progressive change.	12
7	Any change for the sake of joining the crowd is unjustified.	12

| 1 | 2 | 3 | 4 | 5 | 6 | 7 | 8 | 9 | 10 | 11 | 12 |

63D **Problem Typing Measurement:** TABLES ⑳ 10′ for getting ready and proofreading; 20′ timing

Problem 1: Three-Column Table

Full sheet; DS; reading position; 8 spaces between columns; correct errors

PAINTINGS BY NINETEENTH CENTURY ARTISTS			Words
		TS	8
Artist	Painting	Cost	16
		DS	
J. B. Pyne	Coniston Water	$ 6,250	23
H. H. Parker	The Silent Mill	2,750	30
R. Gallon	Hambledon Weir	550	36
A. Gordon	Henry-on-Thames	500	42
S. Bough	Borrowdale	1,050	48
F. W. Watts	On the Wye	10,250	54
A. A. Glendening	Bettws-Y-Coed	1,225	61
G. A. Williams	A Summer's Evening	2,000	70
Total Cost		$24,575	74

Problem 2: Four-Column Table

Full sheet; DS; exact vertical center; 6 spaces between columns; correct errors

BASEBALL'S HIGHEST SALARY AT EACH POSITION				Words
				9
1973 Season				11
Position	Player	Team	Salary	22
First base	Dick Allen	White Sox	$225,000	30
Second base	Joe Morgan	Reds	90,000	37
Third base	Brooks Robinson	Orioles	110,000	46
Short stop	Luis Aparicio	Red Sox	100,000	54
Catcher	Johnny Bench	Reds	110,000	61
Outfield	Henry Aaron	Braves	200,000	68
Outfield	Carl Yastrzemski	Red Sox	165,000	76
Outfield	Willie Mays	Mets	165,000	83
Pitcher	Steve Carlton	Phils	165,000	90

Problem 3: Business Letter with Table WB p. 77

Modified block with block ¶s, open punctuation; date on Line 17; 60-space line; 6 spaces between columns; SS and center table horizontally; correct errors; address envelope

Time	7%	8%	Words
			68
20 years	$7.76	$8.37	72
25 years	7.07	7.72	76
30 years	6.66	7.34	80

March 15, 19-- | Mrs. Roland Bauer | 1630 ⟨8⟩ Mimosa Street | Amarillo, TX 79107 | Dear ⟨15⟩ Mrs. Bauer (¶ 1) The figures below show the ⟨23⟩ monthly payment required to pay principal ⟨31⟩ and interest on $1,000. For example, on a ⟨40⟩ $1,000 loan at 7% for 25 years, the payment ⟨49⟩ would be $7.07. For a $25,000 loan, it would ⟨58⟩ be 25 times that or $176.75. ⟨64⟩

(¶ 2) To find how large a loan can be carried ⟨88⟩ by a given monthly payment, find the terms ⟨97⟩ you might be offered and divide your planned ⟨106⟩ monthly payment by the indicated figure. | ⟨114⟩ Sincerely yours | Berton Blake, Loan Depart- ⟨122⟩ ment | xx ⟨124/135⟩

16C Proofreading ⑤ Type the ¶ once, making needed corrections as you type.

There are two ways to proofread: (1) by comparing and (2) by verifying.

Comparing. A typist checks his own work by a careful reading of his copy and by checking it against the original when spelling of words or meaning is uncertain or when figures or proper names are encountered.

Verifying (Recommended for Statistical Copy, Stencils, and Spirit Masters). One person reads from the original while another (preferably not the typist) reads the new copy. Tricky words are spelled; punctuation marks are indicated.

Common errors are circled in the sample shown at the right.

How (wellyou) write (mean) just how (deft ly) you
put words together, say what (your) want to say. It
does (now) mean (ho) well you can use a (epn). If you
(you) learn to type well, you can (impove) the clarity
as (will) as (if) the manner of (you) writing.

Line 1. (1) No space, (2) missing letter, (3) faulty spacing
Line 2. (1) Omitted word, (2) added letter, (3) incorrect spacing
Line 3. (1) Uneven left margin, (2) misstroke, (3) omitted letter, (4) transposition
Line 4. (1) Added word, (2) period for comma, (3) strikeover
Line 5. (1) Changed word, (2) added word, (3) changed word

16D Growth Index ⑱ three 3′ writings

Type three 3′ writings; determine *gwam* and number of errors on each one.

Proofread the first two writings by comparing. Proofread the third writing by *verifying*.

All letters are used.

		3′ GWAM
¶ 1 1.2 SI 5.0 AWL 96% HFW	When you write something, read it. Ask yourself these	4 | 35
	questions. Does this have life, does it move, does it take	8 | 39
	you along with it? Or is it a haze of sorry old words that	12 | 43
	really fail to evoke any drive in you? Does it turn you on?	16 | 47
¶ 2 1.2 SI 5.0 AWL 96% HFW	Remember this when writing: Just talk to a reader the	19 | 51
	way you would if you could visit with him in your own home.	23 | 55
	Try it; then see if your style is not more natural. Do not	27 | 59
	expect to hold your reader if your style is cold and stale.	31 | 63

3′ GWAM | 1 | 2 | 3 | 4 |

16E Individual Practice ⑦ Type as directed for 15E, page 31.

1 p x   Mexico package relax piece wrapped placed hoax mixture parts
2 q m   quiet must acquaint rumor quickly request germ quorum mosque
3 z y   hazards graze fly siezed hazy lonely zone youth mainly dizzy
4 n t   fountain tin notice being dent grant country untold not tent
5 b u   bushel shrubs rubbish hub build burn bundle tube jumped burr
6 v ?   Vince Vogt gave verbal orders? Have David and Ervin shaved?

63A Preparatory Practice ⑤ each line at least twice

Alphabet	The grave fire hazards of the job were quickly explained to three men.
Figure/symbol	McNeil's invoice #4296 (our order #750B dated 10/18) comes to $942.30.
Hyphen/dash	Hyphenate a multiword modifier preceding a noun––a hard-and-fast rule.
Fluency	The authority of those in power should be used for the benefit of all.

| 1 | 2 | 3 | 4 | 5 | 6 | 7 | 8 | 9 | 10 | 11 | 12 | 13 | 14 |

63B Technique Practice: RESPONSE PATTERNS ⑦ each line twice; then 1' writings on Lines 3 and 4

Letter response	Afterwards, we all saw him get an award for addressing the most cards.
Word response	If they can find the right guide, they may all go to the ancient city.
Combination	Believe only half of what you hear, but be sure it is the better half.
	Only a few of the members signed the sales contract that was prepared.

| 1 | 2 | 3 | 4 | 5 | 6 | 7 | 8 | 9 | 10 | 11 | 12 | 13 | 14 |

63C Growth Index ⑧ one 5' writing; determine GWAM and errors

All letters are used.

		GWAM 1'	5'

¶ 1
1.5 SI
5.6 AWL
80% HFW

Many people believe that their dreams can have unique results. — 13 | 3 | 45
Thoreau said that if one moved in the direction of his dreams and really — 27 | 5 | 48
tried to live the life he had imagined, he would meet with unexpected — 41 | 8 | 51
success. A dream can make the impossible possible if you do work dili- — 56 | 11 | 54
gently. You must stay awake and make it come true, however. — 67 | 13 | 56

¶ 2
1.5 SI
5.6 AWL
80% HFW

A right idea consciously and persistently held in mind tends to be — 13 | 16 | 59
realized. Frequently, time is needed to have an idea develop; but it — 27 | 19 | 61
will be realized––of that you can be sure. The power of positive thought — 42 | 22 | 64
is far more than a clever slogan: It is latent power that can make the — 57 | 25 | 67
unusual happen. Clear thinking underlies this power. — 67 | 27 | 69

¶ 3
1.5 SI
5.6 AWL
80% HFW

Things that happen to us are consequences, not coincidences. Once — 13 | 30 | 72
a person believes that he can control circumstances by learning to apply — 28 | 33 | 75
his thinking powers consciously, he can become master of his fate. No — 42 | 35 | 78
one is justified in feeling that opportunity comes only by chance. "As — 57 | 38 | 81
a man thinks in his heart, so is he" is a principle that has been tested — 71 | 41 | 84
many times by men of every nation. — 78 | 43 | 85

1' GWAM | 1 | 2 | 3 | 4 | 5 | 6 | 7 | 8 | 9 | 10 | 11 | 12 | 13 | 14 |
5' GWAM | 1 | 2 | 3 |

SECTION 3

The Figure Keys

LESSONS 17-21

Machine Adjustments. *Use a 60-space line.* Set the left margin stop at center — 30. Move the right margin stop to the extreme right side of the scale. SS all sentence drills, with DS between repeated lines. DS and indent paragraphs 5 spaces.

In this section you will type figures and some new punctuation marks. You will also build your basic skills to higher levels. The paragraph copy is rated *easy*.

LESSON 17

17A **Preparatory Practice** ⑧ each line twice; in Line 3, do not type the dividers

Alphabet	Did Evelyn Wellington quiz Peter Jackson about his tax form?
br	brows bright brush broil braid brave brace broom break brisk
Combination resp.	with you|for him|did look|and regard|if it sets|to read well
Fluency	When Rod paid the girls, did he make them sign the new form?

| 1 | 2 | 3 | 4 | 5 | 6 | 7 | 8 | 9 | 10 | 11 | 12 |

17B **Location of 5, 8, and 1** ③

Type 5 with F finger

Type 8 with K finger

1. Locate the new key on the keyboard chart.
2. Find the key on your typewriter keyboard.
3. Study the reach illustration for the new key.
4. Type the drill below for that key.

If your typewriter has a special key for figure 1, reach up to it with the left fourth (little) finger. If your typewriter does not have a special key for figure 1, use the small letter l to type 1.

Reach Technique. Move the controlling finger (not the hand) up to type figures in the top row.

17C **Location Drills for 5, 8, and 1** ⑫ Lines 1, 2, and either 3 or 4 twice for tryout; then each line twice

1	5	f f5f 5f 5f 5f 55 555 55 floors, 555 feet, 5 gallons, 5 rods
2	8	k k8k 8k 8k 8k 88 888 88 knots, 888 kits, 8 inches, 88 and 8
3	Figure 1	a a1a a1 a1 a1 11 111 11 aides, 111 attacks, 1 and 11 quarts
4	Letter l as 1	l ll .l l. .ll l.l. My 11 men worked from May 1 to June 11.
5	Review	Is it Channel 5, 8, or 11? Was the score 5 to 8, or 8 to 5?
6	Review	Three of the 158 men are absent; the other 155 arrived at 5.

| 1 | 2 | 3 | 4 | 5 | 6 | 7 | 8 | 9 | 10 | 11 | 12 |

62D Problem Typing Review ⓷⓪ **Proofread as indicated.**

Problem 1: Word Division

Full sheet; DS; reading position;
6 spaces between columns; proof-
read by comparing; correct errors

ACCEPTABLE POINTS OF WORD DIVISION 7

Application of Guides, Pages 65-66 14

Word	Syllables	Divide	
			22
congratulate	con-grat-u-late	con-grat-u-late	31
elaborate	e-lab-o-rate	(Show the acceptable	38
evaluation	e-val-u-ate	points of division for	44
fundamental	fun-da-men-tal	the remaining words.)	52
historical	his-tor-i-cal		60
impartial	im-par-tial		66
reclassify	re-clas-si-fy		74
self-sufficient	self-suf-fi-cient		84

Problem 2: Uneven Amounts,
Dollar Sign, Total

Full sheet; DS; reading position;
8 spaces between columns; proof-
read by verifying; correct errors

Words

PAYMENTS FOR APPROVED SUGGESTIONS 7

Year Ending April 30, 197– 12

Name	Department	Amount	
			21
Alonzo, Susan B.	Sales	$1,200	27
Alvarez, Anthony	Maintenance	300	34
Appleman, David	Advertising	75	41
Baughman, Elizabeth	Personnel	1,150	48
De La Rocha, Betty	Purchasing	750	56
Jacobsen, Donald	Art	525	61
Jaskiewicz, Thomas	Security	300	68
Melkanoff, Stephen	Construction	900	77
Total		$5,200	80

Problem 3:
Simple Memorandum
with Table

Half sheet; date on Line 7; SS;
65-space line; block style; 6
spaces between columns; proof-
read by comparing; correct errors

Words

January 15, 19–– SUBJECT: Family Magazines │ (¶ 1) Many 10
magazines appeal to both adults and children because of a shared 23
hobby or special interest. Examples of these magazines, with 35
their yearly subscription rates, follow: 43

Audubon	Bimonthly	$10.00	49
Gems and Minerals	Monthly	4.75	55
National Geographic	Monthly	8.50	61
Outdoor Life	Monthly	6.00	67
Skin Diver	Monthly	7.50	71

17D **Technique Practice:** STROKING (10) each line twice

Technique Cue. Reach with your fingers. Reach to the top row without moving your hand, twisting your elbow, or arching your wrist.

Words

1 Tour 851 to the Orient is set to depart on August 15, 8 a.m.   12

2 *Don arrived on Flight 881; he leaves on Flight 151 at 5 p.m.*   12

3 Send Model 1851 in pecan finish. I am returning Model 5588.   12

4 *They paid that bill with check No. 88551, dated November 18.*   12

5 The assignment covers pages 8 through 15 and 88 through 151.   12

6 *These 18 men picked 855 crates of tomatoes in just 15 hours.*   12

17E **Speed/Control Building** (17) one 1' writing on each ¶ for speed; repeat for control
one 3' writing on all ¶s for speed; repeat for control

Exploration (Speed) Level of Practice. Use the *exploration level* when the purpose of practice is to reach out into new speed areas.

Control Level of Practice. When the purpose of practice is to type with ease and control, drop down in rate and type on the *control level*.

All letters are used.

		3' GWAM
¶ 1 1.3 SI 5.2 AWL 90% HFW	Without question this is an age of numbers. Ask someone	4 | 44
	his age, and you receive a number. A number also marks a tax	8 | 48
	return, a class card, or a highway route.	11 | 51
¶ 2 1.3 SI 5.2 AWL 90% HFW	It is thus important that you master the top row on your	14 | 54
	machine. Whether you work as a typist or just type your own	19 | 59
	papers, you will prize highly your skill in typing numbers.	23 | 63
	Begin to build it now.	24 | 64
¶ 3 1.3 SI 5.2 AWL 90% HFW	Numbers are assigned to a good many other things, such	28 | 68
	as your home address, the time of day, or ZIP Code. When you	32 | 72
	go to a food store, a number will determine your turn at the	36 | 76
	counter. We may one day exchange numbers for personal names.	40 | 80

3' GWAM | 1 | 2 | 3 | 4 |

LESSON 62

62A Preparatory Practice ⑤ each line at least twice

Alphabet	Julie began to study the six chapters on vitamins for her weekly quiz.
Figure/symbol	Model #S6-718 (20″ screen) sells for $359; with a 27″ screen, $467.20.
Fractions	Can Jane Beal add these fractions: 2/3, 3/4, 4/5, 5/6, 7/8, and 9/10?
Fluency	The total endowment is not big enough to meet the needs of the school.

| 1 | 2 | 3 | 4 | 5 | 6 | 7 | 8 | 9 | 10 | 11 | 12 | 13 | 14 |

62B Individual Practice ⑩

1. Type each line once. Place a check mark before any lines that seemed difficult.

2. Type 2 or more times each line you checked as difficult.

1	Shift keys	John and Frank spent April in Mexico City and June and July in Brazil.
2	Shift lock	Underline or ALL CAP addressee notations: Hold for Arrival, PERSONAL.
3	One hand	Several facets of test data, based on our abstracts, detected a trend.
4	Adjacent keys	We condemned her notion that power in the past excuses present policy.
5	Special symbols	Carmen corrected her arithmetic error: 245 × 8 − 860 + 128 ÷ 4 = 307.
6	1st row	Have Benny, Mac, and Zora Nixon been on vacation in Brazil and Panama?
7	Double letters	Will Larry Feeser discuss Matt Bell's brilliant book, CURRENT LESSONS?
8	1st/2d fingers	Jeff Briggs may fly with my brother rather than take the flight alone.
9	Long words	This work challenges your competence, resourcefulness, and creativity.
10	Letter response	A few dead trees were scattered among the great grove of orange trees.

| 1 | 2 | 3 | 4 | 5 | 6 | 7 | 8 | 9 | 10 | 11 | 12 | 13 | 14 |

62C Control Building: STATISTICAL COPY ⑤ two 2′ writings for control

1.7 SI
6.0 AWL
70% HFW

	2′ GWAM
From data collected from several sources, Andreson & Company of	6 / 49
New York says that of his 113 waking hours per week, the average adult	13 / 56
American spends 38 hours working and 25 hours eating, dressing, and	20 / 63
commuting. The remaining 50 hours are for leisure. Almost 80% of	27 / 69
these hours are utilized either looking at television (45%) or listen-	34 / 76
ing to the radio (34%). Seeing movies accounts for 0.5%; reading books,	41 / 84
only 0.2%.	42 / 85

2′ GWAM | 1 | 2 | 3 | 4 | 5 | 6 | 7 |

LESSON 18

18A Preparatory Practice ⑧ each line twice

Alphabet	Wilbur Jamieson packed the very large box of quartz mineral.
1 5 8	The numbers of the lockers in question are 15, 58, and 1581.
Combination resp.	on the|with my|this date|for you|go to him|and they saw only
Fluency	Would he like to know how the men who work for us save time?

```
|   1   |   2   |   3   |   4   |   5   |   6   |   7   |   8   |   9   |   10  |   11  |   12  |
```

18B Location of 2, 0, and : (Colon) ③

Type 2 with S finger

Type 0 with ; finger

Colon. Type the : (colon) by shifting the ;. Do not space before or after the colon to separate hours and minutes in stating time; space twice after the colon in other uses.

18C Location Drills for 2, 0, and : ⑫ Lines 1, 2, and 3 once for tryout; then each line twice

1	2	s s2s 2s 2s 2s 22 222 22 sets, 222 shots, 22 stops 222 sacks
2	0	; ;0; 0; 0; 0; 00 000 10 poles, 50 lines, 80 loads, 505 oars
3	:	; ;:; :; :; :; 8:01 1:15 5:10 Call at 5:15; arrive at 8:10.
4	Review	Get there by 8:00 or 8:05; the opera begins at 8:15 or 8:20.
5	Review	One of these models will be in stock: 28, 202, 505, or 805.

18D Technique Practice: STROKING ⑩ each line twice

Words

1		Whether you are 20 or 50, each workday there begins at 8:15.	12
2		*Her flight, No. 258, lands at 10 p.m. on Thursday, March 15.*	12
3		You ordered No. 508, but you may wish to change to No. 2015.	12
4	Space twice after colon	*I suggest you try one of these models: 2001, 5002, or 8112.*	12
5		If you arrive by 8:15 a.m., we can set the meeting for 8:20.	12

```
|   1   |   2   |   3   |   4   |   5   |   6   |   7   |   8   |   9   |   10  |   11  |   12  |
```

61D Problem Typing: TABLES IN A LETTER AND A MEMORANDUM (25)

Problem 1: Letter with Table
WB p. 75

Modified block with block ¶s, open punctuation; date on Line 12; 60-space line; SS and center the table horizontally; 10 spaces between columns; correct errors

	Words
February 28, 19--	Dr. Charles B. Maxwell	Lincoln Towers	11
Annex	17832 Grayson Avenue	Trenton, NJ 08619	Dear	21
Dr. Maxwell	24

(¶ 1) Our customers tell us they like our creativity, our quality, 36
and our savings. Because we design our own equipment and make 49
most of it, you won't see it in other stores. When you shop 61
at Dan's Radio City, experience pays off for you—in better se- 73
lection and in the latest features and technology. 83

(¶ 2) As there are no middleman markups, you can always be sure 95
of low prices. Here are just a few examples of the low prices 108
in our Indoor Antenna Department: 114

Telescoping antenna	$15.95	120
Dual rotating UHF antenna	9.95	126
Tabletop UHF antenna	5.29	132
Lennox hideaway antenna	12.79	138

(¶ 3) After we design and engineer our products, they undergo a 150
quality-inspection procedure that's superb. All products must 162
pass thorough tests before we approve them for production. 174

(¶ 4) Informed and interested salespeople know how to answer 185
your questions. They make product recommendations that fit 197
your needs. Our Anniversary Catalog lists more than 1,200 audio 210
and communications items. Just call us if you want a copy. 222

Sincerely yours | William Berger, Manager | xx   230/246

Problem 2: Simple Memorandum with Table

Half sheet; 65-space line; block style; SS; date on Line 7; SS and center the table horizontally; 16 spaces between columns; correct errors

	Words
February 28, 19--	SUBJECT: Job Expectations (¶ 1) Dr. S. I.	11

Hayakawa recently made a study to determine what students 23
wanted in a job. His findings are listed below: 32

Self-expression	78%	36
Challenge	63	39
Security	25	41
Money	13	42

As the educational level of our people increases, so too does 55
their expectation level. Dr. Hayakawa's findings are more 67
evidence that young people's attitude toward work has changed. 79

18E Skill-Transfer Typing ⑰

Type two 1' writings on each ¶. Compare *gwam* on the two ¶s. Type two more 1' writings on the ¶ with the lower *gwam*.

Finally, type two 3' writings on both ¶s. Determine *gwam*. Compare your better 3' *gwam* with the best 1' *gwam* on each of the two ¶s.

All letters are used.

		GWAM		
		1'	3'	
¶ 1 1.3 SI 5.2 AWL 90% HFW	We are told that people in business fall into three	10	3	38
	large classes. In the first class is the worker who has to	22	7	42
	be told in detail everything to be done. This person is a	34	11	46
	heavy burden to the company. Basic skills and a mind that	46	15	50
	thinks for itself are lacking.	52	17	52
¶ 2 1.3 SI 5.2 AWL 90% HFW	The worker in the next class is little better. He does	11	21	56
	just what is required, then quits and fiddles. This person	23	25	60
	has some ability, but he lacks a sincere interest in what he	35	29	64
	is doing. An interested man can size up a job, decide what	47	33	68
	must be done, and do it.	52	35	69

1' GWAM | 1 | 2 | 3 | 4 | 5 | 6 | 7 | 8 | 9 | 10 | 11 | 12 |
3' GWAM | 1 | 2 | 3 | 4 |

LESSON 19

19A Preparatory Practice ⑧ each line twice

Alphabet   Mary very quickly mixed a big jar of soap for the new prize.

0 :   On June 10, Flight 20 left at 2:20 with 10 men and 20 women.

Combination   and the case|for they saw|to do my|if they join|it is on the
response
                | 1 | 2 | 3 | 4 | 5 | 6 | 7 | 8 | 9 | 10 | 11 | 12 |

19B Technique Practice: STROKING ⑩ each line twice

1 Direct   bright muscle verb exceed serve debt gravy hurry brush nurse
2 reaches   Grace Hunter made delectable braised celery and great gravy.

3 Adjacent report enter mast sulk people respond balk column opens true
4 keys   We said that poised talk has triumphed over violent actions.

5 Double   account appears sudden merry common sunny eggs supply buffet
6 letters   Ann Hobbs will collect puzzles, books, buttons, and glasses.

7 Figures   Read: Unit 5, 8 pages; Unit 8, 20 pages; Unit 10, 12 pages.
8   What is the sum of 5 and 55 and 585 and 188 and 881 and 558?

LESSON 61

61A Preparatory Practice ⑦ each line at least twice; then 1' writings on Line 4

Alphabet	Except on Friday, Joe works all day at that big aquarium in Vera Cruz.
Figure/symbol	Ben's policy #718426 for $49,300 has been renewed for another 5 years.
Special symbols	Frank is sure this problem is correct: 369 × 7 + 125 − 840 ÷ 4 = 467.
Fluency	To qualify for the job, he must be able to write short, clear letters.

| 1 | 2 | 3 | 4 | 5 | 6 | 7 | 8 | 9 | 10 | 11 | 12 | 13 | 14 |

61B Control Building: RATE CONTROL ⑧ five 1' writings

1. Select a goal: 40, 50, 60, or more *wam*. Type at your goal rate for each writing—no slower, no faster.

2. When you have typed to your goal word or letter on 2 writings as time is called, advance to the next goal.

NOTE: Your instructor may call the ¼ or ½ minutes to guide you.

All letters are used.

		2' GWAM
1.4 SI 5.4 AWL 85% HFW	Some workers can't do anything unless they are told just what to do	7 | 55
	and how to do it. Although they may be good at routine jobs, they are	14 | 62
	lacking in imagination, in creativity, and in the urge to explore new	21 | 69
	methods and solutions for their problems. Even great ability is inade-	28 | 76
	quate because quick hands must be guided by a reflective head, a fact	35 | 83
	that many workers may fail to recognize. Learn now to match your skills	42 | 90
	with a desire to find a better way of doing your work.	48 | 96

2' GWAM | 1 | 2 | 3 | 4 | 5 | 6 | 7 |

61C Composing and Typing ⑩ 70-space line; DS

1. Type the ¶ as given below. Proofread your copy; circle errors.

2. In a second ¶, summarize in 3 or 4 lines the idea conveyed in the first ¶.

3. Revise your copy as necessary. Retype the 2 ¶s.

What our country needs most is within each of us as individuals.

A cleaner neighborhood begins with your broom. A more beautiful city

begins with a seed in your own garden. A more just society begins in

your own heart. To make this a finer land, we cannot wait for others––

we must begin, ourselves, as individuals.

19C Location of 3, 6, and / (Diagonal) ③

Type 3 with D finger

Type 6 with J finger

Diagonal. Move the right fourth (little) finger down to ? (question) and without shifting, type /.

Space once between a whole number and a fraction typed with the diagonal: 3 1/3.

19D Location Drills for 3, 6, and / (Diagonal) ⑫ Lines 1, 2, and 3 once for tryout; then each line twice

1	3	d d3d 3d 3d 3d 33 333 33 disks, 333 dams, 33 steps, 33 and 3
2	6	j j6j 6j 6j 6j 66 666 66 jars, 6 jobs, 66 helpers, 666 years
3	/	; ;/; /; /; /; 1/8 or 1/5 Type this copy: 2 1/2 6 1/6 1/6.
4	Review	Read pages 33, 66, and 363. Give Al 10, 20, 30, or 50 feet.
5	Review	Take No. 62 for 5 1/3 miles; then follow No. 6 for 12 miles.

19E Sentence Guided Writing ⑰

1. Type Line 1 as a 1' writing, with the call of the line ending each 15, 20, or 30". Then, try to type Line 2 at the same rate. Repeat 1' writings on the figure line as time permits.

2. Type each of the other pairs of lines in this way.

All letters and all figures learned are used.

		G W A M
		30" 20" 15"
1	Did Rex see Van and Max at the new pool?	16 24 32
2	We have these sizes: 8, 10, 11, and 12.	16 24 32
3	John Quick may meet the mayor of Troy in May.	18 27 36
4	Ship 26 feet of No. 58 and 18 feet of No. 60.	18 27 36
5	You can live in luxury at the Mayflower in Dayton.	20 30 40
6	I can see you before 10:15 a.m. or after 2:20 p.m.	20 30 40
7	He may dine at any restaurant and simply sign the bill.	22 33 44
8	Please send us 16 5/8 feet of No. 3820 canvas covering.	22 33 44
9	To learn more about this unique car, visit your dealer soon.	24 36 48
10	The car has a V8 engine, disc brakes, and 15 optional items.	24 36 48

| 1 | 2 | 3 | 4 | 5 | 6 | 7 | 8 | 9 | 10 | 11 | 12 |

Problem 1

Full sheet; DS; reading position; 10 spaces between columns

center { ALL CAP Personal Consumption Expenditures

(In Billions of Dollars)

Type of Product	1960	1970	Words
			7
			12
	1960	1970	21
Food, beverages, and tobacco	87.5	142.9	30
Clothing, accessories, and jewelry	33.0	62.3	38
Personal care	5.3	10.1	43
Housing	46.3	91.2	47
Household operations	46.9	85.6	53
Medical care expenses	19.1	47.3	59
Personal business	15.0	35.5	65
Transportation	43.1	77.9	70
Recreation	18.3	39.0	74
Private education and research	3.7	10.4	82
Religious and welfare activities	4.7	8.8	91
Foreign travel and other, net	2.2	4.8	99

Problem 2

Half sheet; DS; center vertically; 6 spaces between columns

all caps
Work Improvement Committee
1975-76 ←DS
←TS

Name	Dept. (spell out)	Room	Words
			5
			7
			15
Crowder, Enos (chairman)	Sales	1640	22
Glenwood, Denis	Purchasing	28	29
LeClaire, Marie	Accounting Bookkeeping	2104	35
Sanchez, Norbert	Advertising	1744	42
Yuen, Harry Henry	Data Processing	1509	48

LESSON 20

20A Preparatory Practice (8) each line twice

Alphabet	Max Quigley hopes Dick Webster can leave for Zurich in July.
Figures	Type the figures that follow: 58, 20, 16, 33, 20, 616, 310.
Fractions	Now type these fractions: 1/3, 5/6, 2/5, 3/8, 1/6, and 5/8.
Fluency	There is little doubt in his mind that he can make the trip.

| 1 | 2 | 3 | 4 | 5 | 6 | 7 | 8 | 9 | 10 | 11 | 12 |

20B Technique Practice: RESPONSE PATTERNS (7) each line twice; Lines 1, 3, and 5 from dictation

1	Word	the right form │they may go │it is due │to work at │for that man
2	response	It is the duty of men to work; their wish, to make a profit.
3	Letter	only you │after my │you saw │my tax case │refer to our │were ever
4	response	As you are aware, my estate tax case was, in fact, deferred.
5	Combination	if they look │when the facts │if they imply │they also serve to
6		He treated the data with care; he stated my case with vigor.

| 1 | 2 | 3 | 4 | 5 | 6 | 7 | 8 | 9 | 10 | 11 | 12 |

20C Technique Practice: TAB MECHANISM AND FIGURES (10) Type the drill twice, DS.

Procedure for setting tab stops

Clear all tab stops. (See page 18, if necessary.) For Column 1, set the left margin stop for a 60-space line. For Column 2, set a tab stop 8 spaces from the left margin. For Column 3, set a tab stop 8 spaces from the first tab stop.

Set stops for remaining columns in a similar manner. When the left margin stop and all tab stops have been set, operate the tab mechanism for a full line without typing.

Technique emphasis

Nonelectric. Depress and hold down the tab bar or key until the carriage stops. Move quickly back to home position and type the next item.

Electric. Flick the tab key or bar lightly. Return the controlling finger to its home position at once.

Eyes on copy during return

Reach with the fingers								
	to	it	do	if	go	so	the	did
	15	85	55	88	15	51	185	558
	as	no	be	on	we	in	you	pat
	55	88	15	18	51	81	888	555
	be	of	an	me	by	as	row	now
	88	55	11	85	58	18	151	881

KEY | 2 | 6 | 2 | 6 | 2 | 6 | 2 | 6 | 2 | 6 | 2 | 6 | 3 | 6 | 3 |

60A Preparatory Practice ⑦ each line twice; then 1' writings on Lines 1 and 4

Alphabet   Can the judge quiz the lawyer from Iowa about extensive profit taking?

Figure/symbol   On May 17, we shipped Lukin & Decker 6 cars of #932Y valued at $5,480.

Shift keys   On June 2, Ted Kuhn and George Lyon left for Italy, Greece, and Spain.

Fluency   I like to get his letters because they are short, clear, and friendly.

| 1 | 2 | 3 | 4 | 5 | 6 | 7 | 8 | 9 | 10 | 11 | 12 | 13 | 14 |

60B Technique Practice: COMBINATION RESPONSE ⑧ each line once from the book; twice from dictation

to you | to your | to our | to have | to him | like to | to be | of the | in the | to us

to the | for the | on the | with the | and the | from the | that the | at the | by the

is the | you will | you have | you are | you can | and you | that you | to you | it is

for your | of your | to your | in your | we are | we have | we will | we would | to be

of the | of our | this is | of this | one of | we can | in this | should be | that the

60C Skill-Transfer Typing ⑤ 60-space line; SS; two 1' writings on each line; compare GWAM; in Line 4, type the correct words for the circled words

Words

Straight copy   Hold the arms very still; just let your fingers do the work.   12

Script   New ideas will come to you as you give your ideas to others.   12

Corrected copy   With faith enough, work enough, we can do almost anything.   12

Proofreading   They make the forms four they men to us for there feild work.   12

60D Control Building ⑤

1. Type two 1' writings for *control*. Circle errors; note the *gwam* on the writing with the fewer errors.

2. Type a 2' writing for *control*. Compare *gwam* and number of errors with the better 1' writing.

All letters are used.

	2' GWAM
1.5 SI If you always try to put first things first in the jobs you do, you	7 | 45
5.6 AWL 80% HFW can expect to win the prize you seek. This is especially important if	14 | 52
your goal is that of improving your skill in typewriting. Many factors	21 | 60
enter into the development of skill at the typewriter. Most critical,	28 | 67
however, are the use of correct techniques and the efficient use of the	35 | 74
operative parts of the machine.	38 | 77

2' GWAM | 1 | 2 | 3 | 4 | 5 | 6 | 7 |

20D Location of 4 and 9 ③

Type 4 with F finger

Type 9 with L finger

Technique Cue. Reach to the top row of keys without moving the hand to the figure row and without twisting the elbow outward or arching the wrist. Try to hold the other fingers over their home keys.

20E Location Drills for 4 and 9 ⑩ Lines 1 and 2 once for tryout; then each line twice

4	f f4f 4f 4f 4f 44 444 44 feet, 4 fields, 444 files, 44 firms
9	l l9l 9l 9l 9l 99 999 99 lines, 9 leads, 99 oars, 99 leaders
Review	The clerk checked Items 14, 19, and 94 on pages 194 and 249.
Review	On June 19 we sent Check 4991 to 4926 Lynn Street, Portland.

20F Skill-Transfer Typing ⑫

Type two 1' writings on each ¶. Compare *gwam* on the two ¶s. Type two more 1' writings on the ¶ with the lower *gwam*.

Finally, type one 3' writing on both ¶s. Determine *gwam*. Compare your 3' *gwam* with the best 1' *gwam* on each of the two ¶s.

All letters are used.

		GWAM		
		1'	3'	
¶ 1	You guessed it. In the third class are the individuals	11	4	40
1.3 SI	who do the job assigned to them. They do not require close	23	8	44
5.2 AWL	attention. You know they will do good work. They have a	35	12	48
90% HFW	sincere interest in their jobs and will try to find new and	47	16	52
Straight copy	better ways of doing them.	52	17	54
¶ 2	Neither the age of a person, nor his size, nor the exact	11	21	57
1.3 SI	number of years he attended school has much to do with job	23	25	61
5.2 AWL	commitment. People under 25 or 30 with no more than 12 or	35	29	65
90% HFW	13 years in school are often more resourceful than are those	47	33	69
Statistical	over 50 or 30 with 15 or 16 years of education.	57	36	72

1' GWAM | 1 | 2 | 3 | 4 | 5 | 6 | 7 | 8 | 9 | 10 | 11 | 12 |
3' GWAM | 1 | 2 | 3 | 4 |

59D Problem Typing: THREE-COLUMN TABLES Ⓐ25

Problem 1

Full sheet; DS; reading position; 10 spaces between columns

In a money column, use a dollar sign before the top item and a total, if given. If the top item is not the longest number in the column, the dollar sign may be placed 1 space to the left of the horizontal starting point of the longest number (which may be the *total* number).

Underline the last item; DS and type the total, indenting the word *Total* 5 spaces.

OGLETHORPE COLLEGE BUILDING FUND

Contributions Received in First Quarter

Name	State	Amount	Words
			7
			15
Name	State	Amount	21
George Anderson	New York	$ 1,750.00	29
Edward O. Babcock	Idaho	500.00	35
Myron D. Bailey	Maryland	1,500.00	42
Marilyn O. Cross	Indiana	200.00	49
D. Wesley Dodds	Ohio	15,000.00	55
Allien Gratz	Iowa	1,250.00	60
N. R. Howell	Utah	75.50	65
Arthur McDonald	Illinois	2,500.00	72
Sylvia Schwartz	Indiana	1,250.00	79
Oscar P. Sweeney	Maine	560.00	85
Edward O. Welsh	Vermont	1,500.00	94
		DS	
Total		$26,085.50	97

Problem 2

Full sheet; DS; reading position; 10 spaces between columns

DEL MONACO PRODUCTS, INCORPORATED

Annual Conference Costs

Item	1974	1975	Words
			7
			12
Item	1974	1975	17
Conference rooms	$ 1,200	$ 1,200	23
Demonstration materials	750	620	30
Exhibits	1,940	1,450	35
Entertainment	470	675	40
Handouts	92	140	45
Hotel accommodations	11,430	12,740	50
Meals for conferees	17,840	18,820	54
Travel	10,690	10,870	61
Total	$44,412	$46,515	66

21A Preparatory Practice ⑧ each line twice

Alphabet	James quickly helped fix a latch to be given to Ezra Wilson.
4 9	The 44 men had 99 days in which to make 494 No. 1499 wagons.
Figure review	What is the sum of 5 and 30 and 26 and 84 and 93 and 95 1/8?
Fluency	There are more ways than one to do a job; use the right one.

| 1 | 2 | 3 | 4 | 5 | 6 | 7 | 8 | 9 | 10 | 11 | 12 |

21B Typing from Dictation ⑤ once with the book open, once with it closed

the them lend land for form go got he held their light sight

Do not type the dividers it is the|to do the|go with them|and wish to|and do the work

and lend|the form|they held|to go with|for them|with the bid

21C Location of 7 and – (Hyphen) and –– (Dash) ③

Type 7 with J finger

Type – with ; finger

Dash. Type the dash with two hyphens without spacing before or after, as in: His speed––50 mph––was not excessive.

21D Location Drills for 7 and – ⑫ Lines 1, 2, and 3 once for tryout; then each line twice

1	7	j j7j 7j 7j 7j 7 77 777 77 jars, 77 jets, 777 units, 7 for 7
2	–	; ;-; -; -; -; co-op, up-to-date book, first-class newspaper
3	––	; –– ; –– Use a 6-inch line––60 pica spaces––for your paper.
4	Review	His speed––50 mph––was not excessive; he made 476 3/8 miles.
5	Review	FOR SALE: 8-room, 3-bath house––4/5 acre at 290 Pine Drive.

| 1 | 2 | 3 | 4 | 5 | 6 | 7 | 8 | 9 | 10 | 11 | 12 |

59A Preparatory Practice (5) each line twice; then 1' writings on Line 4

Alphabet | Jenny Saxon left my squad last week and gave back a prize she had won.
Figure/symbol | Is that last-minute (!) report on bill #6753-48 due on April 19 or 20?
Quotation marks | "Have 'sunglow' all winter," I typed, "with a Magic Sunlamp by Solco."
Fluency | The civic group may ask for a formal audit of the records in February.

| 1 | 2 | 3 | 4 | 5 | 6 | 7 | 8 | 9 | 10 | 11 | 12 | 13 | 14 |

59B Technique Practice: COMBINATION RESPONSE (5) each line twice

which is | of these | of course | amount of | number of | some of | part of | on our
it will | have to | for this | that this | at this | on this | to this | this letter
this matter | this time | that this | that it | so that | hope that | it was | if we
there are | it would | for this | that it | in order | will not | as you | thank you
as well | as well as | as soon | as soon as | we will | we will be | thank you for

59C Speed/Control Building (15)

1. Type each of the following ¶s as two 1' writings, once for speed and one for control.

2. Type a 5' writing on the 3 ¶s. Proofread by comparing. Determine *gwam*.

All letters are used.

		GWAM		
		2'	5'	
¶ 1 1.4 SI 5.4 AWL 85% HFW	In this class--and likely in your English classes as well--you have	7	3	35
	been taught the importance of selecting just the right word to convey	14	6	38
	the meaning you are after. You may have put the idea into practice in	21	8	41
	composing papers that are to be graded.	25	10	42
¶ 2 1.4 SI 5.4 AWL 85% HFW	You should also realize how important it is that you choose care-	31	13	45
	fully the words that you use in your daily conversation. Not only will	39	15	48
	such a habit help you to build a larger and more interesting vocabulary,	46	18	51
	but it will also require you to pause and think a bit before you speak.	53	21	54
¶ 3 1.4 SI 5.4 AWL 85% HFW	How can we expect our heads of state to communicate perfectly when,	60	24	56
	as most of us learn, a good friend at a casual get-together may react in	67	27	59
	some surprising way to a remark that, to the speaker, has been clearly	74	30	62
	stated? Better communications should start at the one-to-one level.	81	32	65

2' GWAM | 1 | 2 | 3 | 4 | 5 | 6 | 7 |
5' GWAM | 1 | 2 | 3 |

21E Growth Index ⑩

Type two 3′ writings on these ¶s. Proofread by comparing. Circle errors. Determine *gwam*. Compare results on the two writings.

Proofreading Cue. Read for meaning, catching changed, omitted, or repeated words in your copy. Check tricky words such as *finesse* with the book for spelling.

All letters are used.

		3′ GWAM
¶ 1	Just how well can you speak and write? Is it almost	4 | 40
1.3 SI		
5.2 AWL	impossible for you to put your own ideas into words that	7 | 44
90% HFW		
	others can understand? If so, you can learn how to use them	11 | 48
	with finesse and ease. The odds are in your favor; your	15 | 52
	chances are excellent.	17 | 54
¶ 2	Some people believe that it is essential to use complex	20 | 57
1.3 SI		
5.2 AWL	terms to impress others; but it is the correct choice of word,	25 | 61
90% HFW		
	not the size of the word, that is important. Be as concise as	29 | 66
	possible in your quest to enhance your writing. Use as many	33 | 70
	words as you need--but only that many--to state your points.	37 | 74

3′ GWAM | 1 | 2 | 3 | 4 |

21F Individual Practice ⑫

1. Type each line once. Place a check mark before each line that seemed difficult.

2. Type 2 or more times each line you checked as difficult.

1 1 6 :   By 11:16 a.m., he reread these pages: 16, 66, 116, and 166.

2 2 7   She ordered 27 pens, 72 notebooks, 227 maps, and 772 rulers.

3 3 8 -   Buy 3- and 8-yard lengths--not those that are 33 or 88 feet.

4 4 9   They can also use Items 44, 49, 494, 949, and 994 very soon.

5 5 0   In just 5 years, we made 50 changes in Models 5005 and 5055.

6 Fractions   The rods come in these sizes: 14 3/8 inches and 6 1/5 feet.

7 Shift lock   The editors will review THE ODESSA FILE and OPERATION RHINO.

| 1 | 2 | 3 | 4 | 5 | 6 | 7 | 8 | 9 | 10 | 11 | 12 |

58C Problem Typing: TABLES WITH COLUMN HEADINGS (33)

Problem 1

Full sheet; DS; 32 spaces between columns; reading position (p. 59); proofread by verifying

		Words
U.S. PERSONAL AND PER CAPITA INCOME		7
DS		
Ten Highest by State--1971		13
TS		
State	Amount	17
Tab stop———→	DS	
New York	$5,000	21
Connecticut	4,995	24
Alaska	4,875	27
Nevada	4,822	30
New Jersey	4,811	33
Illinois	4,775	36
Hawaii	4,738	39
Delaware	4,673	42
California	4,640	45
Massachusetts	4,562	49

13 | 32 | 6

Problem 2

Full sheet; DS; 24 spaces between columns; center vertically; proofread by verifying

		Words
TEN LARGEST COUNTRIES		4
DS		
In Square Miles (1970 Data)		10
TS		
Country	Area	15
Tab stop———→	DS	
Soviet Union	8,647,249	20
Canada	3,850,789	23
Mainland China	3,690,546	28
United States	3,614,254	33
Brazil	3,294,110	36
Australia	2,967,108	40
India	1,261,482	43
Argentina	1,071,879	47
Sudan	967,243	51
Algeria	919,352	54

14 | 24 | 9

Problem 3

Full sheet; DS; 18 spaces between columns; exact center; proofread by verifying

			Words
TWELVE MOST POPULOUS CITIES			6
DS			
Figures Given for Latest Year Available			13
TS			
City	Population	Year	21
Tokyo	9,005,000	1969	26
New York	7,798,757	1970	30
London	7,703,400	1969	35
Moscow	6,942,000	1970	39
Shanghai	6,900,000	1957	44
Bombay	5,700,358	1970	48
Sao Paulo	5,684,706	1968	53
Cairo	4,961,000	1970	57
Rio de Janeiro	4,206,332	1968	64
Peking	4,010,000	1957	68
Seoul	3,794,959	1966	72
New Delhi	3,772,457	1970	77

14 | 18 | 9 | 18 | 4

SECTION 4

The Basic Symbol Keys

LESSONS 22-26

In this section you will learn to type symbols. You will also improve figure control and build higher basic skill. Some of the copy will be presented in rough draft.

Machine Adjustments. Use a 60-space line (set the left margin stop at center — 30; move the right margin stop to the extreme right of the scale). SS all sentence drills with DS between repeated lines. DS and indent paragraphs 5 spaces.

Lessons 22 and 23. The symbols presented in these lessons are located on the same keys for both nonelectric and electric typewriters. The same fingers control the keys.

LESSON 22

22A Preparatory Practice ⑦ each line twice

Alphabet	Jenny Quarry packed the zinnias in twelve large, firm boxes.
Figures	The box is 6 5/8 by 9 1/2 feet and weighs 375 to 400 pounds.
Tricky spelling	occur excels forty tempt oblige using yield siege relic rely
Fluency	It is great to have talent; it is tragic not to use it well.

| 1 | 2 | 3 | 4 | 5 | 6 | 7 | 8 | 9 | 10 | 11 | 12 |

22B Location of $, &, ( ) [Left and Right Parentheses] ⑤

$ (Dollars). The $ is the shift of **4**. Type it with the *f* finger: f4f f$f

& (Ampersand or "And"). The & is the shift of **7**. Type it with the *j* finger: j7j j&j

([Left Parenthesis]. The (is the shift of **9**. Type it with the *l* finger: l9l l(l

) [Right Parenthesis]. The) is the shift of **0**. Type it with the *;* finger: ;0; ;);

22C Location Drills for $, &, (, and) ⑮ Lines 1, 3, and 5 once for tryout; then each line twice

1	$	f4f f$f $f $f for $488, from $427 to $832, a balance of $144
2		We received checks for $488 and $744 from them on August 14.
3	&	j7j j&j &j &j Brown & Nelson, H. B. Jones & Son, Bye & Colts
4		D. K. Jones & Company sold the plant to Boswell & Carpenter.
5	( )	l9l l(l (l (l ;0; ;););); due in 90 (ninety) days (May 15)
6		Most of the companies (129 to be exact) have tried the plan.

| 1 | 2 | 3 | 4 | 5 | 6 | 7 | 8 | 9 | 10 | 11 | 12 |

57D Problem Typing: ALIGNING FIGURES IN COLUMNS ⑳

Problem 1

Half sheet; SS; 16 spaces between columns; center the problem vertically, the headings and columns horizontally; proofread by comparing

		Words
MANPOWER NEEDS IN THE 1970'S		6
DS		
Annual Average by Office Occupations		13
TS		
Accountants	31,200	17
Bank tellers	14,700	21
Bookkeepers	74,000	25
Cashiers	64,000	28
Office machine operators	20,800	34
Programmers	34,700	38
Stenographers/secretaries	247,000	45
Systems analysts	22,700	50
Typists	61,000	53

| 25 | 16 | 7 |

Problem 2

Half sheet; SS; 20 spaces between columns; center the problem vertically, the headings and columns horizontally; proofread by comparing

		Words
FIRST SEMESTER ENROLLMENTS--1975		7
DS		
By Colleges and Schools		11
TS		
Art	218	13
Business Administration	1,505	19
Education	980	22
Engineering	453	25
Letters and Science	5,225	30
Library Science	91	34
Music	174	36
Public Health	47	40
Theater Arts	117	43

| 22 | 20 | 5 |

LESSON 58

58A Preparatory Practice ⑦ each line twice; then 1′ writings on Lines 2 and 4

Alphabet	Jane Fox owns a copy of the book Zelma Quade has given to all members.
Figure	Please turn to page 530 and answer Items 2, 4, 6, 7, 8, 9, 10, and 16.
Apostrophe	Is the notation on this memorandum Bob's, Dick's, Ralph's, or R. J.'s?
Fluency	A good student knows: the brighter he is, the more he needs to learn.

| 1 | 2 | 3 | 4 | 5 | 6 | 7 | 8 | 9 | 10 | 11 | 12 | 13 | 14 |

58B Centering Column Headings ⑩

To determine the center of a column

From the beginning point of a column, space forward once for each two strokes (letters, figures, or spaces) in the longest line in the column. Disregard a leftover stroke.

To type the column heading

From the center of the column, backspace once for each two spaces in the heading. Disregard a leftover stroke. Begin to type where the backspacing ended.

Type the drill below on a half sheet; DS; 10 spaces between columns; center the column headings over the columns, underlined.

Name	Birthday
George Washington	February 22, 1732
Ulysses Simpson Grant	April 27, 1822

22D Proofreading: IDENTIFYING ERRORS ⑤ Type each line once, making needed corrections as you type.

1 Spacing, punctuation
2 Misstrokes
3 Omissions
4 Strikeovers, transpositions
5 Word substitution
6 Review

How canwe become true, happy; viv acious, genuine, and free?

Not by chance, not bu magic, not byy just hopinf and waiting.

We get thes things, meetin joyful, genuine, free people

You cah leatn ot distinguish between hte true and hte phony.

Best of all, he will learn it become an honest humane being.

You can then life in har mony with yourslf and your friends.

22E Skill-Transfer Typing ⑭

1. Type a 3′ writing beginning with ¶ 1 and typing until time is called. Proofread by comparing. Circle errors. Determine *gwam*.

2. Type two 1′ writings on each ¶.

3. Repeat Step 1. Compare results.

All letters are used.

Difficulty controls for "mixed" copy (words and figures) are determined for the words only. Punctuation marks and symbols used with words, such as quotation marks and parentheses, are considered to be a part of the word with which they are typed. See ¶ 2.

		3′ GWAM
¶ 1	You need to have a special goal for each writing. If	4 | 38
1.3 SI	the immediate aim is to improve your speed, move quickly	7 | 42
5.2 AWL		
90% HFW	from word to word. If control is a problem, drop back in	11 | 46
Straight		
copy	speed to type with greater ease. Adjust the rate to the	15 | 49
	purpose of the practice.	17 | 51
¶ 2	How many GWAM can you type today: 18, 20, 22, 24, or	20 | 55
1.3 SI		
5.2 AWL	more? You may be able to add some words to your rate by	24 | 58
90% HFW		
Statis-	stressing the right kind of typing habits. Do not freeze	28 | 62
tical		
	as you type. Instead, space very quickly and begin the next	32 | 66
	word at once. Type without pausing.	34 | 69

3′ GWAM | 1 | 2 | 3 | 4

22F Control Building: RATE CONTROL ④ four ½′ writings

1. Type ¶ 1 in 22E, above. This time, type at a specific, predetermined rate: 20, 30, or 40 words a minute (*wam*). Select your rate.

2. With light pencil marks, mark your ¼′ and ½′ goals, based on your selected rate.

3. Your instructor will call the ¼ and ½ minutes. Control your rate so that you will be typing your goal word just as the signals are given.

LESSON 57

57A Preparatory Practice ⑦ each line twice; then 1' writings on Line 4

Alphabet   Dr. Robert Wachs received a quaint onyx ring from Jack Pelz of Venice.

Figure/symbol   Did Ned pay $4.81 to $4.95 (less <u>6%</u> discount) for 37 ft. of #260 wire?

Long words   Today, car buyers are knowledgeable about performance characteristics.

Fluency   Hand the proxy forms to the chairmen so that they can sign the titles.

| 1 | 2 | 3 | 4 | 5 | 6 | 7 | 8 | 9 | 10 | 11 | 12 | 13 | 14 |

57B Speed/Control Building ⑬ two 1' writings on each ¶; then one 3' writing on both ¶s on the SPEED level and one 3' writing on the CONTROL level

All letters are used.

		GWAM	
		1'	3'

¶ 1
1.4 SI
5.4 AWL
85% HFW

You would not expect a sizable response to a mailing late in the spring of a letter promoting snow tires. Nor should you expect a letter written in less than standard language to be effective if it has been mailed to a group of college professors.

1'	3'	
13	4	41
28	9	46
42	14	51
50	17	54

¶ 2
1.4 SI
5.4 AWL
85% HFW

A good knowledge of words is vital to a writer, but so is a clear knowledge of the reader. To style your message to your reader's taste and to direct it to his vocabulary range are basic requirements of good writing. The writer is just the first half of the communication process. The reader is the other.

1'	3'	
13	21	58
27	26	63
42	30	67
57	35	72
61	37	74

1' GWAM | 1 | 2 | 3 | 4 | 5 | 6 | 7 | 8 | 9 | 10 | 11 | 12 | 13 | 14 |
3' GWAM | 1 | 2 | 3 | 4 | 5 |

57C Aligning Figures in Columns ⑩

To align columns of figures at the right

Follow the backspace-from-center method (page 95) to determine the left margin stop, backspacing once for each 2 strokes in the longest item in each column and intercolumn.

For the remaining columns, set a tab stop for the digit in each column that will require the least forward or backward spacing. To type the columns, tabulate and space forward or back as appropriate.

Type the drill below twice as shown; 60-space line.

	Margin		Tab		Tab		Tab
	1890		1398		6901		4901
Space twice →	76 2/3		7193	→	723 5/6		5781
	4650		1533		1475	←	65210
	1390	Backspace once ←	71155		1944	→	617

| 4 | 14 | 5 | 14 | 4 | 14 | 5 |

LESSON 23

23A Preparatory Practice ⑦ each line twice

Alphabet   Willis Garvey put a dozen quarts of jam in the box for Jack.

$ &   Bond & Rossi gave us checks for $50.12, $489.75, and $20.63.

( )   The Zorn & Son check (dated June 15) was sent to 315 Oak St.

Fluency   One of these new problems can be solved at our next meeting.
        | 1 | 2 | 3 | 4 | 5 | 6 | 7 | 8 | 9 | 10 | 11 | 12 |

23B Location of #, %, ½, ¼ ⑤ (same location on all typewriters)

 # (Number or Pounds). The # is the shift of **3**. Type it with the *d* finger: d3d d#d

NOTE: Before a figure, # stands for *number*; after a figure, it stands for *pounds*. See Line 2 of 23C below.

% (Percent). The % is the shift of **5**. Type it with the *f* finger: f5f f%f

½ (Fraction Key). Type ½ (at the right of the letter *p*) with the ; finger. No shift: ;½; ;½;

¼ (Fraction Key). The shift of ½ is ¼. Type it with the ; finger: ;½; ;¼;

23C Location Drills for #, %, ½, ¼ ⑮ Lines 1, 3, and 5 once for tryout; then each line twice

1 **#**   d3d d#d #d #d deed #389, lot #372 for lot No. 372, #921, #33
2   Ship order #365 for 33# of Compound #72 as soon as possible.

3 **%**   f5f f%f %f %f at a 5% rate, 55% are used, the city tax of 6%
4   Will the 6% rate be changed to 7% or possibly to 8% by June?

5 **½ ¼**   ;½; ½; ½; 23½, 57½, 31½ and 4½, ;¼; ¼; ¼; 12¼ and 7¼ and 13¼
6   Type fractions in the same way: 1/2 and 2/3--not ½ and 2/3.

7 **Review**   His 7½% note (for $300) was paid on April 29 by check #4658.
        | 1 | 2 | 3 | 4 | 5 | 6 | 7 | 8 | 9 | 10 | 11 | 12 |

23D Individual Practice ⑩ Use 21F, page 41.

1. Type each line once. Place a check mark before any line on which you made more than 1 error.

2. Type 2 or more times each line you checked. Type slowly; think of the individual strokes.

56D Problem Typing: MAIN AND SECONDARY HEADINGS FOR TABLES ㉚

Problem 1: Three-Column Table

Full sheet; DS; 8 spaces between columns; center the problem vertically, the headings and columns horizontally

Note the spacing of the main and secondary headings when both are used.

Use the word-division guides on pages 65-66 and a dictionary to complete the third column. In typing the words, use a hyphen at the acceptable point or points at which a word may be divided. (The longest word in the third column will contain 12 strokes.)

Check your work against the key below the table.

			Words
Main heading → **ACCEPTABLE WORD-DIVISION POINTS**			6
DS			
Secondary Heading → Application of Guides			11
TS			
adamant	ad-a-mant	ada-mant	16
additional	ad-di-tion-al	(Show acceptable	24
addressing	ad-dress-ing	division points for	31
beginning	be-gin-ning	remaining words.)	37
biennial	bi-en-ni-al		44
century	cen-tu-ry		49
confidence	con-fi-dence		56
legality	le-gal-i-ty		62
material	ma-te-ri-al		69
self-reliant	self-re-li-ant		77
superior	su-pe-ri-or		83
typically	typ-i-cal-ly		90

| 12 | 8 | 14 | 8 | 12 |

Problem 2: Two-Column Table from Rough Draft

8½" by 5½" half sheet; SS; 10 spaces between columns; center the problem vertically and the headings and columns horizontally; proofread by verifying

		Words
HALL OF FAME FOR GREAT AMERICANS		7
Inventors with Dates Elected ←DS		12
←TS		
Alexander Graham Bell	1905	18
Thomas Edison	1930	22
~~Robert fulton~~	~~1900~~	
Robert Fulton	1900	25
Elias Howe ~~Thayer~~	1951	29
Samuel Finley Breese Morse	1900	35
George Westinghouse	1910	40
Eli M. Whitney	1900	43
Orville wright	1965	47
Wilbur Wright	1965	51

| 26 | 10 | 4 |

Problem 3: Table with Two-Line Main Heading

Follow the directions for Problem 2. Because the heading is long, type it in 2 SS lines, centering one below the other. (Break long headings into logical word groups.) Proofread by verifying.

center each line of heading

			Words
OFFICE ASSIGNMENTS AND TELEPHONE			8
(NUMBERS) OF DEPARTMENT CHAIRMEN			13
Westwood Branch ←DS			16
TS			
Albert, Fred A.	793	394-8973	22
Chambers, George	722	394-8927	28
Field, James A.	729	394-8941	34
Hughes, J. Dean	650	394-8959	40
Irwin, William	656	394-8801	45
Manicotti, Joseph	727	394-8080	52
Scott, John Bird	618	394-3389	58
Tierman, William	704	394-8900	63
Upjohn, Bernard ~~Leonard~~	714	394-8970	69
yasaki, Robert F.	677	394-8000	76

| 17 | 10 | 3 | 10 | 8 |

23E Skill-Transfer Typing ⑬

1. Type three 1' writings on each ¶. Compare the *gwams* for the best writing on each ¶.

2. Type a 3' writing. Proofread by verifying. Circle errors. Determine *gwam*.

		GWAM
		1' 3'

All letters are used.

¶ 1
1.3 SI
5.2 AWL
90% HFW

	1'	3'
Some of us worry so much about our writing style that we	11	4	39
fail to get the job under way. Remember this about style:	23	8	43
Once you have a message to convey, your words will seem to	35	12	47
flow in a simple, direct way. Style results from knowing the	48	16	51
idea that you want to express.	54	18	53

¶ 2
1.3 SI
5.2 AWL
90% HFW

	1'	3'
Organize your ideas; write. If you know what to write,	11	22	57
you will not have to worry about style. You will have it.	23	26	61
Put fresh ideas into your work. If you do not have anything	35	30	65
novel to say, you are not ready. In writing, it is quality,	48	34	69
not volume, that counts.	52	35	71

1' GWAM | 1 | 2 | 3 | 4 | 5 | 6 | 7 | 8 | 9 | 10 | 11 | 12 |
3' GWAM | | 1 | | 2 | | 3 | | 4 | |

LESSON 24

24A Preparatory Practice ⑦ each line twice

Alphabet	Doug Zola expects to fly to Quebec to visit with Jack Monti.
# %	Ship 233# of your #316A bulbs. Bill me at retail, less 15%.
½ ¼	His 6½% and 7¼% notes (for $950 and $300) are due next week.
Fluency	The work is done, and they will leave by the end of the day.

| 1 | 2 | 3 | 4 | 5 | 6 | 7 | 8 | 9 | 10 | 11 | 12 |

24B Control Building: RATE REDUCTION ⑩

Type two 3' writings on 23E, above. Type at a rate that is 4 to 8 words lower than the rate you made on the 3' writing in Lesson 22. Circle errors. Compare the number of errors on writings in the two lessons.

Lessons 24 and 25. The symbols and special characters in these lessons are located on different keys on non-electric and electric typewriters. Learn key locations and controlling fingers for your typewriter.

56A Preparatory Practice ⑦ each line twice; then 1′ writings on Lines 2 and 4

Alphabet	Mr. Brown was dazzled by the quick jumps of the five or six young men.
Figure/symbol	Send the following items: 3 sets K-217F @ $6.75; 4 prs. M826 @ $9.20.
One hand	The union referred only a few of my cases to the referee for decision.
Fluency	It is the wish of the chairman to have all the workmen at the meeting.

| 1 | 2 | 3 | 4 | 5 | 6 | 7 | 8 | 9 | 10 | 11 | 12 | 13 | 14 |

56B Technique Practice: COMBINATION RESPONSE ⑧ each line once from the book; twice from dictation

1 I am│I have│I would│I will│I hope│I can│that I│that we│and we│with you
2 will be│would be│to us│to make│to do│to me│able to│as to│is to│wish to
3 up to│and to│as the│about the│have the│you may│you would│as you│is not
4 for you│from you│with your│on your│and your│we do│we hope│if we│all of
5 which we│as we│not be│as to│be able│be in│is to│is in│there is│are not

56C Proofreading Procedures ⑤

Typing statistical copy

Copy containing figures must be typed and proofread with great care. For typing statistical copy, use the following guides:

1. Type columns of figures horizontally, using the tabulator bar or key.

2. Use a ruler to aid in reading the figures correctly across the columns. Read across; then move the ruler down for the next line.

3. In reading the numbers for typing, mentally group them into logical divisions whenever possible. For instance, read *1235* as *twelve thirty-five*, not *one, two, three, five.*

Proofreading statistical copy

Use these guides to check the accuracy of your copy:

1. If possible, use the *verifying method*. Read aloud from the original while someone else checks the new copy.

2. If you must proofread your own work, place the original copy and the new copy as close together as possible, matching the numbers on a horizontal plane. Read a number from the original copy first; then compare it with the corresponding number in the new copy.

3. Proofread columns of figures vertically; that is, column by column. Use the procedures given below in reading copy for proofreading.

Guide	Number	Mental or Spoken Procedure
Read figures in logical groups whenever possible.	12	Twelve
	1234	Twelve thirty-four
	1,234	One two thirty-four
When a number is repeated, read the number; then say *twice, three times,* etc.	416	Four sixteen—twice
	416	
For a series of consecutive numbers, read all the digits in the first number but—in the series—only the digits that change. Indicate by your tone of voice that you are reading a series.	2471	Twenty-four seventy-one, two, three, four, five
	2472	
	2473	
	2474	
	2475	

24C Location of ', ", ! ⑤ (located on different keys for nonelectric and electric)

Nonelectric—top row only

Electric—top three rows only

Spacing Rule. Space twice after an exclamation point at the end of a sentence.

' (Apostrophe) Nonelectric. The ' is the shift of **8**. Type it with the *k* finger: k8k k'k

' (Apostrophe) Electric. The ' is at the right of the semicolon key. Type it with the *;* finger. No shift: ;'; ;';

" (Quotation) Nonelectric. The " is the shift of **2**. Type it with the *s* finger: s2s s"s

" (Quotation) Electric. The " is the shift of **'**. Type it with the *;* finger: ;'; ;";

! (Exclamation Point) Made. Type ' and backspace; then type a period. (!).

! (Exclamation Point) Special Key. If your machine has a key for ! (usually the shift of the special figure 1), type it with the *a* finger: Try! Don't stop!

24D Location Drills for ', ", ! ⑮ Line 1 or 2, Line 3 or 4, and Lines 5 and 6 once for tryout; then same lines twice

```
1   ' (Nonelectric)   k8k k'k 'k 'k It's here.  I'm ready.  It can't be 4 o'clock.
2   ' (Electric)      ;'; ;'; '; '; It's here.  I'm ready.  It can't be 4 o'clock.

3   " (Nonelectric)   s2s s"s "s "s He typed "its" for "it's" and "see" for "sea."
4   " (Electric)      ;"; ;"; "; "; He typed "its" for "it's" and "see" for "sea."

5   !                 Jump!  Don't stop!  Great!  Type faster!  Type with control!

6   Review            The principal said, "It's right!  Stand by your principles!"
                    |   1   |   2   |   3   |   4   |   5   |   6   |   7   |   8   |   9   |  10   |  11   |  12   |
```

24E Sentence Guided Writing ⑬

1. Type a 1' writing on each sentence. Determine *gwam*. Compare rates on each pair of sentences.

2. Type additional 1' writings on the figure and symbol sentences with the greatest differences in rates.

		Words in Line
1	Please send this order to our plant in Boise.	9
2	See the first 29 pages of our 1974-75 report.	9
3	The papayas were shipped air express from Florida.	10
4	I paid the 7½% note by check #93--on the date due.	10
5	The price does not cover shipping charges or insurance.	11
6	We hold Reed & Long's note for $3,000 (dated March 12).	11
7	I look forward to hearing from you soon about the paintings.	12
8	When it's on time, Flight 568 leaves Des Moines at 6:15 a.m.	12

```
|   1   |   2   |   3   |   4   |   5   |   6   |   7   |   8   |   9   |  10   |  11   |  12   |
```

55E Problem Typing: TWO- AND THREE-COLUMN TABLES ⑳

Guides for horizontal placement of columns (backspace-from-center method)

1. Move margin stops to ends of scale. Clear all tabulator stops.

2. Move carriage (carrier) to center of paper.

3. Decide on spacing between columns (if spacing is not specified)—preferably an even number of spaces (4, 6, 8, 10, etc.).

4. From center of paper, backspace once for *each 2 strokes* in the longest line of each column and for *each 2 spaces* to be left between columns.

As you backspace, count any extra stroke (that may occur at the end of the longest line of a column) with the space between columns. Likewise, if an extra space occurs at the end of an intercolumn, count it with the next column.

5. Set the left margin stop at the point where you complete the backspacing.

6. From the left margin, space forward *once for each stroke* in the longest line of the first column and for each space to be left between the first and second column.

7. *Set the tab stop at this point for the second column.*

8. Follow this procedure for each column in the table.

Problem 1: Two-Column Table

Use an 8½″ by 5½″ half sheet; DS; leave 20 spaces between columns. Center the problem vertically (see p. 59). Center the columns horizontally (see guides above).

NOTE: After setting the margin and tab stops by backspacing from center, check the placement by using the boxed key below the problem.

Words

OFFICERS OF HORIZON INDUSTRIES — 6

TS

Margin stop →	Tab stop	
Victor Potter	President	11
Ben F. Edwards	Vice President	17
Eva M. Baker	Vice President	23
Kenneth Hoffman	Treasurer	28
Axel Hansen	Secretary	32
Melvin Hauser	Asst. Secretary	38

15   20   15

Problem 2: Three-Column Table

Full sheet; DS; 14 spaces between columns; center the problem vertically, the heading horizontally, and the columns horizontally

Technique Cue. Tabulate from column to column without looking up from the copy. Reach to the tab bar or key without moving the hand out of typing position.

Evaluate Your Work. Use your stroke and line-space ruler to check top, bottom, and side margins and the number of spaces between the columns.

Words

SOME STATE NAMES AND THEIR ABBREVIATIONS — 8

TS

Arizona	Ariz.	AZ	11
California	Calif.	CA	15
Connecticut	Conn.	CO	19
Delaware	Del.	DE	22
Illinois	Ill.	IL	25
Indiana	Ind.	IN	28
Louisiana	La.	LA	32
Michigan	Mich.	MI	35
New York	N.Y.	NY	38
Pennsylvania	Penn.	PA	42
Tennessee	Tenn.	TN	46
Washington	Wash.	WA	50

12   14   6   14   2

LESSON 25

25A Preparatory Practice ⑦ each line twice

Alphabet	Fire hazards of the job were quickly explained by Mr. Novig.
' !	That's the way to do this job! It's simple if you know how!
"	"This," the man said, "is the right way to make a decision."
Fluency	He can always see those antique chairs at our downtown shop.

`| 1 | 2 | 3 | 4 | 5 | 6 | 7 | 8 | 9 | 10 | 11 | 12 |`

25B Location of *, ¢, @, and Underline ⑦ (located on different keys for nonelectric and electric)

Nonelectric—top three rows only

Electric—top row only

Spacing Rules. (1) Space before and after typing @, which is used in typing bills. **(2)** Do not space between ¢ and the figure preceding it. **(3)** Do not space between a figure and #, $, %, /.

To Underline. Backspace (or move carriage by hand) to the first letter of the word; then type the underline once for each letter in the word.

* (Asterisk) Nonelectric. The * is the shift of -. Type it with the ; finger: ;-; ;*;

* (Asterisk) Electric. The * is the shift of 8. Type it with the k finger: k8k k*k

¢ (Cent or Cents) Nonelectric. The ¢ is at the right of the ;. Type it with the ; finger. No shift: ;¢; ;¢;

¢ (Cent or Cents) Electric. The ¢ is the shift of 6. Type it with the j finger: j6j j¢j

@ (At) Nonelectric. The @ is the shift of ¢. Type it with the ; finger: ;¢; ;@; ;¢; ;@;

@ (At) Electric. The @ is the shift of 2. Type it with the s finger: s2s s@s

_ (Underline) Nonelectric. The _ is the shift of 6. Type it with the j finger: j6j j_j

_ (Underline) Electric. The _ is the shift of the hyphen. Type it with the ; finger: ;-; ;_;

25C Location Drills for *, ¢, @, Underline ⑮ appropriate line of each pair once for tryout; then same lines twice

1	*	(Nonelectric)	;-; ;*; *; *; My first * refers to page 129, ** to page 307.
2	*	(Electric)	k8k k*k *k *k My first * refers to page 129, ** to page 307.
3	¢	(Nonelectric)	;¢; ;¢; ¢; ¢; The prices Jones quoted are 57¢, 79¢, and 94¢.
4	¢	(Electric)	j6j j¢j ¢j ¢j The prices Jones quoted are 57¢, 79¢, and 94¢.
5	@	(Nonelectric)	;¢; ;@; @; @; Ship 56 lbs. @ 7¢ a lb. and 16 lbs. @ 9¢ a lb.
6	@	(Electric)	s2s s@s @s @s Ship 56 lbs. @ 7¢ a lb. and 16 lbs. @ 9¢ a lb.
7	_	(Nonelectric)	j6j j_j _j _j Use a quick stroke. Please think as you type.
8	_	(Electric)	;-; ;_; _; _; Use a quick stroke. Please think as you type.

`| 1 | 2 | 3 | 4 | 5 | 6 | 7 | 8 | 9 | 10 | 11 | 12 |`

SECTION 9 Simple Tables

LESSONS 55-63

LESSON 55

Goals. When you complete these lessons, you should be able to type a variety of tables. You will also improve your typing speed and control.

Errors. Correct errors in problem solutions as noted in directions. Your instructor will tell you how to handle errors in other problems.

Machine Adjustments. 70-space line; SS sentence drills; DS and indent ¶s 5 spaces; space problem copy as directed. For problems and ¶ copy, use an adjusted right margin.

55A Preparatory Practice ⑦ each line twice; then 1' writings on Lines 2 and 4

Alphabet   Maude Parker will visit the Chicago zoo before joining Alexis Quigley.

Figure   Paul typed page 29 on May 7, page 30 on May 14, and page 65 on May 18.

Figure/symbol   Baxter & Moore's check for $974.20 (check #1305) was cashed on July 7.

Fluency   He will do well to try one or more of the very fine pens for the work.
                | 1 | 2 | 3 | 4 | 5 | 6 | 7 | 8 | 9 | 10 | 11 | 12 | 13 | 14 |

55B Technique Practice: STROKING ⑤ each line 3 times

Home row   Hal Skaggs had a bad fall as he made a gallant dash to raise the flag.

1st row   Zeal or zest can bring much more success next time than luck ever can.

Double letters Ella was puzzled by the letter that followed the offer of a free book.

Adjacent keys   Last Wednesday, Lew Polk threw the ball to Sam Hopper for an easy out.

55C Technique Practice: RESPONSE PATTERNS ⑧ each line 3 times; then 1' writings on Lines 3 and 4

Letter response The executive expects the expert to explain his actions to an auditor.

Word response   The aid the men got from us did much to help them get their work done.

Combination   Nine seniors pointed to the easy quiz questions to support their case.

                A good many workers of this world surely need to have a faith lifting.
                | 1 | 2 | 3 | 4 | 5 | 6 | 7 | 8 | 9 | 10 | 11 | 12 | 13 | 14 |

55D Speed/Control Building ⑩ two 1' writings for speed; two 1' writings for control; one 2' writing for speed; one 2' writing for control

All letters are used.

1.4 SI
5.4 AWL
85% HFW

	GWAM 1'	2'
Tabulating is just an extension of centering, which you have been	13	6	49
doing for quite some time; so it is not new to you. When you were typing	28	14	57
words or figures in columns in past lessons, you were told the number of	43	21	64
spaces to leave between the columns. You will likely use guides for the	57	28	71
horizontal placement of columns until you learn to plan a table without	72	36	79
help; then you will use your own judgment in typing an attractive table.	86	43	86

1' GWAM | 1 | 2 | 3 | 4 | 5 | 6 | 7 |
2' GWAM | 1 | 2 | 3 | 4 | 5 | 6 | 7 | 8 | 9 | 10 | 11 | 12 | 13 | 14 |

25D Skill-Transfer Typing ⑬ each line twice

1. Type two 1' writings on each ¶. Compare your *gwams* on the better writing on each ¶.

2. Type a 3' writing on all ¶s. Proofread by verifying. Circle errors. Determine *gwam*.

All letters are used.

		GWAM 1'	3'

¶ 1
1.3 SI
5.2 AWL
90% HFW
Straight
copy

```
        Just one year ago today you opened an account with us,     11   4
so this is a suitable time to express our thanks for your          23   8
friendship and business.  Serving you, Mr. Smith, has been a       35  12
pleasure.  All of us here hope that you will always find a         47  16
helping hand in our store.                                         52  17
```

¶ 2
1.3 SI
5.2 AWL
90% HFW
Figures

```
        You can hear almost anything you want to hear about the    11  21
dazzling speed of new copiers.  Claims range from 30 to 75 or      24  25
more copies a minute.  The new 824 makes 65 good, clean copies     36  29
a minute; and it works for days without a stop.                    46  32
```

¶ 3
1.3 SI
5.2 AWL
90% HFW
Figure/
symbol

```
        We are pleased to reserve one double room for July 26 to   11  36
30.  If you plan to arrive after 4 o'clock, please forward a       24  40
deposit of $18.50 to hold the room.  We look forward to serving    36  45
you and hope you will enjoy your Quebec visit.                     46  48
```

1' GWAM | 1 | 2 | 3 | 4 | 5 | 6 | 7 | 8 | 9 | 10 | 11 | 12 |
3' GWAM | 1 | 2 | 3 | 4 |

25E Typing from Corrected Copy ⑧ Study the correction symbols; then type each drill line twice.

Errors are often circled in copy that is to be retyped. The typist must know what corrections to make. Sometimes correction symbols are used. Those at the right are quite common.

Symbol	Meaning	Symbol	Meaning
Cap ≡	Capitalize	#	Add horizontal space
∧ ℓ	Insert	lc /	Lowercase letters
ℓ	Delete (take out)	⌒	Close up space
⌐_	Move to left	⌣	Transpose

1   our problem that they day begins with first half hour.

2   Without question, the worst Boss can we have bad habit.

3   Use quick, light, sure strikes to build useable skill.

4   the hand writing wall is often unheeded by must of su.

5   Thus, facing the truth can alter the direction of our life.

6   it is to decide on a risd then is it two life with it.

54D Problem Typing Measurement ㉚

Get Ready to Type . . .	4'
Timed Production . . .	20'
Proofread	6'

In the problems below, punctuation marks have been omitted in the opening and closing lines. Add those needed. Correct your errors.

Materials Needed. 3 letterheads, 4 copy sheets, 2 sheets of carbon paper, and 3 large envelopes

Problem 1 *(WB p. 61)*

Modified block, block ¶s, mixed punctuation; 1 cc; 60-space line; date on Line 17; SS and indent listed items 5 spaces; address an envelope

	Words
April 5 19-- │ Mr H M Polaski President │	9
Victor Research Corporation │ 1560 Union	16
Street │ Denver CO 80215 │ Dear Mr Polaski	25
(¶1) Our electronic message-switching sys-	32
tem directs--with computer │ speed and pre-	40
cision--the transmission and reception of mes-	49
sages │ and data. Our system can control a	57
mixture of private lines, │ dial-up circuits, and	67
high-speed data communication channels.	75
(¶2) The system can make your message	82
switching more efficient and │ can reduce your	91
communication costs in several ways. It:	100
1. Eliminates lost messages	105
2. Makes routing flexible	111
3. Monitors the network	116
4. Simplifies operations	121
(¶3) For more information, write or call us.	129
Better still, pay us │ a visit. Our exhibit and	139
demonstration of this superb system │ will	147
interest you. │ Sincerely yours │ Alva M Hil-	156
gers │ Sales Promotion │ xx	160/178

Problem 2 *(WB p. 63)*

Block style, open punctuation; 1 cc; 60-space line; date on Line 17; center the all-cap statement; address an envelope

	Words
Current date │ Fordham Manufacturing Co │ 109	9
Northeastern Boulevard │ Nashua NH 03060 │	17
Gentlemen (¶1) High-speed microfilming can	25
change the way you look at filing. │ The Reli-	34
able 600 Microfilmer records more than 200	42

	Words
letters a │ minute. (¶2) Microfilming is the	50
practical alternative to paper filing. │ Micro-	59
filming is fast, accurate, and safe. The Reliable	69
600 │ makes "filing" almost as easy as taking a	78
snapshot.	80

TAKE A CLOSER LOOK	84

	Words
(¶3) Return the enclosed card for our infor-	92
mative booklet on the │ Reliable 600, or ask to	101
have a representative call. There is │ no obli-	110
gation. │ Yours very truly │ John D Marvin │	118
Sales Manager │ xx │ Enclosure	123/137

Problem 3 *(WB p. 65)*

Block style, open punctuation; 2 cc; 60-space line; date on Line 17; address an envelope

	Words
Current date │ Miss Mabel Lampel President │	9
Mobile Filing Systems Co │ 1467 Coral Way │	17
Miami FL 33145 │ Dear Miss Lampel (¶1)	24
A master key that can be copied for 50 cents	33
means that your │ security is worth even less.	42
You can change your locks, but │ this takes	51
time and costs money. (¶2) Safecard Elec-	58
tronic Keys can't be copied. They can be can-	67
celed │ by simply pushing a button. A Safecard	76
is an invisibly coded │ plastic card that opens	85
your doors when it is inserted into a │ mag-	93
netically controlled slot. This card is rewriting	103
the book │ on security systems. (¶3) For a	111
free demonstration of this amazing device,	119
write or call │ toll free: (800) 423-4100. │ Sin-	128
cerely yours │ Mrs Maxine Strong │ Security	137
Systems │ xx │ cc Mr H L Stone	143/160

LESSON 26

26A Preparatory Practice ⑦ each line twice

Alphabet We have six men doing quick flying jumps on the trapeze bar.

* ¢ Use the * (asterisk) for your footnote. Send 57¢ in stamps.

@ - Send <u>only</u> 189 qts. @ 46¢ a qt. Read the book <u>Jungle Cowboy</u>.

Fluency These cash benefits are yours to use for every kind of bill.

| 1 | 2 | 3 | 4 | 5 | 6 | 7 | 8 | 9 | 10 | 11 | 12 |

26B Location of = (equals) and + (plus) symbols ③

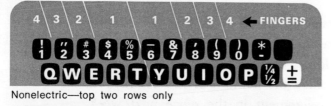

Nonelectric—top two rows only

Electric—top row only

Some typewriters have = and + symbols at the right end of either the top row or the third row. The + is the shift of =. Type with the ; finger: ;=; ;+;

If your typewriter does not have this key, make the symbols.

Plus: + (diagonal; backspace; hyphen)

Equals: = (hyphen; backspace; roll platen forward slightly; hold it in position; type hyphen; return to line position)

A space precedes and follows each of the symbols.

26C Location Drills for = and + ⑩ each line twice

1 = + The answer: 827 + 64 = 891. My solution: 536 + 904 = 626.

2 Review Beverly bought 16 7/8 yards @ $3.92 and 5 2/3 yards @ $4.00.

3 Review Space after @, but not between the figure and ¢, %, #, or $.

4 Review "Truth," a man once said, "doesn't hurt unless it <u>ought</u> to."

5 Review O'Neil & Bond's $750 note (due 4/29) was paid by check #625.

6 Review Ford & Rhode's $739.25 check (check #194) is dated March 16.

26D Typing from Corrected Copy ⑥ Type once, making needed corrections as you type.

	Words
If ~~this~~ these advantage makes any sense, ~~to you~~, you should not try	11
the <u>Journal</u> for a few weks on a regular bases? Your ~~may~~ I can	22
start right now. just select as many weeks as you for like	34
just ~~83~~ 80 cents a week for a minmum of 15 weeks. we pay the	46
postage to your home or office.	53

LESSON 54

54A Preparatory Practice ⑦ each line twice; then 1′ writings on Lines 2 and 4

Alphabet   Ben Jackson will save the money required for your next big cash prize.

Figure/symbol   The 6½% interest of $81.08 on my $1,247.35 note (dated May 29) is due.

Rule for
word division   Never divide contractions like "don't," "didn't," "wasn't," and so on.

Fluency   If you wish to write well, use those words that we all can understand.

| 1 | 2 | 3 | 4 | 5 | 6 | 7 | 8 | 9 | 10 | 11 | 12 | 13 | 14 |

54B Technique Practice: STROKING ⑤ each line at least twice

1 One hand   In my opinion, it was foolish to race up that hill as fast as you did.

2 Balanced hand   Did the chairman say the visit of the men will aid the endowment fund?

3 Combination   We mailed your statement to the address given on the card you sent us.

4 Adjacent keys   As Sadie said, few are they who excelled the points Portia Powers won.

5 Double letters   Lynn will see that Jill accepts an assignment in the office next week.

| 1 | 2 | 3 | 4 | 5 | 6 | 7 | 8 | 9 | 10 | 11 | 12 | 13 | 14 |

54C Growth Index ⑧ one 5′ writing; determine GWAM and errors

All letters are used.

	GWAM
	2′ | 5′

¶ 1
1.5 SI
5.6 AWL
80% HFW

The most alive, engaging, and capable people of every age are those (7 / 3) with the clearest view of their personal as well as business goals. Ask (14 / 6) anyone who fits this description, and he will probably be able to tell (21 / 8) you exactly what he intends to do. Most people can achieve reasonable (28 / 11) goals, so why not set yours high enough to keep your mind and body alert (35 / 14) and flexible? The most satisfactory goal must be well beyond your pres- (43 / 17) ent ability. It must be one, however, that you can attain with the (49 / 20) right kind of planning and effort. A goal should make you acquire in- (56 / 23) sights into new situations; it should make you use some unique talents. (64 / 25)

¶ 2
1.5 SI
5.6 AWL
80% HFW

To make goal setting a really meaningful project, why not start by (6 / 28) writing a comprehensive story of the rest of your life? You will dis- (14 / 31) cover much from this exercise. Turn your imagination loose, but be (20 / 34) practical. Write an honest report of the direction you want your life (27 / 37) to take. As you write, ask yourself some penetrating questions: What (34 / 39) kind of person do I want to be? What type of occupation do I want to (41 / 42) pursue? What do I expect to get from it? Will I be satisfied with (48 / 45) myself when I fulfill my expectations? What are the things I really (55 / 48) want to accomplish? Answers to these puzzling questions will help you (62 / 50) to formulate your goals. (65 / 51)

| 2′ GWAM | 1 | 2 | 3 | 4 | 5 | 6 | 7 |
| 5′ GWAM | 1 | | 2 | | 3 | |

26E Growth Index (14)

1. Type a 3' writing. Proofread by comparing. Circle errors. Determine *gwam*.
2. Type two 1' writings on each ¶, typing once for speed and once for control.

3. Type a second 3' writing on the *control level*. Proofread by comparing. Circle errors. Determine *gwam*. Compare your rate and number of errors with those on the first writing.

All letters are used.

		3' GWAM
¶ 1 1.3 SI 5.2 AWL 90% HFW	Novelty in everything is prized, perhaps too much, as	4 | 42
	an end in itself. There is a quest for a "sense of self" in	8 | 46
	the way we think and act. We don't like the feeling of being	12 | 50
	put together by a production line. We demand things that fit	16 | 54
	our personal wishes.	17 | 55
¶ 2 1.3 SI 5.2 AWL 90% HFW	Take the case of cars, for example. They are made by	21 | 59
	factory methods to keep costs down. We can get them, however,	25 | 63
	with variety in color, size, body style, and number and kind	29 | 67
	of extras. They meet our own personal taste. The job a man	33 | 71
	has must meet the same test. It must give him a chance to	37 | 75
	express himself.	38 | 76

3' GWAM | 1 | 2 | 3 | 4 |

26F Individual Practice (10)

1. Type each line once. Place a check mark before any line that seemed difficult.

2. Type 2 or more times each line you checked as difficult.

1	Lesson 22	Was Hale & Gordon's check (or was it Mr. Hale's) for $2,500?
2	$ & ( )	Kahn & Bail, Inc., gave checks of $350 and $275 to the club.
3	Lesson 23	The 10% discount on bill #1592 for cassettes comes to $7.25.
4	# % ½ ¼	Please send us 15 dozen envelopes which are 9½ by 4¼ inches.
5	Lesson 24	O'Hanlon doesn't know the difference between "to" and "two."
6	' ! "	Ken's father said, "Might won't make right!" He's so right!
7	Lesson 25	The * refers to item #17. Send 72 tubes of glue @ 79¢ each.
8	* ¢ @ _	The Master Spy and Decision at Sea are on your reading list.

| 1 | 2 | 3 | 4 | 5 | 6 | 7 | 8 | 9 | 10 | 11 | 12 |

53B Skill-Transfer Typing ⑩

65-space line; 1' writing on each line; compare GWAM
In Line 5, type the correct words for those that are circled.

		Words
1 Straight copy	Can a new van move the six heavy zinc boxes to their local plant?	13
2 Statistical	My order #73649 totals $528.90 and must be shipped by January 14.	13
3 Script	*The two artists worked steadily on in spite of the stifling heat.*	13
4 Corrected copy	Ed ex⌐pected the quiz be to very dificult for the twelve boys.	13
5 Proofreading	They shall by most please to recieve you comments on the giude.	13

53C Problem Typing Review ㉝ Correct or circle errors, as directed.

In the problems below, punctuation marks in the letter address, salutation, complimentary close, and signature lines have been omitted. Provide those needed.

Materials Needed. 2 letterheads, 3 copy sheets, 2 sheets of carbon paper; 2 large envelopes

Problem 1 (WB p. 51)

Modified block style, block ¶s, mixed punctuation; 60-space line; date on Line 17; 1 cc; address envelope

	Words
Current date ｜ Raymond Laboratories Co ｜ 1673	9
Como Avenue ｜ St Paul MN 55108 ｜ Gentle-	17
men (¶ 1) Anyone can run the Lusk Dupli-	24
cator and turn out clear, sharp ｜ prints fast--	33
for a fraction of a cent a copy! Sure, it's ｜	42
easy to punch the "On" button of a photo-	50
copier; but it is the ｜ slow, high-cost way to	59
make copies. (¶ 2) With a Lusk Duplicator	66
you can quickly and very inexpensively ｜ print	75
all the copies you want, when you want	83
them--in color ｜ if you wish. You can use	91
almost any paper or card stock and ｜ get up	99
to 140 copies a minute. Use the Lusk Dupli-	108
cator for ｜ price lists, bulletins, catalog pages,	118
and routine forms-- ｜ and use your regular	126
office staff. (¶ 3) Lusk Duplicators come in	134
many models to fit all needs. Send ｜ the en-	142
closed coupon for complete information. ｜	150
Yours very truly ｜ Alva M Hilgers ｜ Sales Pro-	159
motion ｜ xx ｜ Enclosure	163/175

Problem 2 (WB p. 53)

Block style, open punctuation; date on Line 14; 2 cc; address envelope

	Words
Current date ｜ Ms Charlotte Mueller ｜ Office	8
Manager ｜ Columbia Corporation ｜ 1539 Au-	16
waiolimu Street ｜ Honolulu HI 96813 ｜ Dear	24
Ms Mueller (¶ 1) What can an editing type-	31
writer do? (¶ 2) --It can turn out perfect	38
copy very quickly no matter how many ｜ re-	46
writes, changes, deletions, and additions you	55
have made. (¶ 3) --It corrects a typo simply	63
by backspacing to the point where ｜ the typo	71
was made and typing in the correction. (¶ 4)	79
--It finds coded paragraphs, sentences, and	88
pages and types ｜ them in the order you spec-	97
ify. (¶ 5) --It permits the storage of complex	105
format information so that ｜ edited material is	114
typed out in the required style. (¶ 6) Does	121
the editing typewriter sound like something	130
your office ｜ can use? Write or telephone us	139
for more information. ｜ Yours very truly ｜	147
John D Marvin ｜ Sales Manager ｜ xx ｜ cc Mr	155
Bruce Hofstra	157/176

SECTION 5
Basic Skills Improvement

LESSONS 27-30

Purpose. Use the lessons in this section to improve your basic stroking skills and your use of the operative parts of the machine. The techniques to be used are those stressed in earlier lessons.

Machine Adjustments. 60-space line; set the left margin at center — 30. Move the right margin stop to the extreme right side of the scale. SS drills unless otherwise directed; DS and indent ¶s 5 spaces.

LESSON 27

27A Preparatory Practice ⑦ each line twice

Alphabet	John Quick believes the campaign frenzy will excite Dorothy.
Figure	Your 3:15 p.m. show drew 49 men, 72 women, and 680 children.
Figure/symbol	Bob's 5½% note for $375 was discounted at the bank on May 8.
Fluency	Learn about these prices and services from any travel agent.

`|  1  |  2  |  3  |  4  |  5  |  6  |  7  |  8  |  9  |  10  |  11  |  12  |`

27B Technique Practice: STROKING ⑮

1. Type each line twice for practice, keeping in mind the technique cue at the right.

2. Type a 1' writing on Lines 2, 4, and 6. Determine the *gwam* on each writing.

> **Technique Cues.** Sit erect. Curve the fingers; hold wrists low. Strike the keys squarely.

All letters are used.

| 1 | Home row | glad flag dash half shall salad ask flask gash lad gall lash |
| 2 | | As Galahad, he held a flag. Jake had Gale add half a glass. |

| 3 | 1st row | can bomb zinc cave nimble box examine men bank cab club numb |
| 4 | | The six nimble men can examine the bomb in an old zinc mine. |

| 5 | 3d row | too tower rope you quote power write troup rewrite trip pert |
| 6 | | Terry wrote two reports to Peter on the proper way to start. |

`|  1  |  2  |  3  |  4  |  5  |  6  |  7  |  8  |  9  |  10  |  11  |  12  |`

27C Technique Practice: RESPONSE PATTERNS ⑮ each line 3 times

Lines 1-2. Read a word letter by letter. Type at a controlled pace. Center stroking in the fingers. Keep wrists and elbows quiet.

Lines 3-4. Try for "chained" response. Read and type a syllable, word, or short phrase at a time. Type without pauses.

Lines 5-6. Type short, easy words by word response; longer or more difficult words letter by letter. Work for flowing rhythm pattern.

| 1 | Letter | to see, to see him, as you, as you are, we only, we only saw |
| 2 | response | After the new rate was set, we detected a decrease in taxes. |

| 3 | Word | and the, and then, if they, they did, to them, when they did |
| 4 | response | It is right for them to sign the forms; Rod may do so, also. |

| 5 | Combination | for the jump, if the grade, and the only, with the only case |
| 6 | | She agreed to get the draft for the chairman if it is ready. |

`|  1  |  2  |  3  |  4  |  5  |  6  |  7  |  8  |  9  |  10  |  11  |  12  |`

Problem 2 (WB p. 47)

Letterhead; 2 sheets of carbon paper; 2 sheets of copy paper; 1 large envelope; 60-space line; date on Line 17; address an envelope. Type the listed items at the left margin, SS with DS above and below the list.

Words

February 21, 19-- | Miss Vivian Hartshorn | 8
3129 Kaskaskia Street | Springfield, IL 62702 | 17
Dear Miss Hartshorn (¶1) Mrs. Lee has 23
asked me to send you the following payroll 32
record | forms to be completed before you 40
report for work on March 15: | 1. Employee's 49
Withholding Exemption Certificate | 2. Health 58
insurance application | 3. Personal data card 67
(¶2) We certainly are pleased that you have 75
decided to join our | company when you move 84
to Chicago next month. We shall do what- | 92
ever we can to make your adjustment to new 100
surroundings smooth | and pleasant. Please 109
let us know how we can help. | Cordially 116
yours | Miss Beverly Newburg | Secretary to 124
Mrs. Lee | Enclosures | cc Mrs. Alma Reed 132
Lee 133/146

Problem 3 (WB p. 49)

Letterhead; carbon paper; 1 copy sheet; large envelope; 60-space line; date on Line 18; address an envelope

Words

February 23, 19-- | Christ Chialtas Com- 7
pany | 7720 Jefferson Street | Nashville, TN 16
37208 | Gentlemen (¶1) This letter will con- 23
firm our telephone conversation of yesterday | 32
morning. We shall appreciate your sending 41
us information on | any electronic calculators 50
you have available for sale. (¶2) We are 57
particularly interested in printing calculators, 67
recon- | ditioned or in "as is" condition. They 76
should, however, be | operable. (¶3) Let us 83
hear from you soon about the machines you 92
now have in | stock. Keep us in mind when 100
additional printing or nonprint- | ing elec- 108
tronic calculators, copying machines, or edit- 117
ing type- | writers become available. We rent 125
such machines to offices | that we service and 134
have a heavy demand for them. | Sincerely 142
yours | Allan Wunsch | Purchasing Depart- 150
ment | xx 151/164

52D Evaluate Your Work ⑤

Compare your typed letters with the model on page 88. With your stroke and line-space ruler, check the vertical placement of the letter parts.

Check the side margins. They should be about equal in width. Proofread by comparing. Have all errors been neatly erased and corrected?

LESSON 53

53A Preparatory Practice ⑦ each line twice; then 1' writings on Lines 1 and 4

Alphabet	We expect to solve the jigsaw puzzle more quickly than Bud Franks did.
Figure/symbol	The Idaho Utility 6 3/4% bonds (due June 20, 1980) now sell at 75 3/8.
Rule for figures	Type order numbers in figures: Order #839462 was sent to Day & Burns.
Fluency	The chairman thought the audience should take part in the discussions.

| 1 | 2 | 3 | 4 | 5 | 6 | 7 | 8 | 9 | 10 | 11 | 12 | 13 | 14 |

27D Skill-Comparison Typing ⑬

1. Type a 1' writing on each ¶; compare *gwam* and number of errors.
2. Type two or more 1' writings on the slower ¶. Try to equal or exceed the rate on the faster ¶.

3. Type one or more 1' writings on the ¶ on which you made the most errors. Try to equal or exceed your accuracy on the more accurate ¶.
4. Type a 3' writing on both ¶s; compute and record *gwam*.

All letters are used.

		3' GWAM
¶ 1	What is the effect of music on the way we think and	3 | 45
1.2 SI	work? Many writers hold that it will improve the way we	7 | 49
5.0 AWL		
95% HFW	work with others. Some say that we can get more done with	11 | 53
	less effort. Some say that music will take our attention	15 | 57
	off the easy jobs we do. A great many say that it will	19 | 60
	make us think eloquently.	20 | 62
¶ 2	Does music improve the quality of office work? At	24 | 65
1.4 SI	least a dozen experts say it does if the music is pleasant	28 | 69
5.4 AWL		
85% HFW	and if the jobs do not require careful thought. On simple	32 | 73
	jobs, music does reduce tension and fatigue. Even on these	35 | 77
	jobs, a strong case can be made for having periods when the	40 | 81
	music is actually turned off.	42 | 83

3' GWAM | 1 | 2 | 3 | 4 |

LESSON 28

28A Preparatory Practice ⑦ each line twice

Alphabet	Bob realized very quickly that jumping was excellent for us.
Figure	Please type these figures: 92 and 101 and 85 and 47 and 36.
Rule of style	Underline words printed in <u>italics</u> when you type from print.
Fluency	Hold your arms quite still and let your fingers do the work.

| 1 | 2 | 3 | 4 | 5 | 6 | 7 | 8 | 9 | 10 | 11 | 12 |

28B Building Speed/Control ⑮ 1' writing on ¶ 1 to establish base rate; 1' writing on ¶ 2 to establish base rate

1. Type two 1' guided writings on ¶ 1 of 27D, above for speed (base rate plus 6-8 words).
2. Type two 1' guided writings on ¶ 2 for control (base rate minus 6-8 words).

3. Type a 3' writing on both ¶s combined. Determine *gwam* and errors.
4. Compare the 3' *gwam* with that typed in Lesson 27.

LESSON 52

52A Preparatory Practice ⑦ each line twice; then 1' writings on Lines 2 and 4

Alphabet   The audience was amazed by the report John F. Maxwell gave so quickly.

Figure/symbol Net income for the year 1974 credited to earned surplus is $2,536,800.

Hyphen   Here is an up-to-date reference for those out-of-this-world questions.

Fluency   The worker ranks appreciation of his good work as of first importance.

| 1 | 2 | 3 | 4 | 5 | 6 | 7 | 8 | 9 | 10 | 11 | 12 | 13 | 14 |

52B Speed/Control Building ⑩ two 1' writings for speed; two 1' writings for control one 2' writing for speed; one 2' writing for control

All letters are used.

1.4 SI
5.4 AWL
85% HFW

The size of a business may not indicate the number of its owners.
A large company may be owned solely or by several partners on an equal
basis. On the other hand, a small corporation may belong to a relatively
large number of stockholders whose rights extend just as far as the number of shares they own.

	GWAM	
	1'	2'
	13	7	37
	28	14	44
	42	21	52
	57	28	59
	61	31	61

1' GWAM | 1 | 2 | 3 | 4 | 5 | 6 | 7 | 8 | 9 | 10 | 11 | 12 | 13 | 14 |
2' GWAM | 1 | 2 | 3 | 4 | 5 | 6 | 7 |

52C Problem Typing: BUSINESS LETTERS IN BLOCK STYLE, OPEN PUNCTUATION ㉘ Correct or circle errors, as directed.

Problem 1 WB p. 45

*Letterhead; carbon paper; 1 copy sheet; large envelope;
60-space line; date on Line 12; address an envelope*

Words

February 19, 19-- | Mr. Harold F. Janowski | 8
Manager, Actron Corporation | 6530 North 16
Lincoln Avenue | Chicago, IL 60645 | Dear 24
Mr. Janowski (¶ 1) Thank you for telephon- 31
ing this morning to discuss the possi- | bility of 40
our providing some temporary office help dur- 49
ing | the months of April and May. We shall 57
be glad to work with | you in any way that 66
will be beneficial. (¶ 2) We can furnish on 73
short notice any typists, stenographers, | and 82
bookkeepers required. All operators are ex- 91
perienced. | They are capable of using stan- 99
dard equipment. If you need | operators for 108

Words

specialized equipment, we shall make every | 116
effort to provide them. (¶ 3) The enclosed 124
brochure describes our functions and outlines | 133
briefly our methods of operation. The table 142
of pay rates for | various job classifications 151
will give you a good idea of the | cost of the 160
work you want to have done. (¶ 4) Mr. Albert 167
Valdez, one of our work-relations coordi- 175
nators, | will call you early next week to 183
arrange an appointment to | consider your job 192
requirements in detail. You will find him | 201
helpful in matching the worker to the job. | 209
Sincerely yours | John D. Marvin | Sales 217
Manager | xx | Enclosure 221/240

28C Technique Practice: WORD RESPONSE ⑩ each line 3 times from dictation

Do not type the dividers

of the | is the | by the | and the | to the | to them | for the | for them

it is | to do | of us | by me | or go | if he | if he did | and do | and did

if it is | if it is the | to do | to do the | and go | and go | to do it

and the | and they | and if they | and if they go | for the | for them

28D Skill-Transfer Typing ⑩ three 1' writings on each ¶; compare GWAM

1' GWAM

¶ 1
1.4 SI
5.4 AWL
85% HFW

The purposes of business letters are many and varied.   11
Letters are used to seek or inform, to direct or explain, to   23
gain or retain goodwill--to name only a few functions. Their   36
value is great; the cost is vital, too.   43

¶ 2
1.4 SI
5.4 AWL
85% HFW

The biggest factor in letter cost is labor. Reduce the   11
cost of this human factor--increase the production of the one   24
who dictates and the one who makes notes and types--and you   36
reduce a major cost of writing letters.   43

¶ 3
1.4 SI
5.4 AWL
85% HFW

An ~~excellent method~~ *easy way* to cut cost*s* is to write ~~sounder~~ *shorter* letters.   11
[____] many are loaded with dry, usless phrases. Study *this* one   23
example: ~~Please~~ *Kindly* be advise*d* that ~~that~~ *the* copy was put in*t*o the   35
~~mills~~ *mail* today. ~~Now~~ how about: we send the letter to*t*day?   45

28E Tabulating and Figure-Typing Practice ⑧ Type the drill twice; DS; 60-space line; 7 spaces between columns

1. Clear all tab stops. (See page 18, if necessary.)

2. For Column 1, set the left margin stop for a 60-space line.

3. For Column 2, set tab stop 10 spaces from the left margin.

4. For Column 3, set a tab stop 10 spaces from the first tab stop.

5. For Column 4, set a tab stop 11 spaces from the second tab stop.

6. Set the remaining stops in a similar manner.

Clear and set tab stops

121	111	1639	15.70	5:30	79,288
161	444	1752	28.00	2:40	80,260
414	666	1973	47.25	1:45	86,205
818	999	5720	50.50	8:47	92,036

KEY | 3 | 7 | 3 | 7 | 4 | 7 | 5 | 7 | 4 | 7 | 6 |

Communications Design Associates

801 JACKSON STREET, WEST   CABLE: COMDA
CHICAGO, ILLINOIS   60607   TELEPHONE: (312) 342-9753

		Words in Part	Total Words

Dateline February 14, 19-- *Date on Line 18* · 4 · 4

Operate return 4 times

Letter address
Mr. Martin McKensie · 8 · 8
McKensie Brothers, Inc. · 12 · 12
7829 Robertson Street · 17 · 17
Abilene, TX 79606 · 21 · 21
DS

Salutation Dear Mr. McKensie · 24 · 24
DS

Body of letter
This letter is typed in block style with open punctuation. · 36 · 36
The simplicity of this style has made it increasingly popular · 49 · 49
among business firms. The streamlined appearance seems to · 60 · 60
typify today's modern, streamlined world--yet the style in- · 72 · 72
cludes all the elements of information normally found in · 84 · 84
business letters. · 87 · 87

Observe that all lines, including the date, inside address, · 12 · 99
salutation, and closing lines, begin at the left margin. The · 24 · 111
spacing between letter parts is standard. As in the modified · 37 · 124
block letter style, the number of line spaces left in the top · 49 · 136
margin varies with the length of the letter. · 58 · 145
DS

Complimentary close Sincerely yours · 61 · 148

Operate return 4 times

Charles Harley Chambers

Typed name Charles Harley Chambers · 66 · 153
Official title Public Service Director · 71 · 158

Reference initials mew · 72 · 159

Style Letter 3: BLOCK STYLE, OPEN PUNCTUATION

Note that with open punctuation, the salutation and complimentary close have no terminal punctuation.

LESSON 29

29A Preparatory Practice ⑦ each line twice

Alphabet	Baxter Fork requested my help in covering the Iwo Jima zone.
Figure	The serial number of Donald's 1974 adding machine is 386502.
Figure/symbol	We received a check from Dodge & Son (dated 10/18) for $550.
Fluency	We should not expect someone else to cure our nation's ills.

| 1 | 2 | 3 | 4 | 5 | 6 | 7 | 8 | 9 | 10 | 11 | 12 |

29B Technique Practice: COMBINATION RESPONSE ⑩ each line 3 times from dictation

Do not
type the
dividers

and the date | if the case | to the only | if it were | and the fact

to him | to my | to look | to see | to test | to pull | to you | to get it

if the only | if they were | and they saw | if they saw | to get him

by the date | by the case | by the only | with him | with great ease

| 1 | 2 | 3 | 4 | 5 | 6 | 7 | 8 | 9 | 10 | 11 | 12 |

29C Skill-Transfer Typing ⑱

1. Type a 1' writing on each sentence. Determine *gwam*. Compare rates on each pair of sentences and on the last 3 lines.

2. Type additional 1' writings on the 2 or 3 sentences on which you made the lowest rates. Work for improvement in keystroking speed.

Words in Line

1	We appreciate your returning the signed form before Tuesday.	12
2	My check for $175 pays Waltz & Walton's bill for provisions.	12
3	This wonderful new device answers your phone when you can't.	12
4	The actual cost of these terminal units is $34.50 (less 6%).	12
5	Hold your arms and wrists quiet as you let the fingers type.	12
6	She can call you before 12:45 p.m. on Tuesday, September 30.	12
7	We have built a new system that grows as your company grows.	12
8	Call (201) 937-3800 and ask for Mr. Redbord or write to him.	12
9 Script	*Write today for the free sample and a booklet worth reading.*	12
10 Corrected copy	here is book let giving your some facts about car insurance.	12
11 Proofreading	The (pamplet) is (four) new friends as (will) as for (are) old ones.	12

| 1 | 2 | 3 | 4 | 5 | 6 | 7 | 8 | 9 | 10 | 11 | 12 |

50D Individual Practice ⑮ each line 3 times; retype any lines on which you made more than 3 errors in the 3 writings

1 One hand   Bart Kimmon was aggravated after only a few union cases were referred.
2 Balanced hand   Bud and eight girls may bicycle to the lake for a trip to Duck Island.
3 Combination   The staff at the car lot wanted him to make a trade after ten minutes.
4 Combination   They may award the contract to a downtown auditor at the minimum rate.
5 Adjacent keys   Three guides were in a column as we went over the trails after a lion.
6 Double letters Bill and Ann will soon see the bookkeeping committee from Mississippi.
7 Figure/symbol   Approximately 10% of the #237 machines were priced incorrectly at $89.
8 Direct reaches Myrtle took to a rummage sale the junk Fred left at the service plaza.
9 1st row   Anna Mae McVay became excited when Calvin Bixmont raced over the line.
10 3d row   Is it true that you were the ones who raised the issue of party lines?

| 1 | 2 | 3 | 4 | 5 | 6 | 7 | 8 | 9 | 10 | 11 | 12 | 13 | 14 |

LESSON 51

51A Preparatory Practice ⑦ each line twice; then 1' writings on Lines 1 and 4

Alphabet   The objective of the tax quiz was clarified by checking samples of it.
Figure/symbol   Interest accumulated in 1974 to $280.56 when the rate increased by 3%.
Rule for figures Type invoice numbers in figures: Invoice #9705 is dated September 26.
Fluency   The chairman said a large bequest had been made to the endowment fund.

| 1 | 2 | 3 | 4 | 5 | 6 | 7 | 8 | 9 | 10 | 11 | 12 | 13 | 14 |

51B Technique Practice: RESPONSE PATTERNS ⑩ two 1' writings on each line; compare GWAM

Letter response We erected a farm house and garage on the best acreage in Union, Ohio.
Word response   To throw their pots, they dug one-eighth ton of clay from Jay's field.
Combination   Our visual display at the civic arts center show was observed by many.
                 We send large packages overseas by surface; small items go by airmail.

| 1 | 2 | 3 | 4 | 5 | 6 | 7 | 8 | 9 | 10 | 11 | 12 | 13 | 14 |

51C Problem Typing: BUSINESS LETTERS IN BLOCK STYLE, OPEN PUNCTUATION ㉝

Problem 1 (WB p. 41)

1. Study Style Letter 3, page 88. Note the placement of the date and closing lines. Note also that open punctuation is used.

2. Type the letter. Use a 60-space line and type the date on Line 18.

3. After typing the letter, proofread it. Check names, addresses, and tricky words with the original. Circle errors.

Problem 2

1. Type a 2' writing on the opening lines and ¶ 1 of Style Letter 3, page 88. Move from part to part quickly to improve your speed.

2. Type a 2' writing on the last ¶ and the closing lines of Style Letter 3.

Problem 3 (WB p. 43)

Retype Style Letter 3. Proofread by comparing. Circle or erase errors, as directed by your instructor.

29D Proofreading: WORD SUBSTITUTION ⑩ each line once, making needed corrections as you type

> **Proofreading Cue.** Word substitution errors are commonly missed in proofreading. To catch them, read the copy for meaning.

1   That's why it (as) so vital that (your) choose the system wisely.

2   (Thank) of the people you (could) have to hire to get work done.

3   You can (us) the system in (quite) rooms; (being) by calling (know).

4   You don't (has) to ask (you) caller (of) you can call him later.

5   Here are (come) features to consider when planning (he) system.

6   You can (by) away (form) your desk (an) still receive your calls.

7   "Pocket paging" (unables) anyone to (contract) a man on the move.

29E Technique Practice: TABULATOR AND RETURN ⑤ at least twice

↓ Center + 10

Tab ⇥ Reach the finger to   *Return*
the tabulator bar or key. ──Tab──▶ Depress it quickly,   *Return*
then move back to home position. ──▶ Reach to the return   *Return*
lever or key quickly, too.

LESSON 30

30A Preparatory Practice ⑦ each line twice

Alphabet   Dwight and Ezra Quick flew over Byrd Peak six times in July.

Figure   These numbers have been designated: 37, 49, 15, 60, and 28.

Long reaches He expects the sunshiny days to check the epidemic of colds.

Fluency   Be ever grateful for luck, but don't lean on it too heavily.
              | 1 | 2 | 3 | 4 | 5 | 6 | 7 | 8 | 9 | 10 | 11 | 12 |

30B Technique Practice: RESPONSE PATTERNS ⑩ two 1' writings each line; compare rates

Word response   Rod makes the forms for the men to use for their field work.

Letter response As you are aware, I look upon Milo Savage as a great trader.

Combination   When I agreed to the rates, he signed the proxy you gave me.

                 Think of the time you would lose without an intercom system.
                 | 1 | 2 | 3 | 4 | 5 | 6 | 7 | 8 | 9 | 10 | 11 | 12 |

49D Growth Index (8) one 5' writing; determine GWAM and errors

All letters are used.

	GWAM		
	1'	2'	5'

¶ 1
1.5 SI
5.6 AWL
80% HFW

If there is any one secret of doing a difficult job well, it is the | 14 | 7 | 3
ability to concentrate. The efficient person does first things first and | 28 | 14 | 6
does them one at a time. This is not so simple as it first appears, in | 43 | 21 | 9
that the busy worker has the most demands upon his time and thus faces | 57 | 27 | 11
a more difficult problem in priorities. To put tasks in the order of | 71 | 35 | 14
their importance requires skill and experience, and to concentrate solely | 86 | 42 | 17
on one job takes patience and a disciplined mind. People with these | 100 | 50 | 20
particular qualities know how to avoid the unnecessary jobs and the use- | 114 | 57 | 23
less efforts and how to apply their time to the really important things. | 129 | 65 | 26

¶ 2
1.5 SI
5.6 AWL
80% HFW

The typical person hurries. Nothing to which he gives attention | 13 | 6 | 28
gets enough time. Capable people do not race. They set an easy pace, | 27 | 13 | 31
but they continue working steadily. Also, the typical person tries to | 41 | 20 | 34
do a dozen tasks at once. As a result, he does not have adequate time | 56 | 28 | 37
for any of the activities on his agenda. If one of his duties must be | 70 | 35 | 40
slighted, his entire program collapses. More often than not, crises-- | 84 | 42 | 43
not people--make decisions. Generally this tactic does not pay, as not | 98 | 49 | 45
enough time is spent on each element in a decision. The able person | 112 | 52 | 48
avoids this trap by doing first things first, one at a time. | 124 | 62 | 51

```
1' GWAM | 1 | 2 | 3 | 4 | 5 | 6 | 7 | 8 | 9 | 10 | 11 | 12 | 13 | 14 |
2' GWAM |   1   |   2   |   3   |   4   |   5   |   6   |   7   |
5' GWAM |       1       |       2       |       3       |
```

LESSON 50

50A Preparatory Practice (7) each line twice; then 1' writings on Lines 1 and 4

Alphabet   J. V. Packard may excel in law, but Hal Ford is quite good in zoology.

Figure   Please turn to page 350 and answer Questions 2, 4, 6, 7, 8, 9, and 17.

Figure/symbol   Order #678 for 24 chairs (@ $10.35 each) was shipped to you on May 19.

Fluency   Think the words as you type, but let your fingers do the work for you.

```
| 1 | 2 | 3 | 4 | 5 | 6 | 7 | 8 | 9 | 10 | 11 | 12 | 13 | 14 |
```

50B Speed/Control Building (18)

1. Type a 5' writing on 49D, above. Determine *gwam* and errors.

2. Type two 1' writings on each ¶ for control.

3. Type a 5' writing. Compare *gwam* and errors with the first writing.

50C Skill-Transfer Typing (10) 60-space line; each line for two 1' writings; compare GWAM

Words

Straight copy   All the girls in this firm work with speed but without rush.   12

Figure/symbol   Order #836 comes to $197.50 and is to be shipped by June 24.   12

Script   *Harley will handle the problem of forms for your firm today.*   12

Corrected copy   the new chair man will not your top sign that amendment.   12

30C Growth Index ⑱

1. Type a 3' writing on both ¶s. Determine *gwam* and number of errors. Proofread by comparing.

2. Type two 1' writings on each ¶. Determine *gwam*.
3. Repeat Step 1 . Compare the *gwam* and number of errors with the first 3' writing.

All letters are used.

		3' GWAM
¶ 1	There is an old saying that recommends: Take care of the	4 | 40
1.4 SI 5.4 AWL 85% HFW	pennies and the dollars will take care of themselves. This is	8 | 44
	very good advice in handling money, and it can also be applied	12 | 48
	quite directly to other phases of life.	15 | 51
¶ 2	For instance, if you learn to accept or conquer each of	19 | 55
1.4 SI 5.4 AWL 85% HFW	your little frustrations as they occur every day, you will	23 | 58
	develop the ability to face personal crises if and when they	27 | 63
	arise. You will also learn to maintain a clear head and not	31 | 67
	be panicked by the size of the next major problem that may	35 | 71
	block your progress.	36 | 72

3' GWAM | 1 | 2 | 3 | 4 |

30D Individual Practice ⑮

1. Type each line once. Place a check mark before any line that seemed difficult.

2. Type 2 or 3 times each line you checked as difficult.

1 Backspacer   Does Ruth often spell <u>ninty</u> for <u>ninety</u> and <u>fourty</u> for <u>forty</u>?

2 Shift keys   The names of the winners are these: Jay, Ted, Ben, and Pam.

3 Long words   determine alteration parallel population excessive centering

4 One hand   John Reed read my opinion in July. Lum Wertz was in Warsaw.

5 Double letters   Ellis can sell all the green tweed wool on the loom to Bess.

6 1st/3d rows   Many a man never quite wins the big prize of complete peace.

7 3d/4th fingers   This quaint puzzle was used as a quiz; it was quite popular.

8 Direct reaches   Why must Mervyn Youngman bring the check from Pike Brothers?

9 Adjacent keys   The report asked for opinions from people opposing reunions.

| 1 | 2 | 3 | 4 | 5 | 6 | 7 | 8 | 9 | 10 | 11 | 12 |

49A Preparatory Practice ⑦ each line twice; then 1' writings on Lines 1 and 4

Alphabet   Next week qualified judges will have to analyze our club performances.

Figure/symbol   Kauffman's invoice #3278 for $461.50 (less 2%) was paid on November 9.

Rule for figures   Type exact ages in figures: June is 18 years 4 months and 9 days old.

Fluency   It is now thought that the men in business who read more achieve more.

| 1 | 2 | 3 | 4 | 5 | 6 | 7 | 8 | 9 | 10 | 11 | 12 | 13 | 14 |

49B Word-Division Drill ⑩ half sheet; 1½" top margin; DS; 60-space line; 6 spaces between columns

The words in the second column indicate *all* syllables. As you type the words in the third column, show the acceptable division points for typewritten work.

ACCEPTABLE POINTS OF WORD DIVISION
TS

advertisement	ad-ver-tise-ment	adver-tise-ment
carefully	care-ful-ly	
determination	de-ter-mi-na-tion	
economic	eco-nom-ic	
elementary	el-e-men-ta-ry	
self-satisfied	self-sat-is-fied	
synonymous	syn-on-y-mous	

KEY   14   6   17   6   16

49C Problem Typing: BUSINESS LETTERS IN MODIFIED BLOCK STYLE, BLOCK ¶s ㉕

Problem 1 (WB p. 37)

Letterhead; carbon paper; 2 copy sheets; large envelope; small envelope; 60-space line; date on Line 15; mixed punctuation; address small envelope for cc as indicated; correct or circle errors, as directed by your instructor.

Words

October 27, 19-- | Ms. Gladys F. Woodman,   8
Dean | Lakeview College of Business | 943   16
North Burbank Avenue | Milwaukee, WI   23
53224 | Dear Ms. Woodman: (¶1) We are   29
pleased to send you today a complimentary   37
copy of our | communications layout guide: 46

DS and center

STYLED TO THE READER'S TASTE   52

DS

(¶2) This little booklet has become a popular   60
item on the shelves | of many college book-   68
stores. (¶3) After you have used the guide   75
as a reference for a few days, | you will prob-   84
ably want each of your students to have one.   93
It | is available at $1.50 a copy from Mr.   102

Words

George Peters, Reference | Books, Inc., 1285   110
Ramayne Avenue, Racine, Wisconsin 53402.   118
(¶4) Thank you for your interest in our com-   126
munication practices. | We shall be pleased to   135
receive any comments and suggestions | you   143
may have for the improvement of our layout   152
guide. | Sincerely yours, | John D. Marvin | 160
Sales Manager | xx | Enclosure | cc Mr.   166
George Peters   169/190

Problem 2 (WB p. 39)

On plain paper, compose a reply to the letter in Problem 1 for Ms. Woodman's signature. John Marvin's address is Communications Design Associates (see page 81). Thank him for sending the layout guide, comment on the attractive illustrations, and inform him that you are ordering 50 copies of the guide.

Use the directions for Problem 1. Compose the letter; correct it; adjust placement; retype it on a letterhead with 2 carbon copies; address a large envelope.

SECTION 6
Basic Copy-Placement Procedures

LESSONS 31-37

Goals. In this section you will learn the basic rules of centering copy and of applying these rules in typing announcements and short reports. You will also learn some guides for dividing words and sentence parts at the ends of lines. In addition, you will continue to improve your skills at the typewriter.

Machine Adjustments. 70-space line (with left margin stop set 35 spaces left of center of page). Set right margin stop at end of scale unless otherwise directed. SS sentence drills; DS and indent ¶s 5 spaces; space problem copy as directed.

Special Supplies Needed. 5″ by 3″ and 6″ by 4″ cards.

LESSON 31

31A Preparatory Practice ⑦ each line twice; then 1′ writings on Lines 1 and 4 to compare GWAM

Alphabet   Did Blair expect to solve the jigsaw puzzle more quickly than Francis?

Figure   Bob moved 720 cardboard boxes, 395 of which went to Rooms 146 and 188.

Figure/symbol Our check for $1,275, dated February 18, was sent to O'Donnell & Sons.

Fluency   You may thus enjoy trying to do the tasks that others find hard to do.

| 1 | 2 | 3 | 4 | 5 | 6 | 7 | 8 | 9 | 10 | 11 | 12 | 13 | 14 |

31B Technique Practice: RESPONSE PATTERNS ⑩ each line 3 times; then 1′ writings on Lines 3 and 4

Letter response   We were regarded as the team to beat after winning only three debates.

Word response   A sure way to raise his speed is to study the way he strikes the keys.

Combination   Thank you for taking the time to write us about the error on the form.

                  We were pleased to learn that you received the shipment in good order.

| 1 | 2 | 3 | 4 | 5 | 6 | 7 | 8 | 9 | 10 | 11 | 12 | 13 | 14 |

31C Horizontal Centering ⑩ 8½″ by 5½″ half sheet; DS; begin on Line 11 from the top

1. Check placement of paper guide. Turn to Reference Guide page iii for directions. Insert paper with the short edge at the left (at **0** on the paper guide scale).
2. Move both margin stops to the ends of the scale. Clear all tabulator stops. Move the carriage to the center point; set a tab stop here to use for each line.
3. From the center point, backspace once for each 2 spaces in the line to be centered. Disregard a leftover stroke.
4. Begin to type where you complete the backspacing.

	Words
DR. ROBERT DUNHAM	4
TS	
Announces the Location of His	10
DENTAL OFFICES	13
in the Franklin Medical Center	19
3200 Santa Monica Boulevard	24

48B Control Building: ERRORLESS TYPING ⑤ each line once without error or 3 times with no more than 1 error

Each day's work calls for the application of preceding days' learning.

Do yourself a favor: Put things away as soon as you finish with them.

Time is like money——the less of it we have, the further we make it go.

| 1 | 2 | 3 | 4 | 5 | 6 | 7 | 8 | 9 | 10 | 11 | 12 | 13 | 14 |

48C Assembling, Inserting, and Erasing a Carbon Pack ⑩ 60-space line; DS; 5-space ¶ indention

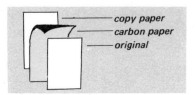

copy paper
carbon paper
original

1. Read ¶ 1 at the right and assemble a carbon pack as directed.

2. Read ¶ 2; then insert the pack as directed.

3. Starting on Line 17, type the copy at the right. Proofread; erase and correct errors.

ASSEMBLING, INSERTING, AND ERASING A CARBON PACK
TS

Place on the desk the sheet on which the carbon (file) copy is to be made; then place a sheet of carbon paper, carbon side down, on the paper. Finally, place the sheet for the original on top of the carbon paper.

Pick up the papers and tap the bottom edges lightly on the desk. Insert the pack with the carbon side toward you as you insert the papers. Roll in the pack until the feed rolls have gripped the papers; then operate the paper release lever to prevent possible wrinkles.

To erase errors, pull the original sheet forward and place a small card in front of the carbon sheet. Erase the error on the original with a hard (typewriter) eraser; remove the card. With a soft (pencil) eraser, erase the error on the file copy.

48D Problem Typing: BUSINESS LETTERS IN MODIFIED BLOCK STYLE, BLOCK ¶s ㉘

Problem 1 *(WB p. 33)*

Letterhead, carbon paper, copy sheet; large envelope; 1 cc; date on Line 17; 60-space line; mixed punctuation; erase and correct errors on original and carbon copies.

	Words
November 16, 19-- │ Dr. R. D. Redford, Chair-	8
man │ Business Department │ Jourdan Com-	15
munity College │ Chicago, IL 60620 │ Dear Dr.	24
Redford: │ (¶ 1) We are processing the em-	31
ployment application of Anne Morris, │ who	39
lists you as one of her references. We should	48
like to │ have your personal assessment of her.	58
(¶ 2) The job requires someone who is compe-	65
tent in shorthand, type- │ writing, filing, Eng-	74
lish, and mathematics. As dictation must │ be	83
taken from several people, we need someone	92
who can adapt │ to different situations. She	101

	Words
must be able to work under │ a great deal of	109
pressure at times. (¶ 3) In your opinion, would	118
Miss Morris be able to handle this │ job? We	127
shall appreciate your giving us this informa-	135
tion │ either on the enclosed form or by letter.	145
│ Sincerely yours, │ Mrs. Alma Reed Lee │ Per-	153
sonnel Officer │ xx │ Enclosure	158/177

Problem 2 *(WB p. 35)*

On a plain sheet 8½″ by 11″, compose for Dr. Redford's signature a reply about Miss Morris and the job to which Problem 1 refers. The address of Alma Reed Lee is Communications Design Associates (see page 81).

Use the directions for Problem 1. Compose the letter; correct it; retype it on a letterhead with a carbon copy, adjusting the top margin to give good balance on the sheet. Address a large envelope.

31D Problem Typing: CENTERED ANNOUNCEMENTS ⓩ⓪ each problem on a half sheet, short edge at the left

Problem 1: Unarranged Copy	**Problem 2: Corrected Copy**

DS; begin on Line 8; center each line

DS; begin on Line 10; center each line

	Words
CORRECT TYPING POSITION	5
TS	
Eyes on Copy; Copy at Right of Typewriter	13
Body Erect; Sit Back in Chair	19
Feet on Floor, One Ahead of the Other	27
Forearms Parallel to Slant of Keyboard	35
Fingers Curved over Second Row of Keys	42
Wrists Down, Not Arched	47
Front Frame of Machine Even with Desk Edge	56
Table Free of Unneeded Books	62

	Words
ALMOND SON'S ←TS	2
IS	3
Proud to ~~Announce~~ Present	6
Felix de Vega Couture Collection	13
Exciting, Beautiful Fashions, Exotic	20
Wednesday, September 27, 19--	26
Sunset Boulevard at Hampton court	33

31E Evaluate Your Work ③

1. Examine your finished copy. Compare your solution lines to those above and below them. Do the numbers of extended or indented strokes at the ends of lines appear to be equal?
2. Is the spacing between lines correct?

NOTE: For an exact check of your spacing, use a regular ruler. A special stroke and line-space ruler can be obtained from the publisher of this textbook. With this ruler, you can measure the number of strokes and the number of typewritten lines.

LESSON 32

32A Preparatory Practice ⑦ each line twice; then 1' writings on Lines 1 and 4 to compare GWAM

Alphabet	Owens thinks freezing prices at July fixed levels may be questionable.
Figure	On January 29 they ordered 186 books, 370 pens, and 45 reams of paper.
From dictation	if they, if they go, if they go to do, it is, it is the, it is the job
Fluency	If they do this job when they should, they may stay at the large lake.

| 1 | 2 | 3 | 4 | 5 | 6 | 7 | 8 | 9 | 10 | 11 | 12 | 13 | 14 |

32B Technique Practice: RESPONSE PATTERNS ⑩ each line 3 times; then 1' writings on Lines 3 and 4

Letter response	We are aware that the union monopoly case is exaggerated by the staff.
Word response	They can handle their profit problem if they do their work with vigor.
Combination	He may find the basic elements of the problem too subtle to determine.
	A wise neighbor said that most of us have potential that we never tap.

| 1 | 2 | 3 | 4 | 5 | 6 | 7 | 8 | 9 | 10 | 11 | 12 | 13 | 14 |

47D Problem Typing: BUSINESS LETTERS IN MODIFIED BLOCK STYLE, BLOCK ¶s (28) 2 letterheads / 2 large envelopes

Problem 1 *WB p. 29*

60-space line; date on Line 16; standard spacing of letter parts (as shown on p. 81); mixed punctuation; address a large envelope

Words

Current date 3

Ms. Beverly N. Montez | Supervisor, Office Services | V. V. Hil- 15
lotte & Company, Inc. | 14339 Maryland Avenue, N.E. | St. Peters- 27
burg, FL 33703 | Dear Ms. Montez: (¶ 1) A personal title, 37
such as Mr., Mrs., Miss, or (if a woman's | marital status is 51
unknown) Ms., should precede the names of | individuals in 62
letter addresses. Such professional titles | as Dr., Professor, and 78
Reverend may be used instead of the | personal titles. (¶ 2) In 91
letter closings, a personal or professional title never | precedes 104
a man's name in the signature; however, a considerate | woman 116
writer indicates an appropriate title, either typed | without 128
parentheses in the signature line or written with | parentheses 140
preceding her handwritten signature. | Sincerely yours, | Mrs. 152
Eva St. Clair | Associate Editor | xx 159/185

Problem 2 *WB p. 31*

60-space line; date on Line 18; standard spacing of letter parts (as shown on p. 81); mixed punctuation; address a large envelope

Words

Current date 3

Mrs. Anne Longworth | Vogel-Sanderson Company | 7302 13
Shertz Street | Peoria, IL 61611 | Dear Mrs. Longworth: 23
(¶ 1) The U.S. Postal Service encourages the use of the two- 34
letter | ZIP abbreviation (without periods or spaces) for state 46
names. | These abbreviations, however, may be used only with 58
ZIP Codes. (¶ 2) If the ZIP abbreviation is unknown, the stan- 69
dard abbreviation | may be used; or the state name may be 81
spelled in full. Good | arrangement of address data is the decid- 93
ing factor. (¶ 3) A report of state names and their ZIP abbrevia- 105
tions is en- | closed for your reference. | Sincerely yours, | Charles 117
Harley Chambers | Public Service Director | xx | Enclosure 127/143

LESSON 48

48A Preparatory Practice (7) each line twice; then 1' writings on Lines 2 and 4 to compare GWAM

Alphabet   Tex queried Kipp and Vince about your jewel boxes for the zircon gems.

Figure/symbol   He ordered 48 boxes of #573 @ $2.69, less 10%, from O'Brien & Company.

Rule for figures   In even amounts of money, omit decimal and ciphers: I sent $85 today.

Fluency   He will be named as chairman for the next meeting of your study group.

| 1 | 2 | 3 | 4 | 5 | 6 | 7 | 8 | 9 | 10 | 11 | 12 | 13 | 14 |

32C Typing Outside the Margins ③ 60-space line   left margin: center − 30
right margin: center + 30

1. Depress the **margin release** or **margin bypass (25)**, and backspace 5 spaces into the left margin.
2. Type the sentence below. When the carriage locks,

depress the margin release or margin bypass and complete the typing.
3. Repeat 1 and 2.

The chief rule of teamwork: Be considerate of others in little things.

32D Vertical Centering: MATHEMATICAL METHOD ⑧ 8½″ by 5½″ half sheet

1. Count the lines and blank line spaces in the copy.
2. Subtract lines needed from 66 for a full sheet or from 33 for a half sheet.
3. Divide by 2 to get top and bottom margins. If a fraction results, disregard it in computing the top margin.
4. To leave the correct *blank* space, space down from the top edge of the paper 1 more than the number of lines in the top margin.

Alternate Procedure. Before inserting the paper, use your stroke and line-space ruler to mark with a dot the starting line.

> **Reading position**
>
> For *reading position*, which is above the exact vertical center, subtract 2 from the exact top margin.

DS; center each line horizontally;
center entire report vertically

	Words
VERTICAL CENTERING	4
TS	
Count the lines to be centered.	10
Count 2 for the triple space after heading.	19
Count 1 for each blank line space in double-spaced lines.	31
Subtract total lines from 66 (full sheet) or 33 (half sheet).	44
Divide the result by 2 for top margin.	52
If a fraction results, disregard it.	59
Space down that number plus 1.	65

32E Problem Typing: CENTERED ANNOUNCEMENTS ⑱

Problem 1: Exact Center

On a half sheet, type the announcement at the right, DS. Center the lines horizontally and the entire announcement vertically.

Problem 2: Reading Position

On a full sheet, type the announcement at the right, DS. Center the lines horizontally and the entire announcement in *reading position* vertically.

	Words
THE VINCENT BARNES ART GALLERY	6
TS	
cordially invites you to attend a	13
reception and preview showing	19
of the new Lynwood Village store	25
Thursday, August tenth, five to seven	33
930 Lynwood Boulevard	38

32F Evaluate Your Work ④ Use your stroke and line-space ruler.

1. Proofread by comparing; circle errors.
2. For Problem 1, are there an equal number of line spaces in the top and bottom margins?
3. For Problem 2, are there 4 fewer line spaces in the top margin than in the bottom?
4. Compare your solution lines to those above and below them. Do the numbers of extended or indented strokes at the ends of lines appear to be equal?
5. Is the spacing between the lines correct?

47A Preparatory Practice ⑦ each line twice; then 1' writings on Lines 1 and 4 to compare GWAM

Alphabet   Our unexpected freezing weather may have killed John Quinley's shrubs.
Figure   Walford reported on the following rooms: 6, 10, 25, 37, 129, and 148.
Figure/symbol   Miller & Southeby (local grocers) sold 1,256# of bananas @ 24¢ per lb.
Fluency   Of the major elements, I think the first is by far the most important.

| 1 | 2 | 3 | 4 | 5 | 6 | 7 | 8 | 9 | 10 | 11 | 12 | 13 | 14 |

47B Technique Practice: RESPONSE PATTERNS ⑩ two 1' writings on each line; compare GWAM

Letter response   Did you regard my opinion of the minimum reserve rates as regrettable?
Word response   Six or eight of their men lent a hand with the work of the city audit.
Combination   Their union steward may draft a formal statement to the next chairman.
                  A man must learn to control himself before he tries to control others.

| 1 | 2 | 3 | 4 | 5 | 6 | 7 | 8 | 9 | 10 | 11 | 12 | 13 | 14 |

47C Addressing a Large Envelope and Folding a Letter ⑤

Large (No. 10) envelopes are used for letters of 2 or more pages or letters with enclosures. In practice, large envelopes are frequently used for full-size 1-page letters as well.

Type state names in full; use the standard abbreviation; or, with a ZIP Code, the special 2-letter abbreviation (without periods or spaces). See Reference Guide p. viii.

SS all addresses, regardless of number of lines. Study the illustration, and observe the placement and spacing notations. Type an envelope from the illustration.

> Type addressee notations (*Hold for Arrival*, *Personal*, *Please Forward*, and the like) a triple space below the return address and 3 spaces from the left edge of the envelope. Underline or use all capitals.

> Type mailing notations in all capitals, (AIRMAIL, SPECIAL DELIVERY, REGISTERED, and the like) at least 3 line spaces above the envelope address and below the stamp position.

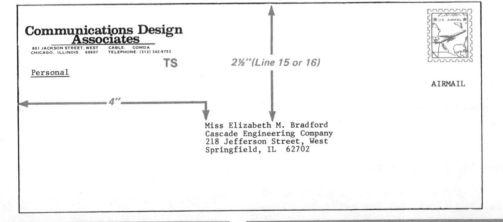

Folding a letter for a large envelope

Step 1. With the letter face up on the desk, fold slightly less than 1/3 of the sheet up toward the top.

Step 2. Fold down the top of the letter to within ½" of the bottom fold.

Step 3. Insert the letter into the envelope with the last-creased edge toward the bottom.

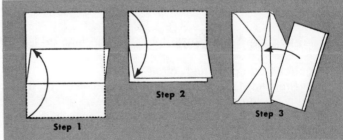

LESSON 33

33A Preparatory Practice ⑦ each line twice; then 1' writings on Lines 1 and 4 to compare GWAM

Alphabet — Packard Bigelow may yet fly to Vera Cruz to inquire about his next job.

Figure — Flight 372 will leave at 10:46 a.m. and arrive in Buffalo at 9:58 p.m.

Figure/symbol — Bob's policy #818429 for $49,500 has been renewed for another 3 years.

Fluency — Money spent for knowledge pays high interest. We must learn to think.

| 1 | 2 | 3 | 4 | 5 | 6 | 7 | 8 | 9 | 10 | 11 | 12 | 13 | 14 |

33B Control Building: RATE CONTROL ⑤ six ½' writings

1. Select a goal: 28, 32, 36, or more *wam*. Type at ½ your 1' goal rate for each ½" writing.

2. When you can type your goal word (or letter) on 2 consecutive writings as time is called, advance to the next goal level.

NOTE: Your instructor may call the ¼' to guide you.

1.4 SI
5.4 AWL
85% HFW

Here is our new growth plan: We do well that which we know well. We also make room for ideas that permit us to use our expertise. Such thinking has brought about our emerging as one of the largest makers of photographic equipment in the world, creating dozens of jobs and products that serve the public in many ways.

33C Special Characters ⑩ each line at least twice

NOTE: If your keyboard provides one of the following characters, use it. If not, type the character as described below.

'	*Minutes or feet*	Apostrophe
"	*Seconds, inches, or ditto*	Quotation mark
°	*Degree*	Roll platen forward ½ space; lowercase o; return platen
+	*Plus*	Diagonal; backspace; hyphen

—	*Minus*	Hyphen (leave space before and after)
×	*Times or by*	Lowercase x (leave space before and after)
÷	*Divided by*	Hyphen; backspace; colon
=	*Equals*	Hyphen; backspace; roll platen forward; hyphen; return platen

The 2' speed range, typed with the 15" call of the guide, is 30 to 46.

A rug 15'6" x 18'9" will be just right for a room that is 20'6" x 25'.

His problem is 27 × 89 — 364 ÷ 2. What is the sum of 157 + 509 — 263?

Type: 15 × 90 — 62 + 136 ÷ 2 = 712 and 7 × 284 — 965 + 301 ÷ 2 = 662.

If 32 × 564 — 897 + 109 equals 17,260, what would 57 + 590 — 63 equal?

The boiling point of water is 212° F. and the freezing point is 32° F.

| 1 | 2 | 3 | 4 | 5 | 6 | 7 | 8 | 9 | 10 | 11 | 12 | 13 | 14 |

Communications Design Associates

801 JACKSON STREET, WEST   CABLE: COMDA
CHICAGO, ILLINOIS   60607   TELEPHONE: (312) 342-9753

		Words in Parts	5' GWAM
	↓ Date and closing lines at center point		
Dateline	Line 15 → February 17, 19--	4	1
	Operate return 4 times		
Letter address	Miss Elizabeth M. Bradford	9	2
	Cascade Engineering Company	15	3
	218 Jefferson Street, West	20	4
	Springfield, IL 62702	25	5
	DS		
Salutation	Dear Miss Bradford:	28	6
	DS		
Body of letter	This letter is typed in modified block style with block	11	8
	paragraphs and mixed punctuation, a style widely used in	23	10
	business. The style has a number of distinctive features.	34	13
	The spacing between parts of the letter is standard. The	12	15
	spacing between the top edge of the letterhead and the date	24	17
	is variable. Short letters require leaving more line spaces	36	19
	than do long ones.	39	20
	The date, the complimentary close, and the name and official	12	23
	title of the writer are begun at the horizontal center of the	25	25
	paper. With mixed punctuation, a colon follows the saluta-	36	28
	tion and a comma follows the complimentary close. Notation	48	30
	lines are typed at the left margin, a double space below the	61	33
	last of the closing lines.	66	34
	I am pleased to enclose a booklet describing a number of	11	36
	letter styles and special letter features.	20	38
	DS		
Complimentary close	Sincerely yours,	23	38
Space for handwritten signature	*Operate return 4 times*		
	Charles Harley Chambers		
Typed name	Charles Harley Chambers	28	39
Official title	Public Service Director	33	40
	DS		
Reference initials	mew	34	40
Enclosure notation	Enclosure	35	41
Carbon copy notation	cc Mr. Alvin Meyer, Jr.	40	42

Style Letter 2: MODIFIED BLOCK STYLE, BLOCK PARAGRAPHS, MIXED PUNCTUATION

Mixed Punctuation. With *mixed punctuation*, as illustrated above, a colon follows the salutation and a comma follows the complimentary close.

Open Punctuation. With *open punctuation*, no punctuation follows the salutation and complimentary close.

33D Vertical Centering: BACKSPACE-FROM-CENTER METHOD

Half sheet inserted with short edge at left; DS; center each line horizontally; center report vertically

1. From the vertical center of the paper, roll the platen (cylinder) back once for each *two lines, two blank line spaces, or line and blank space* to be centered. Disregard an odd or leftover line.

2. The vertical center of an 8½″ by 5½″ half sheet is Line 17; of a full sheet 8½″ by 11″, Line 34.

NOTE: To type a problem in reading position, roll the platen back 2 additional lines.

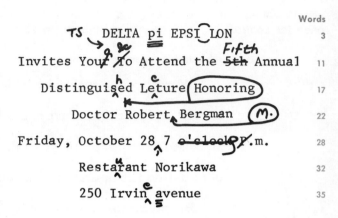

Words

TS   DELTA pi EPSILON   3

Invites You To Attend the ~~5th~~ *Fifth* Annual   11

Distinguised Leture (Honoring)   17

Doctor Robert Bergman (M.)   22

Friday, October 28 7 o'clock P.m.   28

Restarant Norikawa   32

250 Irvin avenue   35

33E Evaluate Your Work ③ Use your stroke and line-space ruler.

1. Examine your finished copy. Is your heading typed on Line 9?

2. Compare your solution lines to those above and below them. Do the numbers of extended or indented strokes at ends of lines appear to be equal?

3. Is the spacing between lines correct?

4. Retype the problem if you are not satisfied with your solution.

33F Problem Typing: CENTERED REPORTS ⑰

Problem 1: Report on a Half Sheet

60-space line; center vertically; TS after heading; SS; indent the 3 items 5 spaces; DS between ¶s and indented items

Words

WRITING NATURALLY   4

Most letters are too wordy. Writing long, involved letters   16
is the letter writer's greatest sin. These three principles   28
can help you cut out useless words: 35

Prefer familiar words to the farfetched.   44

Prefer concrete words to the abstract.   52

Prefer short words to the long.   58

Words that add nothing but weight to your letter should be   70
tossed out. Words are bridges between people. Build this   82
bridge with short, simple words—the kind of words you use   94
when you speak to people.   99

Problem 2: Report on Full Sheet

Type the announcement in Problem 1 on a full sheet in reading position; 60-space line; DS; TS after heading; indent ¶s and the 3 items 5 spaces.

45D Speed/Control Building ㉓

1. Type each of the following ¶s as two 1' writings, once for *speed* and once for *control*.

2. Type two 5' writings on all 3 ¶s. Determine *gwam* and errors for the better writing.

3. Proofread by comparing. Check with the original such commonly misspelled words as *across*, *usable*, and *likely*.

All letters are used.

		5' GWAM
¶1 1.4 SI 5.4 AWL 85% HFW	Words are the tools with which we communicate with others––vocally	3 | 34
	as well as in writing––and like other tools, words must be chosen wisely	6 | 37
	and used with care. In general, prefer a short, simple word to a long	8 | 40
	one; but do not hesitate to use whatever word will convey your meaning.	11 | 43
¶2 1.4 SI 5.4 AWL 85% HFW	Be quick to realize that a large vocabulary is vital to successful	14 | 46
	writing. The more extensive your store of usable words and word mean-	17 | 49
	ings, the more precise your message is likely to be. On the topic of	20 | 51
	words, be sure you have the right ones at hand.	22 | 53
¶3 1.4 SI 5.4 AWL 85% HFW	You must try hard to build a good vocabulary. You must read exten-	24 | 56
	sively, look up the meanings of unfamiliar words, and actively use those	27 | 59
	words. In this way you can learn to produce quickly the exact word to	30 | 62
	get just the effect you seek in your writing.	32 | 64

5' GWAM | 1 | 2 | 3 |

LESSON 46

46A Preparatory Practice ⑦ each line twice; then 1' writings on Lines 2 and 4

Alphabet	Dwight Mystronio lives in a quiet area six blocks from the Jasper zoo.
Figure	David Parker moved from 479 East 135th Street to 228 West 60th Street.
Figure/symbol	Was his 4-year lease (May 23 expiration) renewed May 10 at a 5% boost?
Fluency	Will five of these men work with the foreman for the next eight weeks?

| 1 | 2 | 3 | 4 | 5 | 6 | 7 | 8 | 9 | 10 | 11 | 12 | 13 | 14 |

46B Speed/Control Building ㉓ Repeat 45D, above.

46C Problem Typing: BUSINESS LETTERS IN MODIFIED BLOCK STYLE ⑳ (WB pp. 25, 27)

1. Study Style Letter 2, page 81. Note the placement of the date and closing lines. Read the brief explanations of mixed and open punctuation.

2. 60-space line; modified block with block ¶s; mixed punctuation; date on Line 15.

3. Set a tab stop at horizontal center to indent for typing the dateline and closing lines.

4. After typing the letter, proofread by comparing. Check names, addresses, and tricky words. Make pencil corrections; then retype the letter.

LESSON 34

34A Preparatory Practice ⑦ each line twice; then 1′ writings on Lines 1 and 4 to compare GWAM

Alphabet   When quizzed, Julia Volberg stated she expected no more work for July.
Figure   Our latest inventory includes 958 rings, 3,064 pins, and 172 brooches.
Rule for figures Type invoice numbers in figures: Invoice #5172 is dated September 30.
Fluency   They sent us these ornaments from an ancient temple in a foreign land.

| 1 | 2 | 3 | 4 | 5 | 6 | 7 | 8 | 9 | 10 | 11 | 12 | 13 | 14 |

34B Skill-Transfer Typing ⑩ 60-space line; 1′ writing on each line; compare rates

Words

1	Fluency	When you look, try to see; when you hear, try to understand.	12
2	Figure	If the flight is to leave at 7:45, we must check in by 7:10.	12
3	Symbol	Don't space between ¢, %, or # and the figure typed with it.	12
4	Script	*A letterhead should tell people that your product is unique.*	12
5	Corrected copy	it is such easer todo work right than that to do it ofer.	12
6	Error Recognition	It is will to push hard or speed an drop back four control.	12

34C Centering Data on Special-Size Paper ⑨

To find the horizontal center of special-size paper or cards

1. Insert the paper or card into the machine; add the numbers at the left and right edges of the paper to obtain the number of strokes available on a line.

2. Divide this sum by 2. The result is the horizontal center point for that paper.
3. Follow the steps for horizontal centering on page 57.

Practice Problem

1. Insert a half sheet with the long edge at the left (5½″ by 8½″). For a 3½″ top margin, start on Line 22.
2. Center each line horizontally; DS the lines.
3. Type the information requested at the right.

The name of your college (all caps)
The street address
The city and state address
Your name
Today's date

34D Evaluate Your Work ④ Use your stroke and line-space ruler.

1. Examine your finished copy. Are top and bottom margins approximately equal?
2. Compare your solution lines to those above and below them. Do the numbers of extended or indented lines appear to be equal?
3. Is the spacing between lines correct?
4. If you are not satisfied with your solution, retype the problem as time permits.

34E Centering a Heading on a Horizontal Line ②

With the underline key, type a 3-inch line on your paper. (30 pica or 36 elite strokes). Use the procedure in 34C to determine the center point; then center on the line the heading at the right.

Centered Heading
_____

SECTION 8

Business Letters

LESSONS 45-54

Goal. When you have completed the lessons of this section, you should be able to type modified block and block style business letters with open or mixed punctuation and position them attractively on the page.

Machine Adjustments. 70-space line; SS sentence drills; DS and indent ¶s 5 spaces; space problem copy as directed. For problems and ¶ copy, use an adjusted right margin (see page 64).

Supplies Needed. Large (No. 10) envelopes; carbon paper

LESSON 45

45A Preparatory Practice ⑦ each line twice; then 1' writings on Lines 1 and 4

Alphabet	The king and queen brought dozens of expensive jewels from the colony.
Figure/symbol	Does the 10% discount on Bender & Hunt's invoice #4697 come to $23.58?
Rule for numbers	Type policy numbers without commas: My policy #5923748 is for $6,500.
Fluency	How well did the eight boys do the problems you assigned for homework?

| 1 | 2 | 3 | 4 | 5 | 6 | 7 | 8 | 9 | 10 | 11 | 12 | 13 | 14 |

45B Technique Practice: STROKING ⑩ each line at least 3 times

1	Direct reaches	Mike Goldfarb hunted from jungle to desert for the special king cobra.
2	Double letters	Will Bill sell his sleek-looking car to Miss Nell Pool of Mississippi?
3	One hand	A fast steed's jump at the races deserves to be rewarded with a treat.
4	1st row	Max and Vern Bench expect to be in breezy Vera Cruz, Mexico, next May.
5	3d/4th fingers	Zealous players seldom overlook opportunities to win a valuable prize.

45C Aligning and Typing over Words ⑩

On your typewriter, locate the **variable line spacer (3)** and the **aligning scale (33).**

1. Type the line below, but do not make the return.

Use the aligning scale to align your copy.

2. Move the carriage (or carrier) so that a word with the letter *I* is above the scale. Note that a colored line points to the vertical part of the letter.

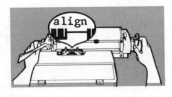

3. Study the relative position of the top, horizontal lines of the scale to the bottom of the descenders of letters like q, y, p, g, and j. Get a visual picture of this relationship to be able to adjust the paper correctly and type over a word with exactness.

4. Remove the paper; reinsert it. To adjust the line so that the bottoms of the letters align correctly with the aligning scale, do this:

- To raise or lower the line of writing, operate the **variable line spacer (3).**
- To center a letter *I* over one of the colored vertical lines, operate the **paper release (16)** to move the paper left or right.

5. Check the accuracy of your alignment by setting the **ribbon control (21)** for stencil position and typing over one of the letters. Make any necessary adjustments. *Return the ribbon control to inking position.*

6. Type over any words in the sentence that contain the letter *I*. Make any further adjustments necessary.

7. Repeat the entire drill. (You will use this procedure frequently to make corrections in your typewritten work.)

34F Problem Typing: CENTERING ON SPECIAL-SIZE PAPER OR CARDS ⑱

NOTE: Laboratory (workbook) materials are available for use with this textbook. The workbook page on which a specific form or stationery item appears is given in the textbook with the appropriate problem. Cards for Problems 1 and 2 are on workbook page 13 (WB p. 13). Students without workbooks should use paper cut to 5″ by 3″ and 6″ by 4″.

Problem 1: Data on 5- by 3-Inch Card

1. Insert 5″ by 3″ card with short edge at the left.

2. Start on Line 5; DS.

3. Center each line horizontally.

4. Evaluate your solution. Use your stroke and line-space ruler to check your work.

Card holders

If your typewriter has adjustable card holders, adjust them as shown above. Paper bail will keep card from slipping.

CENTERING DATA ON SPECIAL-SIZE PAPER
TS

	Words
	7
Insert the card or paper into the machine.	16
Add the scale numbers at both edges.	24
Divide the sum by 2.	28
The result is the horizontal center.	38

Problem 2: Data on 6- by 4-Inch Card

1. Type Problem 1 on a 6″ by 4″ card (or paper) with the short edge at the left. Start on Line 8; DS. Center each line horizontally.

2. Evaluate your solution, using your stroke and line-space ruler.

3. Proofread by comparing.

LESSON 35

35A Preparatory Practice ⑦ each line twice; then 1′ writings on Lines 1 and 4 to compare GWAM

Alphabet · With a fixed goal in mind, quickly size up a job before making a move.

Figure/fraction · A half sheet is 8½ by 5½ inches and has 33 lines (6 lines to an inch).

Figure/symbol · My 90-day note for $2,700 (dated February 10) carries interest at 6¼%.

Fluency · Following a man's advice is far less risky than following his example.

| 1 | 2 | 3 | 4 | 5 | 6 | 7 | 8 | 9 | 10 | 11 | 12 | 13 | 14 |

35B Skill-Transfer Typing ⑧ 60-space line; 1′ writing on each line; correct Line 5 as you type it; compare GWAM

			Words in Line
1		The recent audit proves that their statements are all right.	12
2		The April 16 check for $138.40 should have been for $183.40.	12
3	Script	*To center lines of a problem, we must know the center point.*	12
4	Corrected copy	Back space for ~~every~~ tow speages in ~~the~~ line tobe centred.	12
5	Error Recognition	You brain can stores mush more data then nay large computer.	12

44C Problem Typing Measurement ㉖

Only directions for varying procedures are included for these problems. Standard directions learned in earlier lessons are to be applied. If necessary, refer to earlier lessons for these directions.

Problem 1: Simple Memorandum Form

Half sheet; 60-space line; correct errors; p. 68

	Words
Current date	3

SUBJECT: Summary of Spacing Rules   10

(¶ 1) Space once after a comma, a semicolon,   18
or a period used with | an abbreviation. Space   27
twice after the mark of punctuation | used   36
at the end of a sentence unless it comes at   44
the end of | a line of writing ; in this case, make   54
your return without | spacing. (¶ 2) Do not   61
space between a figure and the following sym-   70
bols : #, | $, %, ¢, * (asterisk), and / (diag-   79
onal). Thus : #13, $50, | 7%, 25¢, and 18*.   87
Exception : In a column of amounts, the | dol-   96
lar sign may be placed one space to the left   105
of the hori- | zontal starting point of the longest   114
line in the column. All | other dollar signs in   124
the column are aligned with it. Thus :   132

	$ 98.50	133
	122.00	135

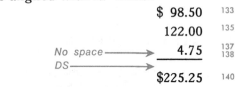

No space →	4.75	137 138
DS →	$225.25	140

Problem 2: Personal Note in Modified Block Style

Half sheet; 60-space line; correct errors; p. 70

	Words
Current date	3

Dear Gil | (¶ 1) Someone once said that the   10
man who builds a better mousetrap | will have   19
a path worn to his door. While I didn't build   29

44D Evaluate Your Work ⑤

Compare your solutions with the model copies on pages 68, 70, and 72. Your vertical placements should be the same as those given in the models.

Get Ready to Type . . .	4′
Timed Production	18′
Proofread	4′

Materials Needed. 2 half sheets, 1 full sheet; small envelope

	Words
a	better mousetrap, I have had a lot of visi-	35

tors lately. The | Music Festival in our city   46
is the chief attraction. (¶ 2) Joel Crane was   54
one such visitor. He inquired about you and | 63
asked me to pass along his greetings the next   72
time I wrote to | you. So a warm hello from   81
Joel. | Regards   84

Problem 3: Personal/Business Letter

Modified block style, open punctuation; 60-space line; return address on Line 16; correct errors; address a small envelope; fold and insert letter; p. 72

	Words
8005 Stewart Street	Albany, New York	8

12205 | June 10, 19-- | Mr. Howard F. Greg-   15
ory | 5829 Thornton Street | Albany, New   23
York 12206 | Dear Mr. Gregory | (¶ 1) You   29
asked me to let you know the nature of the   38
interview and | tests that I took at the Ham-   46
mond Electronics Company. I am | pleased   54
to comply. The tests were practical. They   63
covered | typewriting, English, spelling, and   72
arithmetic. I think I | did well on the tests.   81
(¶ 2) I was also asked about my club activi-   89
ties, hobbies, and | interests. Several times   98
during the interview, I was told | that my   106
attitude toward my job and co-workers would   115
be very | important. The Company fully be-   123
lieves in teamwork. I felt | relaxed and con-   131
fident during the interview. (¶ 3) If I get a   139
call from the Company, I shall let you know   148
the | results. Thank you for all the help you   157
have given me. | Yours sincerely | Miss Mar-   165
sha Siebert   167/180*

* Includes envelope address.

Use your stroke and line-space ruler to check your vertical and horizontal placement. Proofread by comparing. Check names, figures, and tricky words with the original.

35C Control Building: RATE CONTROL ⑫ Type 1' writings at a selected goal rate. Raise your goal rate as directed for 33B, page 60.

All letters are used.

1.5 SI
5.6 AWL
80% HFW

In composing a letter, you may find it hard to recognize that the result need not sound like a corporation. A corporate business does consist of actual people; a message or request to one of them should extend warmth—should project the image that the message is from a living person, not a vague, impersonal name on a letterhead.

35D Setting the Right Margin Stop ⑧

1. Set the margin stops for an exact 60-space line (left: center − 30 | right: center + 30).

2. Type the sentence below; stop on the stroke on which the typewriter bell rings. Instead of typing the remainder of the sentence, type the figures 123 etc. until the carriage locks. The last figure typed is the number of spaces on your typewriter between the bell and the carriage lock.

3. When you are not to type copy line for line, set the right-hand stop for the bell to ring 3 spaces before the desired line ending.

Thus: Subtract 3 from the last figure typed in Step 2. Add the difference to the figure at which the right-hand margin stop would be set for an exact line length.

4. Usually 3 to 7 spaces must be added to the right-hand stop setting, depending upon your typewriter.

REMEMBER YOUR ADJUSTMENT FIGURE.

Example. If your bell rings 9 spaces before the desired line ending, add 6 to the point at which a stop would be set for exact line length.

To get a bell cue, add your adjustment figure to the exact-margin figure.

35E Technique Practice: BELL CUE ⑮ Type the ¶ in 35C 3 times as directed below.

First Typing. 60-space line *plus* your adjustment figure; DS; 5-space ¶ indention. Be guided by the bell to return. If the bell rings and the carriage locks, depress the margin release key; complete the word.

Second Typing. 50-space line with adjustment figure added. Be guided by the bell to return.

Third Typing. 40-space line with adjustment figure added.

Evaluation. Using your stroke and line-space ruler, see if the left and right margins are approximately equal.

LESSON 36

36A Preparatory Practice ⑦ each line twice; then 1' writings on Lines 3 and 4 to compare GWAM

Alphabet   Hugh Wilcox printed five dozen banquet tickets for my meeting in June.
Figure   We are sending 2,795 of the 4,680 sets now and the balance on June 13.
Rule for figures Type weights in figures: The largest box weighs 207 pounds 13 ounces.
Fluency   Keep the right margins of the papers you type just as even as you can.

| 1 | 2 | 3 | 4 | 5 | 6 | 7 | 8 | 9 | 10 | 11 | 12 | 13 | 14 |

43D Folding and Inserting Letters: SMALL ENVELOPES ③

Folding a letter for a small envelope

Step. 1. With the letter face up on the desk, fold from the bottom up to ½″ from the top.
Step 2. Fold the right 1/3 to the left.
Step 3. Folding from left to right, fold the left 1/3 to about ½″ of the last crease to allow for ease of unfolding.
Step 4. Insert last-creased edge first.

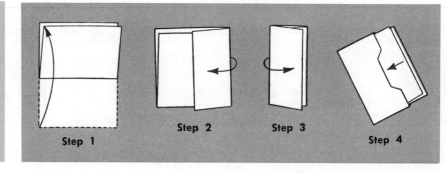

Step 1   Step 2   Step 3   Step 4

LESSON 44

44A Preparatory Practice ⑦ each line twice; then 1′ writings on Lines 1 and 4

Alphabet	Cal Jenkins will have the money required for our next big sales prize.
Figure	Their 1976 sales projection is for 480 Model 2539 heavy-duty tractors.
Figure/symbol	The 2% discount on Robb & Bond's bill #729 amounted to exactly $38.64.
Fluency	They did not include in the report the profits due the firm in August.

| 1 | 2 | 3 | 4 | 5 | 6 | 7 | 8 | 9 | 10 | 11 | 12 | 13 | 14 |

44B Growth Index ⑫ one 3′ and one 5′ writing; determine GWAM; proofread and circle errors

All letters are used.

	GWAM		
	1′	3′	5′

¶ 1
1.5 SI
5.6 AWL
80% HFW

A noted philosopher said that the mind is a very unusual invention. — 14 | 5 | 3
It starts working the instant we are born and never stops until we get up — 29 | 10 | 6
to speak in public. Generally, nobody questions that practice makes per- — 43 | 14 | 9
fect––nor that we can learn and apply codes on which to base that prac- — 57 | 19 | 11
tice according to our needs. — 63 | 21 | 13

¶ 2
1.5 SI
5.6 AWL
80% HFW

While we can memorize rules, the essence of making an excellent — 13 | 25 | 15
talk may still elude us. The truth is, the kind of eloquence that will — 27 | 30 | 18
excite the imagination of listeners may be impossible to acquire. We — 41 | 35 | 21
can learn many things by rules, but a feeling for what will really move — 56 | 40 | 24
people is apparently an inborn trait. — 63 | 42 | 25

¶ 3
1.5 SI
5.6 AWL
80% HFW

A talk about nothing––however eloquent––can become rather tiresome. — 14 | 47 | 28
The speaker must believe in his subject. He must know it very well. The — 29 | 52 | 31
listeners can spot a phony a mile away. A good speech is a short one. — 43 | 56 | 34
Some say that a person who hops to his feet, skips over the introduction, — 58 | 61 | 37
and makes a concluding statement will always get the heartiest applause. — 72 | 66 | 40

1′ GWAM	1	2	3	4	5	6	7	8	9	10	11	12	13	14
3′ GWAM		1		2		3		4		5	
5′ GWAM		1		2		3	

36B Skill-Transfer Typing ⑩ 60-space line; 1' writing on each line; compare GWAM

Words
in Line

1	Fluency	Are your fingers well curved and your wrists low and steady?	12
2	Figure	What is the sum of 22 and 33 and 44 and 666 and 777 and 999?	12
3	Figure/symbol	Will this check #478 for $50.30 pay McDonald & Young's bill?	12
4	Script	*With a service center, the iron you use is the iron you buy.*	12
5	Corrected copy	the booklet is tell you how a service center saves money.	12

36C Problem Typing: WORD DIVISION ㉝

Problem 1: Report on Word Division

1. Center the main heading horizontally. After typing the first line, reset the left margin stop 4 spaces to the right.

Full sheet; 60-space line; center report vertically in reading position; SS; DS between items.

2. To type the numbers for the remaining ¶s, depress the margin release and backspace 4 spaces into the left margin.

3. Proofread by comparing; circle errors; use your stroke and line-space ruler to check top and side margins.

Words

GUIDES FOR WORD DIVISION   5

2 spaces ———————→ ↓ *Reset margin*

1. You may divide words at the ends of lines to keep the	17
right margin as even as possible. Excessive division	27
should, however, be avoided.	33

Use margin release; then backspace 4 spaces ———→

2. Divide words between syllables only, as <u>fore-noon</u> and	46
<u>bom-bard</u>. When in doubt, use the dictionary to help	58
solve word-division problems.	64
3. Do not divide words of only one syllable, such as <u>friend</u>,	78
<u>thought</u>, or <u>trained</u>. Do not separate a syllable without	92
a vowel; as, <u>didn't</u>.	97
4. Do not divide a word of five or fewer letters, such as	109
<u>also</u>, <u>duty</u>, or <u>going</u>.	116
5. Do not separate a one-letter syllable at the beginning	127
of a word; as, <u>enough</u>.	133
6. Do not separate a one- or two-letter syllable at the end	145
of a word; as, <u>ready</u>, <u>largely</u>, <u>higher</u>.	156
7. You may usually divide a word between double consonants;	169
as, <u>cor-rect</u>, <u>mil-lion</u>, <u>mes-sage</u>.	180
8. When adding a syllable to a word that ends in double	191
letters, divide after the double letters of the root	202
word; as, <u>express</u>, <u>express-ing</u>.	212
9. When the final consonant is doubled in adding a suffix,	224
divide between the doubled letters; as, <u>begin</u>, <u>begin-ning</u>.	238

43B Word Division Drill ⑩

1. Half sheet; DS; 1½″ top margin; 70-space line; 10 spaces between columns.
2. Check the points of division (acceptable in typewritten work) by referring to 36C, page 66, and the dictionary.
3. Center WORD DIVISION as the main heading.
4. Type the drill, using a hyphen at all acceptable division points, as in Line 1.

					Words
Tab from column to column	didn't	con-cluded	per-formed	pro-fes-sion	11
	abroad	centrally	supposed	transcribed	19
	lighted	compelled	transmits	performance	28
	across	specially	transcend	conditioned	37
	upon	schedule	troubled	dictation	44

KEY | 7 | 10 | 10 | 10 | 10 | 10 | 13

43C Problem Typing Review ㉚

Directions for only those procedures that vary are included for these problems. Standard directions are not repeated; those learned in earlier lessons of this section are to be applied. If necessary, refer to the page numbers given with the problems before you start to type a problem.

Problem 1: Simple Memorandum Form

Half sheet; 60-space line; correct errors; p. 68

	Words
Current date	3

SUBJECT: Proofreading — 8

(¶ 1) Proofreading is a demanding task re- 15 quiring a great deal of | concentration. A 23 proofreading error that evades many typists | 32 is that in which a word is substituted for an- 41 other word that | appears in the original copy, 50 such as <u>will</u> for <u>well</u>, <u>you</u> for | <u>your</u>, or <u>being</u> 63 for <u>begin</u>. The resulting copy makes very | 73 little sense. (¶ 2) The word-substitution 80 error can be found, all right, if the | copy is 89 read very carefully for meaning. Each word 98 must be | read. Any error found should, of 106 course, be corrected. (¶ 3) Virtually all proof- 114 reading of letters is done by comparing. | In 123 this method a typist checks his own work by 132 carefully | reading his copy and checking it 141 against the original when | any meaning is 149 uncertain. 151

Problem 2: Personal Note in Modified Block Style

Half sheet; 60-space line; correct errors; p. 70

Type the memorandum in Problem 1 as a personal note. Make these changes:

1. Omit the subject line.
2. Use *Dear Sarah* as the salutation.
3. Omit the second paragraph.
4. Provide an appropriate complimentary close.

Problem 3: Personal/Business Letter

Modified block style; return address on Line 17; 60-space line; current date; erase and correct errors; p. 72

Type the memorandum in Problem 1 as a personal/business letter: Make these changes or additions:

1. Type your address as the return address.
2. Address the letter to Miss Carol Winters | 750 Ryerson Street | Paterson, New Jersey 07502.
3. Supply an appropriate salutation and complimentary close. Omit the subject line. Type your name as the writer.
4. Address a small envelope.
5. Fold the letter, and insert it into the envelope. (Use the folding directions described in 43D, page 77.)

Problem 2: Word Division

Half sheet inserted short edge at left; DS; 70-space line; 10 spaces between columns; center the problem vertically

Type the hyphen to show preferred word divisions in typewritten work, as in Line 1. If necessary, refer to Problem 1 or to a dictionary.

WORD DIVISION
TS

Tabulate from column to column	steady	will-ing	blan-ket	quickly
	input	enumerate	luggage	preferred
	afraid	rustproof	cutting	safety
	billed	newsroom	messenger	spirally
	alerted	rectify	skillful	changeable

KEY | 7 | 10 | 11 | 10 | 11 | 10 | 11 |

LESSON 37

37A Preparatory Practice ⑦ each line twice; then 1' writings on Lines 2 and 4 to compare GWAM

Alphabetic A bank gives standardized exams to applicants who qualify for the job.

Figure The test on March 26 will cover the contents of pages 15-49 and 70-83.

Figure/symbol Duggan & Ford's catalog lists item #9137A at $840 (less 10% for cash).

Fluency We should thus know that good habits are as hard to break as bad ones.

| 1 | 2 | 3 | 4 | 5 | 6 | 7 | 8 | 9 | 10 | 11 | 12 | 13 | 14 |

37B Problem Typing Checkup ⑭

Half sheet; 65-space line; DS; exact vertical center; SS and indent numbered ¶s 5 spaces. Align second and following lines of the numbered items as shown.

(This style is "left indention with blocked lines.")

Evaluation. Use your stroke and line-space ruler to check top, bottom, and side margins.

	Words
DIVIDING WORDS AND SENTENCE PARTS	7
TS	

In addition to the guides included on page 65, here are some · · · 19

guides that you should keep in mind: · · · 26

    1. Divide hyphened compounds only at the point of the hyphen. · · · 39
             DS

    2. Avoid dividing abbreviations, numbers, and proper names. · · · 51
       When necessary, separate a surname from the initials or · · · 63
       given name. · · · 66

    3. Separate the parts of a date, if necessary, between the · · · 78
       day of the month and the year. · · · 85

    4. Do not divide the last word on a page. · · · 93

42C Problem Typing: PERSONAL/BUSINESS LETTERS ㉕

Problem 1: Modified Block Style, Open Punctuation

60-space line; return address on Line 14. Using the longest line, center the address in the letter; erase and correct errors

	Words
5003 Columbia Street | Seattle, Washington	8
98104 | April 21, 19— (Operate return 4 times.)	13
Mr. Clark Greenwood, Manager | National	20
Stores, Incorporated | 2349 North Mayfair	28
Street | Spokane, Washington 99207 | Dear	36
Mr. Greenwood | (¶ 1) Last year, during the	43
summer before my senior year at Wash- | ing-	51
ton State University, I worked in the adjust-	60
ment office | of your company. (¶ 2) In June	68
I shall receive a Bachelor of Science degree,	77
and I | have applied for a position with the	85
Hammond Transportation | Company. The	93
job in question will require my contacting |	101
prospective users of a company that is	109
equipped to provide | transportation services	118
by bus, truck, airplane, or ship. (¶ 3) Mr.	125
P. H. Riley, the personnel director, stressed	135
a pleasing, | outgoing personality as well as	143

	Words
stability of character. He | wants a young	152
man who is able to grow with the company.	160
I | shall appreciate your writing to Mr. Riley	169
about your impres- | sions of me. The ad-	177
dress is:	179

	Words
Mr. P. H. Riley, Personnel Director	186
Hammond Transportation Company	192
5892 South Colorado Avenue	198
Seattle, Washington 98134	203

	Words
Sincerely yours (Operate return 4 times.)	206
Joseph P. McDaniel	210

Problem 2: Composing a Letter

Assume that you have received the letter in Problem 1 from Joseph P. McDaniel. Using the directions in Problem 1 and your return address, compose the kind of letter that you would like to have written about yourself.

Correct and retype the letter, adjusting the top margin to give your letter good balance. Erase and correct errors in final typing.

42D Addressing Small Envelopes ⑤ (WB p. 19)

Study the illustration at the right; then address envelopes for the letters typed in Problems 1 and 2. Correct errors.

> **1. Return Address.** Type the writer's name and address in block style, SS, in the upper left corner of the envelope. Start 3 spaces from the left edge on Line 2.
> **2. Envelope Address.** Begin about 2" (on Line 11 or 12) from the top and 2½" from the left edge. Use block style and single spacing. The last line must always be the city, state name or abbreviation, and ZIP Code.

NOTE: Small envelopes are commonly used for half-size stationery or 1-page letters on regular stationery.

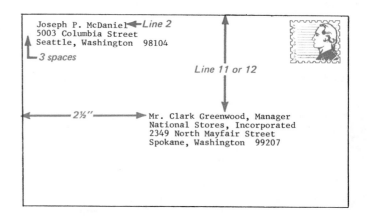

LESSON 43

43A Preparatory Practice ⑦ each line twice; then 1' writings on Lines 1 and 4

Alphabet	Have Wilcox print eight dozen banquet tickets for the meeting in July.
Figure/symbol	Our #30865 pens will cost Knox & Brady $12.97 each (less 4% for cash).
Rule for figures	Type measures in figures: We bought 58¼ gallons of paint for the job.
Fluency	This auditor is the chairman for the next meeting of your study group.

| 1 | 2 | 3 | 4 | 5 | 6 | 7 | 8 | 9 | 10 | 11 | 12 | 13 | 14 |

37C Growth Index ⑫ 70-space line; one 3' and one 5' writing; determine GWAM; proofread; circle errors

All letters are used.

	GWAM		
	2'	3'	5'

¶ 1
1.5 SI
5.6 AWL
80% HFW

What is word processing? It is a new term that identifies the   6 | 4 | 3
effort currently being made to enable an executive to turn his or her   13 | 9 | 5
ideas into letters and reports at top speed, with utmost accuracy, with   20 | 14 | 8
the least work, and at the lowest cost. The equipment that plays the   27 | 18 | 11
most vital part in this process is the automatic typewriter. Many com-   38 | 23 | 14
petent experts report that the frequency of the use of writing papers   41 | 28 | 17
by this new process will multiply by more than four times in just the   48 | 32 | 19
next few years.   50 | 33 | 20

¶ 2
1.5 SI
5.6 AWL
80% HFW

Automatic typewriters have long been used to produce form letters.   7 | 38 | 23
Because the letters are typed instead of printed, they have a personal-   14 | 43 | 26
ized look about them. Another way in which these typewriters are used   21 | 47 | 28
is to record on tape the copy that is typed on paper. The writer edits   26 | 52 | 31
the copy, and the typist changes it by locating the places to be changed   35 | 57 | 34
and inserting the new copy. The final copy, which is then produced from   43 | 62 | 37
the tape at a rapid rate, is correct.   46 | 64 | 39

2' GWAM | 1 | 2 | 3 | 4 | 5 | 6 | 7 |
3' GWAM | 1 | 2 | 3 | 4 | 5 |
5' GWAM | 1 | 2 | 3 |

37D Technique Practice: BELL CUE ⑤ Type ¶ 1, 37C, as directed below.

Use a 60-space line plus your adjustment figure; DS;
5-space ¶ indention. Be guided by the bell to return.

37E Individual Practice ⑫

1. Type each line once. Place a check mark before any line that seemed difficult.

2. Type 2 or more times each line you checked as difficult.

1 3d row   We try to treat the young workers as we treat the top men of our firm.
2 Double letters Will Gregg attempt to sell his three accounting books to Heddy Brooks?
3 One hand   As Frederick Webster swears, they were regarded as brave but defeated.
4 3d/4th fingers As was pointed out by six of the seniors, the quiz questions are easy.
5 Adjacent keys We truly hope you were pleased with the glass dishes I sent as a gift.
6 Hyphen   Bob thinks we have an up-to-the-minute plan for our out-of-town sales.
7 Direct reaches After my brother wrecked my car, Brolen charged for emergency service.
8 Long words   Automatic typewriters are highly effective with repetitive procedures.
9 Shift key   The Laser Bulletin, published in Dayton, Ohio, will be issued in July.

| 1 | 2 | 3 | 4 | 5 | 6 | 7 | 8 | 9 | 10 | 11 | 12 | 13 | 14 |

41D Problem Typing: PERSONAL/BUSINESS LETTERS ㉕ Erase and correct errors.

Problem 1: Modified Block Style, Open Punctuation

*Full sheet; 60-space line; return address on
Line 15; vertical lines indicate line endings*

	Words
3069 Theresa Avenue | Lincoln, Nebraska	8
68504 | February 15, 19-- | *(Operate return 4*	13
times.) Mr. Thomas Rodriguez | Golden Holi-	19
day Tours | 1750 Sewell Street | Lincoln,	27
Nebraska 68509 | Dear Mr. Rodriguez (¶ 1)	34
Let me tell you again how pleased we were	42
with our tour of | the South Pacific, Tour	50
1022. It was a fantastic experience. (¶ 2)	57
Helping to make it so was your efficient tour	67
director, Mr. | Leland Hopkins. He was a	75
superb guide, well organized, clear | in expla-	83
nations, and pleasant. He got us through cus-	92

	Words
toms and | immigration quickly and painlessly.	101
(¶ 3) We saw all the features advertised for	109
the tour--and then | some. We had preferen-	117
tial seating at most of the special | events.	126
There were very few commercial stops. All	135
these | things we liked about the tour and	143
Mr. Hopkins. (¶ 4) Soon we plan to take a	151
trip to South America. If you have a | tour	159
of interesting places there, I should appreciate	169
your | sending me information on it. *(Tab to*	176
center.) Yours sincerely *(Operate return 4 times; tab*	179
to center) Harold Thiel	181

Problem 2: Letter with Changes

Type again the letter in Problem 1. This time omit the last paragraph. Start the return address on Line 17.

Erase and correct any errors you make, using the guides given in 41C, page 73. Proofread by comparing.

LESSON 42

42A Preparatory Practice ⑦ each line twice; then 1' writings on Lines 2 and 4

Alphabet	Clark Wray made several quick jet flights to Peru, Brazil, and Mexico.
Figure	The box is 6 5/8 by 9 1/2 feet long and weighs from 375 to 400 pounds.
Figure/symbol	Order #7849-0 (dated 3/26) must be shipped by May 25 to Sloan & Mason.
Fluency	A light touch is the right touch to use in building good typing skill.

| 1 | 2 | 3 | 4 | 5 | 6 | 7 | 8 | 9 | 10 | 11 | 12 | 13 | 14 |

42B Sentence Guided Writings ⑬ 65-space line; SS; DS between line groups

Type each sentence as a 1' writing, guided by the 20" call of the line ending; then type each sentence as a

1' writing, guided by the 15" call. Try to return the carriage with each call.

		GWAM 20"	15"
1	Hold your fingers lightly just over the keys.	27	36
2	Strike and release the keys and space bar quickly.	30	40
3	The right kind of rhythm will build speed and accuracy.	33	44
4	Your speed will go up as you get rid of the stops in typing.	36	48
5	You can move one finger more quickly than you can move your hand.	39	52

Personal Letters and Composing

Machine Adjustments. 70-space line; SS sentence drills; DS and indent ¶s 5 spaces. Space problems as directed. Use an adjusted right margin stop for problems and ¶ copy.

Supplies Needed. Small envelopes

LESSON 38

38A Preparatory Practice ⑦ each line twice; then 1′ writings on Lines 1 and 4 to compare GWAM

Alphabet	Jack may provide a few extra quiz questions or problems for the girls.
Figure	The 1974 edition of this book has 5 parts, 23 chapters, and 680 pages.
Figure/symbol	Our order dated June 17 reads: Ship 148 bags of 25# ea. @ 39¢ per lb.
Fluency	No problem that we tackle is ever so big as the problem that we evade.

| 1 | 2 | 3 | 4 | 5 | 6 | 7 | 8 | 9 | 10 | 11 | 12 | 13 | 14 |

38B Control Building: ERRORLESS TYPING ⑩ each line twice without error or 3 times with no more than 1 error to a line

One hand	I was not at union headquarters when a new wage contract was defeated.
Shift keys	Send Fields & Marshall ten copies of the new book by Niels and Atwood.
Long words	Analysis of the experimental data provides an estimate of probability.
Fluency	A man should want work enough to do and strength enough to do it well.

38C Problem Typing: SIMPLE MEMORANDUM FORM ㉚ 8½″ by 5½″ half sheets

Problem 1: Memorandum Specifications

60-space line; current date 1″ (Line 7) from the top; Subject line 3 blank line spaces below the date; SS; proofread by comparing; circle errors

NOTE: 3 words (15 strokes) are counted for the date.

	Words
Current date	3
Operate return 4 times	
(3 blank line spaces)	
SUBJECT: Simple Memorandum Form	10
DS	
This is a simple half-sheet memorandum form. In this form	21
the date is always typed one inch (six blank line spaces)	33
from the top. The subject line is typed on the fourth line	45
space below the date.	49
The memorandum is typed in block style. Note that all lines	61
begin flush with the left margin with a double space (one	73
blank line space) between paragraphs. This style is commonly	85
used for memorandums.	90

41A Preparatory Practice ⑦ each line twice; then 1′ writings on Lines 1 and 4

Alphabet   Jackson realized he was required to pay very high taxes for September.

Figure/symbol   Baxter & Garry's check for $679.20 (check #1384) was cashed on July 5.

Rule for figures   Type distances in figures: She drove 579 miles to the annual meeting.

Fluency   We lack the power to stop people from thinking, but we can start them.

| 1 | 2 | 3 | 4 | 5 | 6 | 7 | 8 | 9 | 10 | 11 | 12 | 13 | 14 |

41B Speed/Control Building: RATE CONTROL ⑩ 70-space line; DS; six 1′ writings; 5-space ¶ indention

1. Select a goal: 30, 40, 50, or more *wam*. Type at your goal rate—no slower, no faster.

2. When you can type your goal word (or letter) as time is called, advance to the next goal level.

NOTE: Your instructor may call the ½′ to guide you.

1.4 SI
5.4 AWL
85% HFW

    Under our economic system the customer can choose from many products and services what he wants to buy. The producer can set the price of the product; but if it is too high, the customer will not buy it. So, in effect, he controls the price that a business can charge for its product. The business that does not win customers, fails.

41C Erasing and Correcting Errors ⑧

Type the sentences exactly as shown below, DS. Study the guides for erasing that are given at the right; then erase and correct each error in the 4 sentences.

Eraes lightly, usnig a hard eraser.

Don't dampen eth eraser.

Retype the wrod lightlh.

An eraser sheild prevents smudgee.

Guides for Erasing

1. Use a plastic shield and a hard eraser.

2. Roll the paper forward if the error is on the upper two thirds of the page. Roll the paper backward if the error is on the lower third.

3. Move the carriage (carrier) to the left or right as far as possible to keep dirt out of the mechanism.

4. Use a plastic eraser shield to protect the writing that is not to be erased. Erase lightly—don't scrub the error. Brush any eraser particles away from the page.

5. Return the paper to writing position and type.

Problem 2: Memorandum on Proofreading

Half sheet; 60-space line; block style; SS; 1″ top margin;
Subject line 3 blank lines below date; DS between ¶s; proofread
by comparing; circle errors

Compare all figures with those in original copy.

Words

Current date   3

SUBJECT: Proofreading Figures   9

An undetected error in figures can be embarrassing, if not   21
costly, to a writer. Generally, $150.20 can make as much   33
sense in a letter as can $15.20. As a result, a typist   44
should take great care in checking the accuracy of figures.   56

Compare all figures in your copy with those in the original.   68
If your copy contains numerous figures, consider proofreading   80
by the verifying method. In this method, one person reads   92
from the original while the typist checks the new copy.   103

38D   Evaluate Your Work ③

Compare your solutions with the arranged copies in 38C. Using your stroke and line-space ruler, check spaces in the top margin and between the parts of each solution. Check side margins for equal spacing.

39A   Preparatory Practice ⑦   each line twice; then 1′ writings on Lines 1 and 4

Alphabet   Maxwell Jacks gave the lovely box as a prize to our "Queen for a Day."

Figure/symbol   Is Fred Jackson's report on bill #6735-48 on profits due May 19 or 20?

Rule for figures   Type percentages in figures: She paid 7½% interest on this $500 loan.

Fluency   Most of us, whether young or old, have talent that is never developed.
     | 1 | 2 | 3 | 4 | 5 | 6 | 7 | 8 | 9 | 10 | 11 | 12 | 13 | 14 |

39B   Composing and Typing ⑩   8½″ x 5½″ half sheet; 1″ top margin; 50-space line; DS; 5-space ¶ indention

1. Type the sentences in ¶ form, inserting the needed information. The line endings will differ from those in the copy. Leave uncorrected any errors you make.

2. When you have completed the typing, remove the paper, make pencil corrections, and retype the ¶s on a half sheet with the appropriate top margin.

(¶ 1) My name is *(your name)*. My home address is *(street number and name or P.O. box, city, state, and ZIP Code)*. I am a student at *(name of your school)* in *(city and state)*. I am now living at *(street address, dormitory, or other)*.

(¶ 2) The name of the typewriter I use is *(type the name)*, and the title of my textbook is *(underline the title or type it in all caps)*. I type at approximately *(state the rate in figures)* *gwam*. My greatest difficulty seems to be *(name one, as: too many errors, not enough speed, poor techniques)*.

			Words in Parts	Total Words
		⌐*Tabulate to center to type* ↓ *return address and date*		
Return address	*Line 17*	3981 Montecello Avenue	5	5
		San Jose, California 95125	10	10
Dateline		December 12, 19-- ↑	14	14
		Operate return 4 times ∟*2 spaces*		
Letter address		Mrs. Vincent Meyerson	18	18
		9402 Mohican Drive	22	22
		San Jose, California 95123 DS	28	28
Salutation		Dear Mrs. Meyerson DS	4	31
Body of letter		Because I think that you may be interested in learning about	16	44
		a new project in our community, I should like to introduce	28	55
		you to Hand Art Notes. The response to these notes has been	40	68
		encouraging.	42	70
		A group of students, of which I am a member, design and silk-		82
		screen handmade all-purpose note cards. They are unusual and		95
		attractive, and we can design them to convey your individual		107
		message.		108
		Hand Art Notes can be used for all occasions: party invita-	12	120
		tions, thank-you notes, holiday cards, birthdays, and other	24	132
		types of special events. I think you may enjoy looking at	36	144
		some of the unique sample notes we have prepared. If you	47	156
		will call me at 396-9456, I can arrange to come to your home	60	168
		any evening convenient to you. DS	66	174
Complimentary close		Sincerely yours *Operate return 4 times*	69	177
		Geraldine Phillips		
Typed name		Miss Geraldine Phillips	73	181

↑ *Tabulate to center to type*
| *complimentary close and*
∟*writer's name*

Open punctuation omits marks of punctuation after the salutation and complimentary close. These two elements would not be abbreviated.

Style Letter 1: PERSONAL/BUSINESS LETTER IN MODIFIED BLOCK STYLE, OPEN PUNCTUATION

39C Problem Typing: PERSONAL NOTES (33)

Problem 1: Personal Note in Block Style

Half sheet; 60-space line; SS; DS between ¶s; date on Line 7; salutation on Line 11; proofread by comparing; circle errors

Compare the arrangement of this note with that of the memorandum in Lesson 38.

			Words
7	Date	March 16, 19--	3
8		*Operate the return*	
9		*4 times.*	
10			
11	Salutation	Dear John	5
12		DS	
13	Body	Congratulations on winning a fellowship to study in Munich	17
14		next year. I know of no one better qualified to interact	28
15		with students and community leaders. You have the rare gift	41
16		of putting people at ease when you talk with them.	51
17		DS	
18		See all the interesting places; take a lot of photographs.	63
19		We shall look forward to hearing about your year in Munich	74
20		when you return. Write when you have time.	83
21		DS	
22	Complimentary close	Cordially	85

Problem 2: Personal Note in Block Style

On a half sheet, type the following personal note in the block style illustrated in Problem 1. The placement directions are the same. The vertical lines in the copy indicate line endings. *Do not type these dividers.*

	Words
Current date on Line 7	3
Dear Beth	5
(¶ 1) The Youth Camp Festival was a great	12
success. Our student body raised more than	21
$900. I am tremendously proud. What gen-	29
erous coverage in THE DAILY IOWAN! Please	38
extend my very deepest thanks to your staff.	47
(¶ 2) If I haven't fully thanked you earlier,	55
please be assured that the support given to	64
the Festival by THE DAILY IOWAN was the	72
best ever. Continued best wishes on your job	81
as editor. Your timely editorials are great.	90
Sincerely	92

Problem 3: Note with Centered Title

On the half sheet, type the following note in the style used in Problem 1. All placements are the same. Center the title with one blank line above and below it.

	Words
Current date on Line 7	3
Dear Fran	5
(¶ 1) I have been asked to give a talk on the	13
energy crisis in my speech class. The title	22
of this talk is to be	26
DS	
WHY AN ENERGY SHORTAGE?	31
DS	
(¶ 2) Even with so much coverage of the sub-	38
ject by the press, I am having a difficult time	48
finding articles of official nature. Can you	57
suggest the names of any reliable books or	66
articles? I shall appreciate whatever help	75
you can send me.	78
Sincerely	80

LESSON 40

40A Preparatory Practice ⑦ each line twice; then 1' writings on Lines 2 and 4

Alphabet | Dixie Vaughn acquired the prize job with a large firm just like yours.

Figure | Our store has three locations: 36-40 Grand; 6275 Maywood; 1890 Olive.

Figure/symbol | I am requesting 7 seats @ $2.50, 9 seats @ $3.60, and 8 seats @ $4.15.

Fluency | Giving sound advice to others always works much better than taking it.

| 1 | 2 | 3 | 4 | 5 | 6 | 7 | 8 | 9 | 10 | 11 | 12 | 13 | 14 |

40B Composing and Typing ⑩ 2 full sheets; 2″ top margin; 60-space line

1. Center horizontally the heading SETTING WORLD RECORDS; then triple-space, indent 5 spaces, and type the ¶ below, DS.

2. Type a second ¶ in your own words giving your reactions to setting records of the type described. Why do people set them? Are they of value?

3. Make pencil corrections on your composition; then retype both ¶s from your corrected copy.

	Words
Do you want to be a champion? A man from Ohio lay on a	11
bed of nails for 25 hours 20 minutes. A Kentucky man threw	23
an egg 217 feet 7 inches; another caught it––intact. A Texas	36
student stood in a shower 169 hours. All beat old records,	48
but why? What drives people to set these records?	58

40C Problem Typing: PERSONAL/BUSINESS LETTER IN MODIFIED BLOCK STYLE, OPEN PUNCTUATION ㉘

Problem 1: Style Letter 1, Page 72

On a full sheet type the letter illustrating the modified block style with block paragraphs and open punctuation shown on page 72. Use a 60-space line; follow the spacing directions given on the letter.

Vertical spacing directions are standard for all letter styles—with this exception: The number of blank line spaces in the top margin varies with the lengths of the bodies of the letters.

Become familiar with the terms used to identify the various parts of the letter.

Problem 2: Drill on Letter Parts

Type a 1' writing on each of the following parts of Style Letter 1, page 72:
1. Return address, dateline, and letter address
2. Salutation and ¶ 1
3. Last ¶ and closing lines

Retype the entire letter.

Problem 3: Letter with Changes

Starting the return address on Line 18, retype Style Letter 1, this time omitting the second ¶.

40D Evaluate Your Work ⑤

Compare your 3 letters with the model copy on page 72. Have you used the correct spacing between parts? Using your stroke and line-space ruler, check the number of spaces in the top and side margins. Proofread by comparing. Check proper names, street address numbers, and ZIP Codes with the original. Circle errors.

REFERENCE GUIDE

Typewriter Operative Parts

Typewriters have similar operative parts, the names of which vary somewhat from typewriter to typewriter even when the function is the same. These similar operative parts are identified in the four segments of a typewriter given below and on page ii. Each segment is a composite and not an exact segment of any one typewriter. For this reason, the exact location of a part identified in the segment may be slightly different from that on your typewriter; but the differences are, for the most part, few and slight.

Extra parts that are peculiar to your typewriter can be identified by reference to the instructional booklet distributed by the manufacturer of the typewriter. This booklet can be very helpful to you because its content is directed to the operation of one specific make of machine.

In using the illustrations, follow the line from the number to the part location. Know the function of each part, as explained in the textbook, and learn to operate it with maximum efficiency.

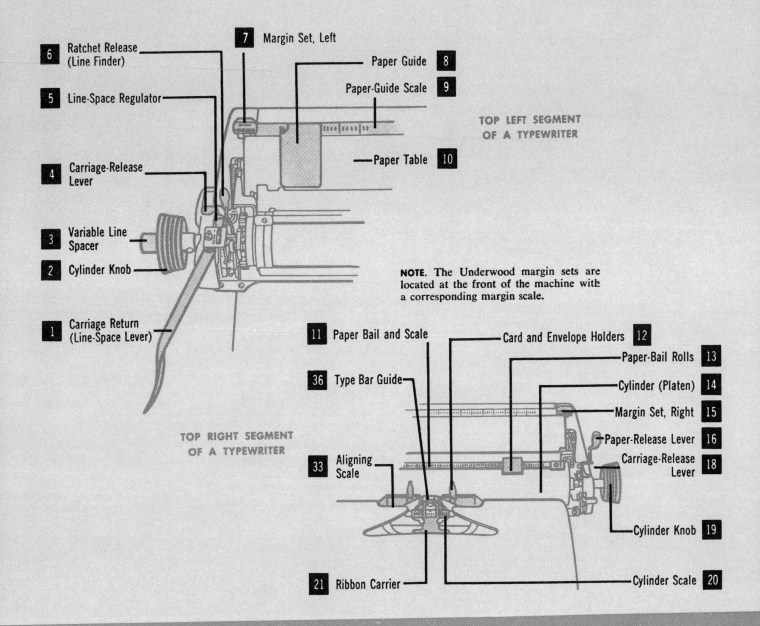

6 Ratchet Release (Line Finder)

7 Margin Set, Left

8 Paper Guide

9 Paper-Guide Scale

5 Line-Space Regulator

TOP LEFT SEGMENT OF A TYPEWRITER

4 Carriage-Release Lever

10 Paper Table

3 Variable Line Spacer

2 Cylinder Knob

NOTE. The Underwood margin sets are located at the front of the machine with a corresponding margin scale.

1 Carriage Return (Line-Space Lever)

11 Paper Bail and Scale

12 Card and Envelope Holders

13 Paper-Bail Rolls

36 Type Bar Guide

14 Cylinder (Platen)

15 Margin Set, Right

16 Paper-Release Lever

TOP RIGHT SEGMENT OF A TYPEWRITER

18 Carriage-Release Lever

33 Aligning Scale

19 Cylinder Knob

21 Ribbon Carrier

20 Cylinder Scale

LOWER SEGMENT OF A MANUAL TYPEWRITER

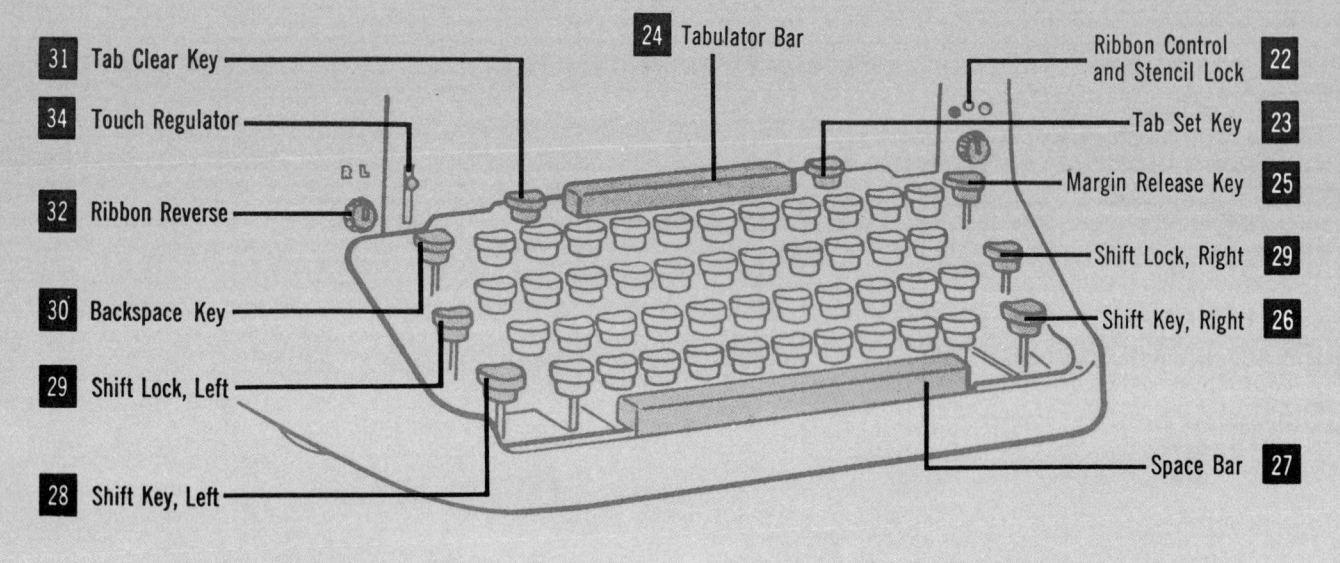

31	Tab Clear Key
34	Touch Regulator
32	Ribbon Reverse
30	Backspace Key
29	Shift Lock, Left
28	Shift Key, Left

| 24 | Tabulator Bar |

Ribbon Control and Stencil Lock | 22
Tab Set Key | 23
Margin Release Key | 25
Shift Lock, Right | 29
Shift Key, Right | 26
Space Bar | 27

LOWER SEGMENT OF AN ELECTRIC TYPEWRITER

CHECK YOUR TYPEWRITER TO SEE IF:

1. The position is different for: ¢ @ * _ (underline)
2. These keys have "repeat" action: *backspace, space bar, carriage return, hyphen-underline*
3. Extra keys are used: **+ = ! 1**

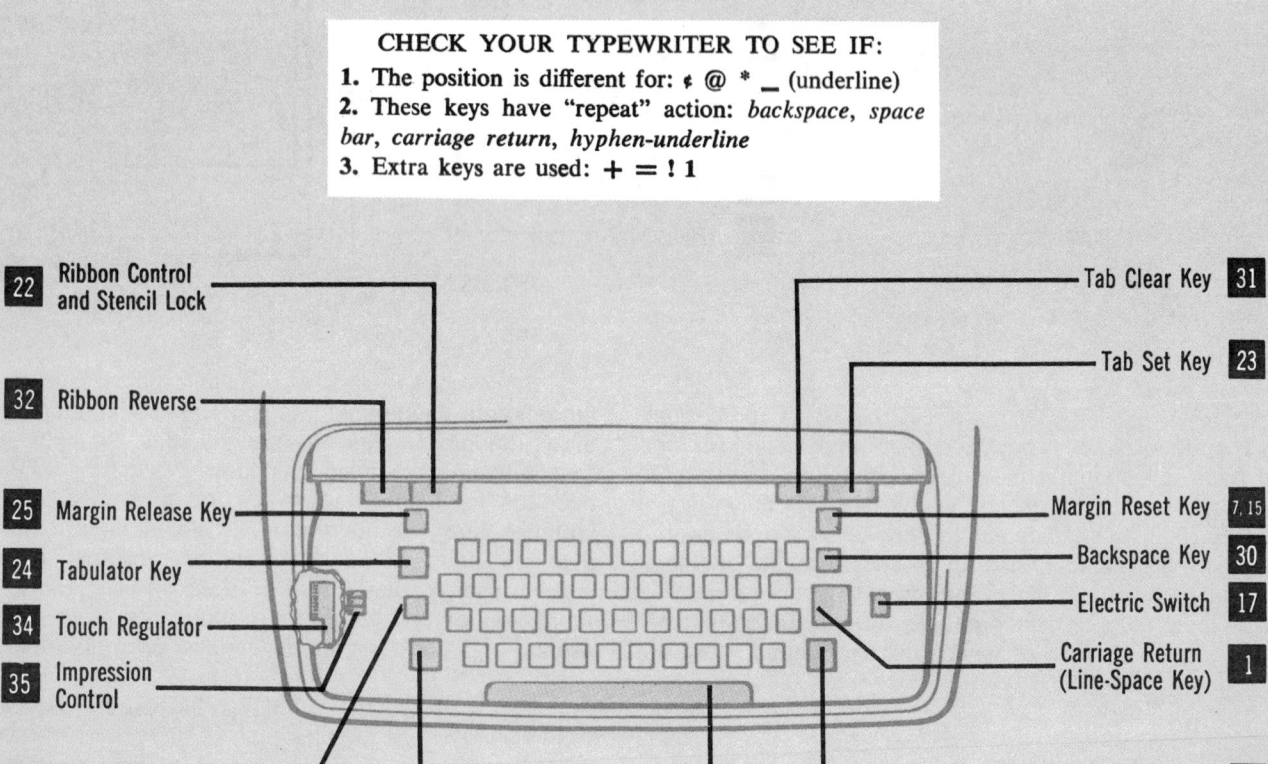

22	Ribbon Control and Stencil Lock
32	Ribbon Reverse
25	Margin Release Key
24	Tabulator Key
34	Touch Regulator
35	Impression Control
29	Shift Lock
28	Shift Key, Left

Tab Clear Key | 31
Tab Set Key | 23
Margin Reset Key | 7, 15
Backspace Key | 30
Electric Switch | 17
Carriage Return (Line-Space Key) | 1
Shift Key, Right | 26
Space Bar | 27

Paper Guide and Centering Point

Typewriters are of 3 types in regard to setting the paper guide and arriving at the center point.

Type 1: Royal, Olympia, Smith-Corona

Set the paper guide on 0 on the paper-guide scale. On 8½" by 11" paper inserted with the left edge against the guide, the centering point is 42 for pica and 51 for elite machines.

Type 2: IBM Model D, Remington

The fixed centering point is 0 for both pica and elite machines. Marks on the paper-guide scale aid the typist in setting the paper guide to center copy correctly.

Type 3: Smith-Corona Nonelectric, IBM Selectric, Olivetti

A variety of marks appear on the paper table or copy-guide scale to aid the typist in setting the paper-guide scale to center 8½" by 11" paper. Marks on the paper-bail scale indicate the center point of the paper.

In the absence of such marks, set the paper guide and insert the paper. Add the carriage scale reading on the left edge of the paper to the reading at the right edge. Divide this sum by 2 for the center point.

Standard Centering Directions

All typewriters have at least 1 scale, usually the cylinder scale **(20)**, that reads from 0 at the left to 85 or more at the right. The spaces on this scale match the spacing mechanism of the machine (pica or elite).

To simplify direction giving, your instructor may ask you to insert paper into your machine so that the left edge corresponds to 0 on the carriage scale. The center point on the carriage scale for 8½" by 1" paper will then be 42 for pica and 51 (or, for convenience, 50, for elite.

Setting the Margin Stops (7, 15)

Center typed material horizontally by setting stops for the left and right margins. Typewriters differ in mechanical adjustments, and the bell rings at different points on different machines; but the carriage locks at the point where the right margin stop is set. After the bell rings, there will be from 6 to 11 or more strokes before the carriage locks, some machines allowing more but none fewer than 6 spaces.

Test your typewriter to determine the number of spaces at which the bell rings before the carriage locks. Take this into consideration when setting the right margin stop. Because the ringing of the bell is a cue to return the carriage, set the right stop 3 to 7 spaces beyond the desired line ending. Then the bell cue will come approximately 3 strokes before the point at which you want the line to end.

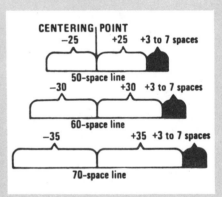

Mechanics of Setting Margin Stops

IBM Model D and Olivetti Electric

To set the left margin stop, depress the return key to return the carriage to the present margin stop. Hold down the margin set key as you move the carriage to the desired new margin point; then release the margin set key.

To set the right margin stop, move the carriage against the present right margin stop. Depress and hold down the margin set key as you move the carriage to the desired new margin position; then release the margin set key.

IBM Selectric

To set left and right margin stops, push in on the appropriate stop and slide it to the desired position on the margin scale; release the stop. Use the space bar to move the carriage out of the way when setting a margin stop to the right of the carrier's present position.

Olympia and Olivetti Nonelectric

To set left and right margin stops, move the left and right margin stops to the desired position on the margin scale.

Remington Electric and Nonelectric

Move the left margin stop to the desired left margin setting. Move the right margin stop to the desired right margin setting.

Smith-Corona Electric and Nonelectric

Depress the left carriage-release button and the left margin button and move the carriage to the desired margin setting. Release the 2 buttons simultaneously. Set the right margin similarly.

Know your typewriter

Your machine may have timesaving features not included in the foregoing discussion of operating parts. Learn these features from a study of the manufacturer's pamphlet that describes and illustrates the operating parts of the typewriter you are using. It will have many ideas for improving your operating manipulations.

You can get such pamphlets without cost from the manufacturer of your typewriter.

Changing Typewriter Ribbons

Techniques for changing ribbons vary from machine to machine. The steps that follow are basic to all machines.

1. Wind the ribbon on 1 spool—usually the right one.

2. Raise and lock the ribbon carrier as follows:

Depress the shift lock. Set the ribbon control for typing on the lower portion of the ribbon. Depress and lock any 2 central keys, such as *y* and *t*.

3. Remove the ribbon from the carrier. Remove both spools from the machine.

4. Hook the new ribbon on the empty spool and wind several inches of new ribbon on it. Be sure that the ribbon winds and unwinds in the correct direction.

5. Place both spools on their holders. Thread the ribbon indicator through the ribbon carrier.

6. Release the shift lock. Return the ribbon indicator to type on the upper portion of the ribbon. Unlock the 2 keys.

7. Clean the keys often to make your work sharp and clear.

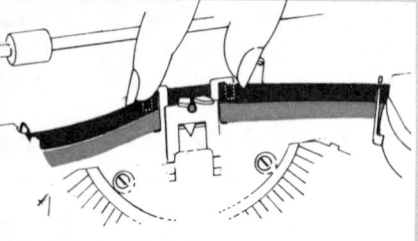

Ribbon threaded through the ribbon-carrier mechanism

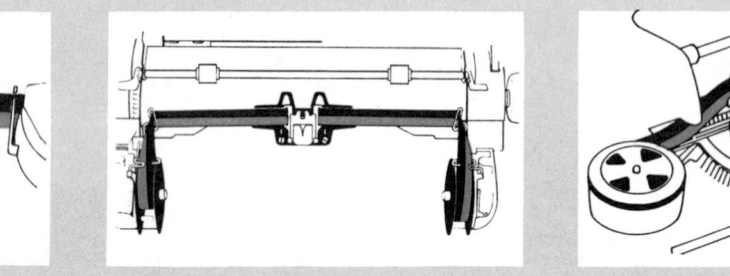

Electric   *Nonelectric*

Path of the ribbon as it winds and unwinds on the 2 spools

Drawing Lines (Rules)

Horizontal Rules. Position the cardholder of the type bar guide at the point at which you want to start the rule. Place the pencil point through the cardholder or on the type-bar guide, depress the carriage-release lever, and draw the carriage across for a line of the desired length.

Vertical Rules. Position the carriage at the starting point desired. Release the line finder. Place the pencil point through the cardholder or on the type-bar guide above the ribbon. Roll the platen up the page until you have a line of the desired length. Reset the line finder.

Communications Design Associates

801 JACKSON STREET, WEST   CABLE: COMDA
CHICAGO, ILLINOIS   60607   TELEPHONE: (312) 342-9753

November 21, 19--

Higgins and Ransom, Inc.
7260 Queen City Avenue
Cincinnati, OH 45238

Attention Mr. Frank Nunn

Gentlemen:

The modified block style has some distinctive features,
as shown in this letter and in the enclosed pamphlet.

The date, the complimentary close, and the name and official title of the dictator begin at the horizontal center
of the paper; thus, one tabulator setting works for all
these lines.

Special lines (reference, enclosure, and carbon copy notations) begin at the left margin, a double space below the
last closing line. When the dictator's name is used in
the closing lines, the reference notation consists of the
typist's initials only. The dictator's initials, if used,
precede those of the typist.

The modified block style is widely used by the clients
for whom we prepare letters. We think you will like it.

Sincerely yours,

Charles Harley Chambers

Charles Harley Chambers
Public Service Director

mew

Enclosure: Styling Business Letters

cc Ms. Alicia LeClair

Modified block. mixed

Communications Design Associates

801 JACKSON STREET, WEST   CABLE: COMDA
CHICAGO, ILLINOIS   60607   TELEPHONE: (312) 342-9753

March 15, 19--

AIRMAIL

Miss Terry Mahle, Office Manager
Standard Steel Equipment Company
270 - 53d Street
Brooklyn, NY 11232

Dear Miss Mahle

The pamphlet about letter formats that you requested
is enclosed. One of the styles described in the pamphlet
is the modified block style with indented paragraphs.
This letter illustrates that style.

A mailing notation is typed at the left margin, a
double space below the date; however, the date and the
closing lines are begun at midpoint of the paper. The
first line of each paragraph is indented five spaces.

We are using open punctuation, which omits punctuation after the salutation and complimentary close.

Although we do not usually use the company name in
the closing lines, we do so here to illustrate the correct
style. We are also omitting the dictator's name in the
closing lines to illustrate the reference notation style
that is then used.

After you have examined your copy of Styling Business
Letters, will you please send us your impressions of it?

Sincerely yours

COMMUNICATIONS DESIGN ASSOCIATES

Charles Harley Chambers

Public Service Director

CHChambers:mew

Enclosure

Modified block, indented ¶, open

Communications Design Associates

801 JACKSON STREET, WEST   CABLE: COMDA
CHICAGO, ILLINOIS   60607   TELEPHONE: (312) 342-9753

February 12, 19--

Miss Doris Marshall
62200 Beacon Hill Road
Waterbury, CT 06716

Dear Miss Marshall

Subject: Styling Business Letters

Thank you for your request of a copy of our letter writing manual. This manual is not yet in print, but I hope
that the mimeographed copies currently available will
meet your needs.

We have adopted the block style of letter, of which this
letter is an example. All lines begin at the left margin, including enumerations. The machine adjustments,
therefore, are simple and save the typist's time.

We hope you will find this little pamphlet helpful. If
you want extra copies when they come off the press, just
let us know.

Sincerely yours

Charles Harley Chambers

Charles Harley Chambers
Public Service Director

mew

Enclosure

The block style may also be used for personal business
letters.

Block, open

Communications Design Associates

801 JACKSON STREET, WEST   CABLE: COMDA
CHICAGO, ILLINOIS   60607   TELEPHONE: (312) 342-9753

October 15, 19--

Mr. Salvadore Palucci
Manager, Apex Company
39501 Bartlett Avenue
Boston, MA 02129

AMS SIMPLIFIED STYLE

This letter is typed in the timesaving simplified style
recommended by the Administrative Management Society.
To type a letter in the AMS style, follow these steps:

1. Use block style.

2. Omit the salutation and complimentary close.

3. Provide a subject line and type it in ALL CAPS a
    triple space below the address. Type the first line
    of the body a triple space below the subject line.

4. Start enumerated items at the left margin, but indent
    unnumbered listed items five spaces.

5. Type the writer's name and title in ALL CAPS on one
    line at least four line spaces below the body of the
    letter.

6. Type only the typist's initials a double space below
    the writer's name.

Correspondents in your company will like the AMS simplified style for the eye appeal it gives letters, as well
as the reduction in letter writing costs it offers.

Klaus Vander Geer

KLAUS VANDER GEER, VICE PRESIDENT

ath

AMS Simplified

LETTER STYLES

Reference Guide

V

Addressing Envelopes

Address Placement and Spacing. Single-space and block the address lines. The bottom line must include the city and state names and the ZIP Code, in that sequence. Leave 2 spaces between the state name or abbreviation and the ZIP Code.

When the ZIP Code is known, use the 2-letter abbreviation (page viii) in all caps without punctuation. If the ZIP Code is unavailable, type the state name in full or use the standard abbreviation.

For a small envelope, start the address lines 2″ from the top and 2½″ from the left edge.

For a large envelope, start the address lines 2½″ from the top and 4″ from the left edge.

Return Address. Start the return address on the second line from the top and 3 spaces from the left edge.

Postal Notations. Type postal notations such as AIRMAIL and SPECIAL DELIVERY, below the space required for the stamp.

Addressee Notations. Type HOLD FOR AR-RIVAL, PERSONAL, PLEASE FORWARD, and the like, a triple space below the return address and 3 spaces from the left edge.

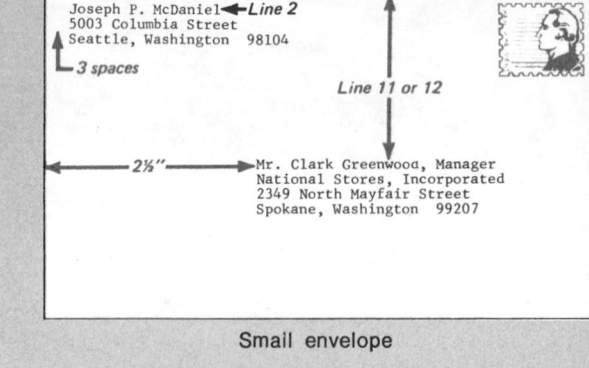

Small envelope

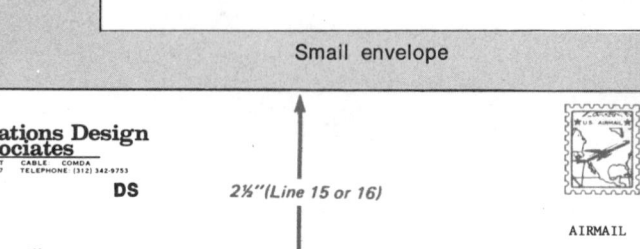
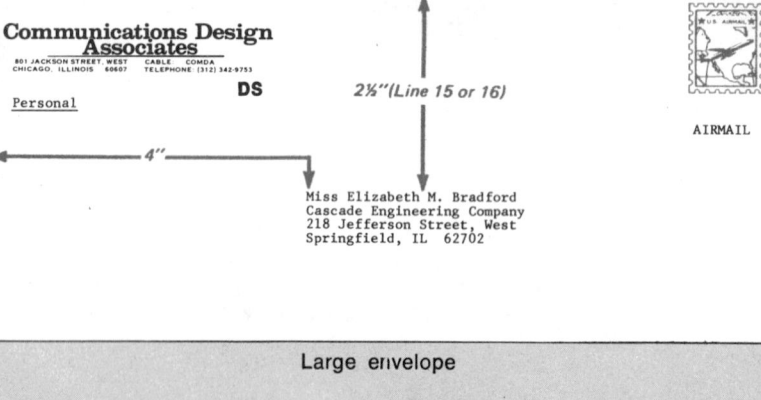

Large envelope

Folding-and-Inserting Procedure

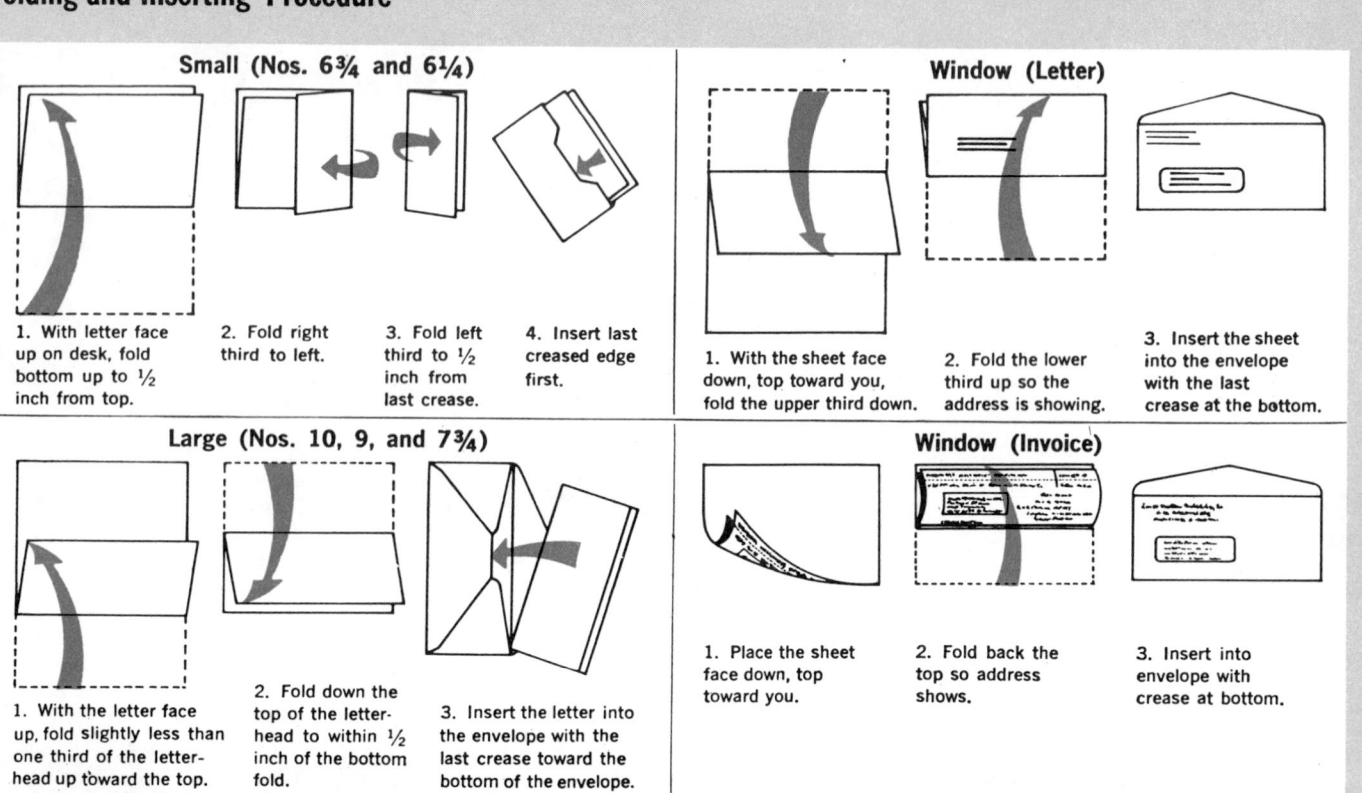

Small (Nos. 6¾ and 6¼)

1. With letter face up on desk, fold bottom up to ½ inch from top.

2. Fold right third to left.

3. Fold left third to ½ inch from last crease.

4. Insert last creased edge first.

Window (Letter)

1. With the sheet face down, top toward you, fold the upper third down.

2. Fold the lower third up so the address is showing.

3. Insert the sheet into the envelope with the last crease at the bottom.

Large (Nos. 10, 9, and 7¾)

1. With the letter face up, fold slightly less than one third of the letter-head up toward the top.

2. Fold down the top of the letter-head to within ½ inch of the bottom fold.

3. Insert the letter into the envelope with the last crease toward the bottom of the envelope.

Window (Invoice)

1. Place the sheet face down, top toward you.

2. Fold back the top so address shows.

3. Insert into envelope with crease at bottom.

Letter-Placement Pointers

LETTER PLACEMENT TABLE

Body of Letter	Letter Length	Side Margins	Dateline on	PUNCTUATION STYLES
Up to 100 words	Short	2″	Line 20	**Mixed punctuation:** Use a colon after the salutation and a comma after the complimentary close.
101 to 300 words	Short-average	1½″	Line 17	
	Average	1½″	Line 15	
	Long-average	1½″	Line 13	**Open punctuation:** Omit these marks.
301 to 350 words	Long	1″	Line 12	
Over 350 words	2-page	1″	Line 12	

The letter-placement table shown above is a *guide*—to be used only until experience has taught the typist to make quick mental judgments regarding the width of the margins and the placement of the dateline.

Dateline. The horizontal placement of the date depends upon the letter style, the design of the letterhead, or a combination of these factors.

In the block and AMS simplified styles, type the date at the left margin.

In the modified block styles, begin the date at the center point or type it to end at the right margin.

Letter Address. Type the first line of the address on the fourth line space below the date. Type an official title, when used, on either the first or the second line—whichever gives better balance.

Attention Line. Type an attention line, when used, at the left margin on the second line below the letter address and a double space above the salutation.

Subject Line. Type a subject line on the second line below the salutation. In block and AMS simplified styles, type the subject line at the left margin. In other styles, type it at the left margin, at paragraph point, or centered. Type the word *Subject* in all caps or with only the first letter capitalized; or omit it.

Company Name in Closing. When the company name is used in the closing lines, type it in all caps on the second line below the complimentary close.

Guides for Word and Sentence-Part Division

Divide—

1. Words at the ends of lines to keep the right margin as even as possible, but avoid excessive division

2. Words between syllables only, using a dictionary or word-division manual as a guide

3. Hyphenated words at hyphens only

4. A word in which the final consonant is doubled when adding a suffix: between the double letters, as *controlling*

5. A word that ends in double letters: after the double letters when adding a suffix, as *will-ing*

6. The parts of a date, if necessary, between the day of the month and the year

Typewritten Name and Official Title. Type the name and official title of the writer of a letter on the fourth line space below the complimentary close or on the fourth line space below the company name when it is used. Except in the AMS simplified style, the writer's title may go on the same line as his name or on the line below his name—whichever gives better balance.

Enclosure Notation. Type the enclosure notation (*Enclosure*, *Enclosures: 2*, or the like) a double space below the reference notation.

Multipage Letters. Leave at least 2 lines of a paragraph at the foot of a page and at least 2 lines at the top of the next page of a mulitpage letter. Start the heading on the second and subsequent pages on Line 7, and leave 2 blank lines below the heading. Use the same side margins on all pages of a letter.

SECOND-PAGE HEADINGS

```
Mr. A. C. Dowling
Page 2
November 4, 19--
```

Block style

```
Mr. A. C. Dowling     2     November 4, 19--
```

Horizontal style

Do not—

7. Divide a word of 5 or fewer letters

8. Separate a 1-letter syllable at the beginning or end of a word

9. Separate a 2-letter syllable at the end of a word

10. Divide the last word on a page or the last word of a paragraph

11. Separate from the rest of a word a syllable without a vowel, as *would-n't*, or numbers typed in figures, as 1,897,-458

Avoid—

12. Dividing names except to separate the initials or given name from the surname

Two-Letter Abbreviations for State, District, and Territory Names

These 2-letter abbreviations, recommended by the U.S. Postal Service, should be used in business addresses for which ZIP Codes are known and used.

Alabama	AL	Illinois	IL
Alaska	AK	Indiana	IN
Arizona	AZ	Iowa	IA
Arkansas	AR	Kansas	KS
California	CA	Kentucky	KY
Canal Zone	CZ	Louisiana	LA
Colorado	CO	Maine	ME
Connecticut	CT	Maryland	MD
Delaware	DE	Massachusetts	MA
District of Columbia	DC	Michigan	MI
Florida	FL	Minnesota	MN
Georgia	GA	Mississippi	MS
Guam	GU	Missouri	MO
Hawaii	HI	Montana	MT
Idaho	ID	Nebraska	NE
		Nevada	NV
		New Hampshire	NH
		New Jersey	NJ
		New Mexico	NM
		New York	NY

North Carolina	NC
North Dakota	ND
Ohio	OH
Oklahoma	OK
Oregon	OR
Pennsylvania	PA
Puerto Rico	PR
Rhode Island	RI
South Carolina	SC
South Dakota	SD
Tennessee	TN
Texas	TX
Utah	UT
Vermont	VT
Virgin Islands	VI
Virginia	VA
Washington	WA
West Virginia	WV
Wisconsin	WI
Wyoming	WY

Assembling a Carbon Pack

Method 1 (desk assembly)

1. Place the second or file copy sheet (on which the carbon copy is to be made) flat on the desk; then place a carbon sheet, *carbon (glossy) side down*, on top of the sheet. Add the original sheet (letterhead or plain sheet) on top of the carbon sheet.

NOTE: For each carbon copy desired, add one "set" (the copy sheet and a carbon sheet).

2. Pick up the carbon pack and turn it so that the second sheets and the glossy sides of the carbon sheets face you.

3. To straighten the pack, tap the top of the sheets gently on the desk.

4. Insert the pack by holding it firmly in one hand while turning the cylinder slowly with the other.

Method 2 (machine assembly)

1. Assemble stationery for insertion into the typewriter (original on top; copy sheets beneath).

2. Insert stationery, turning the cylinder until the sheets are gripped slightly by the feed rolls; then lay all but the last sheet over the top of the machine.

Desk assembly of a carbon pack

3. Place a carbon sheet (*glossy side toward you*) between the last two sheets of stationery; then flip back each sheet of stationery as you add another carbon sheet.

Removing the stationery sheets

After typing the page, roll the platen up to the point at which the stationery is releasable but the feed rolls still grip the carbon sheets. Grasp the top of the stationery pack and remove it; then remove carbon sheets.

Guides for inserting a carbon pack

1. *To keep sheets straight when feeding*, place pack under an envelope flap or in the fold of a plain sheet of paper.

2. To "start" the carbon pack:
   a. Release the paper-release lever,
   b. Feed the pack around the cylinder until sheets appear at the front; then
   c. Reset the paper-release lever.
   d. After thep ack is inserted, remove the envelope or paper fold.

3. *To avoid wrinkling*, release and reset the paper-release lever after the pack has been partially inserted.

Machine assembly of a carbon pack

First page, topbound

First page, unbound

First page, leftbound

Second page, topbound

Second page, unbound

Second page, leftbound

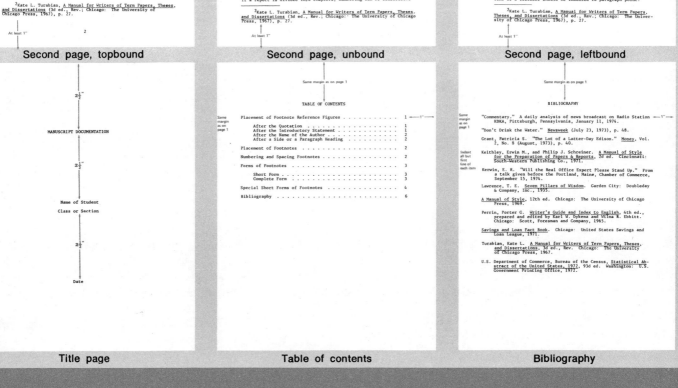

Title page

Table of contents

Bibliography

Correction Symbols (Proofreaders' Marks)

Typed or printed copy can be corrected with proofreaders' marks. The typist must be able to interpret these marks in retyping the corrected copy or *rough draft*. Some commonly used proofreaders' marks are shown below.

꞊ ‿ ‖	Align type
cap ≡	Capitalize
lc /	Use lowercase
⌒	Close up horizontal space
<	Close up vertical space
#	Insert horizontal space
>	Insert vertical space
ℒ	Delete
tr ∽	Transpose

∧	Insert copy shown
∨	Insert apostrophe
⊙	Insert colon
∧	Insert comma
⊙	Insert period
ꙍ ꙍ	Insert quotation marks
ⓙ	Insert semicolon
..... stet	Let it stand; ignore the correction
sp	Spell out

ss	Single-space
ds	Double-space
ts	Triple-space
___	Underline or italicize
⊏	Move left
⊐	Move right
¶	Paragraph
no ¶	No new paragraph
¶ Shift copy	

Centering Summary

Horizontal centering (backspace-from-center method)

Regular headings

1. From the center, backspace once for each 2 strokes in the heading or line to be centered, disregarding an odd or leftover stroke.

2. Start typing where the backspacing ends.

Spread headings

1. From the center, backspace once for each stroke in the heading.

2. From this point, type the heading, spacing once between the letters and 3 times between the words.

Vertical centering

Backspace-from-center method

1. Position the paper at the vertical center:

   8½" by 11": Line 34
   8½" by 5½": Line 17
   5½" by 8½": Line 26

2. Roll the platen back once for each 2 lines (including any blank lines). Disregard an odd or leftover line.

3. Start typing where the roll-back ends.

   (For reading position on a full sheet, roll the platen back 2 additional line spaces.)

Mathematical method

1. Count the lines and blank line spaces in the problem.

2. Subtract that number of lines from the number of lines available on the sheet.

3. Divide the result by 2 to get the number of blank lines in the top margin. Disregard a fraction.

4. Space down from the top edge the number of line spaces for the top margin, plus 1 to reach the first typing line.

Tabulation Summary

Vertical placement of tables

Exact. Count total lines to be used, including any blank lines; subtract total from lines available; divide remainder by 2 (disregarding a fraction). Leave this number of blank lines in the top margin.

Reading Position. Start the material 2 lines above the computed exact center.

Roll-Back Method. Insert the paper; roll it to the vertical center. Roll the cylinder back (toward you) once for every 2 lines in the table. This will place the copy in exact vertical center. For reading position, roll the cylinder back 2 additional lines.

Spacing After Headings. Leave 1 blank line between a main and a secondary heading and between a column heading and its column. Leave 2 blank lines below a main heading, if a secondary heading is not used, or after a secondary heading when both a main and a secondary heading are used.

Horizontal placement of tables

Centered Headings. After determining the top margin and spacing down to the starting line, center the main heading; DS and center a secondary heading, if used; then TS––as noted above.

Columns (Backspace-from-Center Method). Note the longest item in each column. If a column heading is the longest item, count it as such unless judgment indicates otherwise. Decide the number of spaces to leave between columns (preferably an even number).

Backspace from the center of the paper once for every 2 strokes in the longest line of each column and once for every 2 spaces between the columns (the *intercolumns*). Count any odd or leftover stroke with the next column or intercolumn. At the point where you complete the backspacing, set the left *margin* stop for the first column.

From the left margin, space forward once for each stroke in the first column and once for each space between the first and second columns. Set the first *tab* stop. Follow this procedure to set tab stops for the remaining columns.

Column Headings. Center column headings over the columns. When you have counted a column heading as the longest item in a column, you may need to reset the tab stop to center the *column* below the *heading*.

There are several methods of centering a column heading over a column, but probably the easiest is to add the cyclinder-scale figures for the first and last strokes in the column. Dividing this sum by 2 will result in the center point of the column.

Column headings are usually underlined.

Horizontal rulings

Horizontal lines or *rulings* are often used in tables to set off the column headings. Usually, a full-width double ruling is typed above the column headings and a single ruling below them. A single ruling is also typed below the last line of the table.

These rulings can be the exact width of the table, or they can extend several spaces on each side of it. To type rulings the exact width of the table, first determine the placement of the columns. After setting the tab stop for the last column, continue spacing forward once for each stroke in the last column. Immediately after stroking for the last stroke, set the right margin stop to lock the carriage at that point. You can then type rulings across the page until the carriage locks.

Double Rulings. DS from the last line of the centered heading; type the first of the double rulings; then operate the variable line spacer and move the cylinder forward slightly; type the second ruling. DS between this double ruling and the column headings.

Single Rulings. SS from the column headings; type a single ruling; DS and type the first items in the columns. After typing the last items in the columns, SS and type a single ruling.

Source Note (If Used). DS from the last single ruling; type the source note at the left margin or indent 3 to 5 spaces.

Tab stops for columns of figures

Uneven Columns. When a column contains items uneven in length, set the tab stop at a point that will suit the greatest number of entries. After tabulating, backspace for longer items or space forward for shorter ones.

Dollar Signs. In a money column, type a dollar sign before the first amount in the column and before the total, if one is shown. Type the dollar sign before the first amount aligned 1 space to the left of the longest amount in the column, which might be the total.

Totals. Totals are treated as a part of the column. For easier reading, totals are usually separated by a blank line from the last item in the column.

Erasing and Correcting Errors

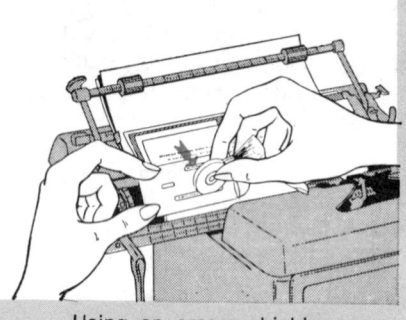

Using an eraser shield

1. Depress the margin-release key and move the carriage to the extreme left or right.

2. To avoid disturbing the type alignment, turn the cylinder forward if the error is in the upper 2/3 of the paper; backward, on the lower 1/3 of the paper.

3. To erase on the original sheet, lift the paper bail and place a 5″ by 3″ card *in front* of the first carbon sheet.

Use a hard (typewriter) eraser and an eraser shield. Brush away eraser crumbs.

4. Move the protective card in front of the second carbon, if more than 1 copy is being made. Use a soft (pencil) eraser.

5. When the error has been erased on all copies, remove the protective card, position the carriage at the proper point, and type the correction.

Squeezing and Expanding Words

Conventional typewriters

In correcting errors, it is often possible to "squeeze" or "expand" words.

1. An omitted letter at the beginning or end of a word:

Erase the entire word and retype it according to the procedure given in No. 2, below.

2. An omitted letter within a word:

Error: a leter within
Correction: a letter within

Corrective steps with a nonrepetitive space bar:

a. Erase the incorrect word.
b. Position the carriage at the space after the letter *a*.
c. Press down and hold the space bar; strike the *l* key.
d. Release the space bar and repeat the process for each remaining letter.

Corrective steps with a repetitive space bar:

Follow the same steps by manually centering the carriage *between* the guides on the cylinder or paper-bail scale.

3. An extra letter within a word:

Error: a lettter within
Correction: a letter within

Follow the same procedure as in Step 2, except start the correction 1 space to the right.

IBM Selectric typewriter

When making corrections, locate the horizontal position of the typing element by using either the black line on the clear-view card holder (circled below) or the red arrow on the margin scale. If you use the card holder as your indicator, position the

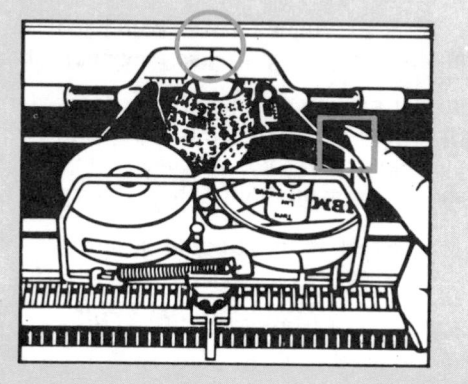

black line at the point on the paper at which you want to insert the new character. Then return to the line of type and insert the correction.

Squeezing Words

Error: the ordr today
Correction: the order today

To crowd the "e" into "ordr," erase the final "r." Backspace until the black line on the card holder is over the space formerly occupied by the final "r." Place the palm of the right hand on the top of the front cover. Reach under the cover and press LEFT against the carrier position post with your finger until the black line is moved back one-half space (as indicated in the illustration). Hold the carrier in this position

and type the "e." Repeat the procedure for the "r."

Expanding Words

Error: He will send
Correction: He can send

To replace "will" with "can," first erase "will." Type "c" in place of "w" and type "n" in the place of final "l."

Position the black line on the card holder over the position occupied by the first "l." Place the palm of the right hand on the top of the front cover. Reach under the cover and press left against the carrier position post with your finger until the black line of the card holder is directly between the "i" and "l." Type "a." Release the carrier and continue to type.

List of Illustrations

List of Drills and Timed Writings

Quarter-minute check points

Use this scale to identify the quarter-minute goals for guided writing. First, decide the goal rate at which you want to type for the minute; then get from the scale the quarter-, half-, three-quarters-, and one-minute goals and check the copy at these points.

The paragraphs in the guided writings are marked with the 4-word count shown in figures and with an in-between count shown by a • (dot). To check the goals, place a small mark above each quarter-minute goal. If your goal is not shown in the copy by a figure or a dot, spot the approximate midpoint between the dot and the figure and check this point. Do not take time to count the exact strokes; rather, estimate the correct placement of the goal check when there is no figure or dot to show the exact count.

Goal	Quarter	Half	Three-Quarters	One
16	4	8	12	16
20	5	10	15	20
24	6	12	18	24
28	7	14	21	28
32	8	16	24	32
36	9	18	27	36
40	10	20	30	40
44	11	22	33	44
48	12	24	36	48
52	13	26	39	52
56	14	28	42	56
60	15	30	45	60
64	16	32	48	64
68	17	34	51	68
72	18	36	54	72
76	19	38	57	76
80	20	40	60	80
84	21	42	63	84
88	22	44	66	88
92	23	46	69	92
96	24	48	72	96
100	25	50	75	100

INDEX